Teacher's Practical Guide for Educating Young Children

TEACHER'S PRACTICAL GUIDE FOR EDUCATING YOUNG CHILDREN

A Growing Program

SYDELLE H. HATOFF
Educational Institutes, Inc.

CLAUDIA A. BYRAM
Program of Auxiliary Services for Students
Philadelphia, Pennsylvania

MARION C. HYSON
University of Delaware

RESEARCH FOR BETTER SCHOOLS, INC.

ALLYN AND BACON, INC.
Boston • London • Sydney • Toronto

Copyright © 1981 by Allyn and Bacon, Inc., 470 Atlantic Avenue, Boston, Massachusetts 02210. All rights reserved. No part of the material protected by this copyright notice may be reproduced or utilized in any form or by any means, electronic or mechanical, including photocopying, recording, or by any information storage and retrieval system, without written permission from the copyright owner.

Library of Congress Cataloging in Publication Data

Hatoff, Sydelle H
   Teacher's practical guide for educating young children.

   Bibliography: p.
   1. Education, Preschool—Handbook, manuals, etc. 2. Creative activities and seat work—Handbooks, manuals, etc. I. Byram, Claudia A., joint author. II. Hyson, Marion C., joint author. III. Title.
LB1140.2.H37   372'.21   80-23334
ISBN 0-205-07126-0

Series Editor: Hiram G. Howard

Printed in the United States of America

Contents

Preface ix

1 YOUR GROWING PROGRAM 1
Finding the Road to Success 2
The Goal: A Growing Program 3
Thinking about Change 5
Steps to Your Growing Program 7

2 GROWING YOUR OWN: A TEACHING PHILOSOPHY 11
A Philosophy: The Map for Your Teaching Journey 12
Why Have a Philosophy? 13
The Hidden Philosophy 16
Our Teaching Philosophy 16
Growing Your Own Philosophy 18
Putting Your Principles into Practice 18

3 PATTERNS OF GROWTH: CHILD DEVELOPMENT AND TEACHING 23
Purpose of This Chapter 24
The Direction of Growth 25
Developmental Milestones 27
The Ingredients of Growth 29
The Many Ways of Growing 32
A Closer Look 37

4 THE GROWING CHILD: OBSERVING AND RECORDING 49
Using Growth Areas 50
Making a Profile of Growth 51
A Final Word 79

5 DIRECTIONS FOR GROWTH: GOALS, OBJECTIVES, AND PLANS 81
Goals 83

Objectives	86
What Next?	92
Plans	92

6 SETTING DIRECTIONS FOR GROWTH: PUTTING GOALS, OBJECTIVES, AND PLANS TO WORK — 97
Setting Directions for Individual Growth through Staffing — 98
Talking about Children — 98
A Final Word: Using Your Plans — 106

7 PLACES FOR GROWTH: ACTIVITY AREAS — 113
How Children Learn — 114
Activity Areas and Play: Harnessing Natural Energy — 114

8 RESOURCES FOR GROWTH: ACTIVITIES AND MATERIALS — 133
Things for Learning: Activities and Materials — 134
Activities — 134
Materials: Ingredients for Learning — 141
Save It! — 150
"Scrounge" List from Small Businesses — 150

9 SUPPORTING CHILDREN'S GROWTH: THE MANY WAYS OF TEACHING — 155
Children Learn through People — 156
What Is Teaching? — 157

10 SPACE AND TIME FOR GROWTH: THE ROOM ARRANGEMENT AND SCHEDULE — 179
The Room: Planning the Use of Space — 180
The Schedule: A Tool in Your Program — 198
A Final Word — 206

11 THE GROWING STAFF: MAKING THE MOST OF YOURSELVES — 209
Using Your Talents in Your Program — 210
Working Together in the Classroom — 214
Working Together in Staff Meetings — 223
A Final Word — 228

12 GROWING TOGETHER: PARENTS, CHILDREN, AND STAFF — 231
Getting Past the Communication Gap — 232
Parents and Their Child — 234
"Problem Parents" and "Problem Teachers" — 239
Parents and the Program — 244
A Final Word — 249

13 DIFFERENCES IN GROWTH: MAINSTREAMING HANDICAPPED YOUNG CHILDREN — 253
Introduction — 253

Handicapped Children   254
Mainstreaming and the Law   255
Why Mainstream?   256
Talking about Handicaps with Children: Some Guidelines   258
Issues in Planning and Implementing a Mainstreamed Program   261
In Summary   268

14 AN END... AND A BEGINNING   271
A Backward Look   272
What's Next?   277

Preface

This book grew out of the belief of Research for Better Schools that the growth of young children is of great importance in our society. Research for Better Schools, a nonprofit corporation, is dedicated to the development and implementation of educational programs for early childhood through adult life.

The book was conceived by Sydelle H. Hatoff and me as an outgrowth of our work in early-childhood education. With the support and encouragement of Robert G. Scanlon, Executive Director of RBS, Inc., a proposal was developed and approved for the preparation of this book. It became a publication objective of the Educational Services Division and has been under development since the summer of 1975.

As the project began, it became obvious that the task was too much for a single author; Claudia Byram and Marion C. Hyson were therefore engaged to be part of the writing team. All three authors are to be highly commended for their outstanding work, which has resulted in this contribution to the field of early-childhood education.

When the project was undertaken, Research for Better Schools intended this effort to add a new educational dimension to those working with young children. We feel confident that the authors have achieved our goal and sincerely hope that you will agree with this assessment.

This text is intended to be a practical guide for teachers, assistant teachers, and teacher's aides; for student teachers and center directors—in short, for all those involved in planning and carrying out activities with three- to five-year-old children. This book will help you create a Growing Program especially suited to the needs of your children. A *Growing Program* is a planned environment of things, people, and activities. But though planned, it is not fixed. A Growing Program changes as the needs of the children in it change. Its growth is the result of planning based on continuous observation of children's progress and problems. Because of this, no two Growing Programs are alike.

Each person has a unique set of beliefs, attitudes, and habits. When reading this book, we believe you will be taking in experiences or ideas that might cause you to change a bit, modifying or shaping your beliefs and attitudes toward young children.

This book will help you develop and use

- *your own* philosphy of education
- *your own* firsthand knowledge of young children
- *your own* plans, activities, and procedures.

The result will be an effective, sensitive, and developing program for your children, and ever-increasing professional and personal rewards for you. And this is real success.

James I. Mason
Director of Educational Services
Research for Better Schools, Inc.

1

Your Growing Program

DO YOU BELIEVE THAT

- children have individual patterns of development?
- children learn through play?
- children want to feel competent?
- children are natural explorers?
- teachers can grow and change along with children?

If these ideas are important to you, this book may be for you.

WOULD YOU LIKE TO PUT THESE BELIEFS INTO ACTION BY

- developing a really useful system for observing each child's growth?
- creating a better, more organized way of using staff time to discuss and plan for children?
- providing an environment that encourages more exploration and independence?
- refining teaching strategies to help children solve their own problems?
- working more cooperatively with parents to support children's growth?

If these are your goals, this book will probably help you reach them.

It's a rainy Monday morning. Jeff walks into the classroom early. He's wet, sleepy, and a little cross. His teacher, Ms. Black, has already set out glue and some bright yellow paper shapes, like the blue ones they used the day before. She notices Jeff's mood and asks him to help her choose a record to play while they're waiting for the others. Then she sits with him for a while and they talk about the rain. When his friend Kevin arrives, the two boys decide to make "rocket pictures" out of the paper. Ms. Black helps them find cotton to glue on for the smoke. She makes a mental note to read a rocket book at story time.

This is a Growing Program. It's a Growing Program not just because of the yellow paper or the record or the cotton or the book, but because of the way Ms. Black and Jeff choose and use these materials. A Growing Program is *people*—teachers and children—growing together in an environment that respects and responds to their needs.

This book is a guide and resource for people who work with young children. It will help them create a program especially suited to the needs of *their* children, *your* children—a *Growing Program* that grows and changes along with the children it serves.

The guidelines and activities in this book are based on our beliefs about what is important in working with young children, no matter who you are or what your level of education or responsibility. The book is for teachers, assistant teachers, and teacher aides. It is for student teachers and center directors. It is for anyone who is involved with planning and carrying out activities with children three to five years of age. Since the book is for so many people in different jobs, we have used the word "teacher" to refer to everyone.

FINDING THE ROAD TO SUCCESS

All around us, advertisers are selling slickly packaged products which claim to meet every human need. From coast to coast, fast-food chains turn out identically mediocre hamburgers. Television talk shows describe "ten easy steps to success" at everything from bread baking to marriage. Educators, too, have been lured by "how-to" books, learning kits, and "teacher-proof" curriculum materials.

There are two things wrong with these formulas for instant success.

- First, they often don't work. After our hopes have been raised by promises of easy answers, we often find that the answers refuse to fit our individual problems and questions. Each oven is different, each marriage is unique, each child is special. Recipes that work in one case fail dismally in another.
- Second, they underestimate your talents. We believe that there is a wealth of

energy and creativity in teachers and children which the "sure-fire" formulas don't even begin to explore. This book will draw on these resources. It will call on you to explore yourselves, as professionals who are also thinking, caring human beings. So you will not find easy answers to difficult problems. You will not find a packaged set of activities for every day of the year. You will find something better.

This book will help you develop and use

- *your own* philosophy of education
- *your own* first-hand knowledge of young children
- *your own* plans, activities, procedures.

The result will be an effective, sensitive, and developing program for your children and ever-increasing professional and personal rewards for you. This is real success.

THE GOAL: A GROWING PROGRAM

What Is a Growing Program?

It is a planned environment of things, people, and activities. It is planned, but not fixed. A Growing Program is one that changes as the needs of the children in it change. Its growth is the result of planning based on continuous observation of children's progress and problems. Because of this, no two Growing Programs can be alike.

Let's take a look at one Growing Program in action, first from a child's point of view, and then from a teacher's point of view. We'll begin with Sarah, a four-year-old child.

The Child's View

Sarah arrives a little late this morning. Ms. Stein, the teacher, comes over to greet her. Her mom couldn't start the car that morning, Sarah says. Ms. Stein sympathizes with Sarah; she often has the same problem. Then Sarah goes off to hang up her jacket, check her name off on the attendance list, and find her friends.

The class has already begun the morning activity period. Sarah looks around for a while, going from one group to another, and then joins some children in the block corner. They busy themselves building a house out of large, hollow blocks, complete with a porch and bedroom. Several times the roof topples, but they finally get it to balance. When Alex announces that he's going to the "store" for food, Sarah interrupts: "No, I am!" An angry exchange follows. The teacher intervenes and helps them figure out a way for both children to go to the store. She suggests that they will need some money. With the teacher's help, Sarah and Alex cut out some "dollars" and find some plastic discs for "pennies." The two children set off for the "store," which they have located in the house corner. Ms. Andrews helps them find some empty cereal boxes and juice cans to stock the store but they need bananas and carrots, too. They think about making them from play dough but finally decide to cut them out of yellow and orange construction paper.

After a while the shopping game runs its course. Ms. Stein invites Sarah and two other children to play an animal lotto game with her. They find a place on the rug to spread out their cards. By the time they're finished, the class is ready to begin cleaning up. Sarah gathers the cards and puts the box back on the game shelf.

She joins the others back on the rug, curling up comfortably while Ms. Andrews reads the story, *Let's Be Enemies*. The teacher asks if any of the children have felt like the boys in the book. Sarah tells the group about the fight she had with her friend Alex and about how they became friends again. Ms. Andrews reminds her that that was the way it was in the story, too. Other children add their tales to the discussion.

Sarah makes sure to sit next to Alex for snack, and she gives him the first cracker as she passes them around the table.

SARAH'S MORNING DIDN'T JUST HAPPEN

It was the result of some careful planning by her teachers, based on what they know about Sarah as an individual and as a four-year-old.

Sarah is growing in this program. Can you reread the description of Sarah's morning and find evidence of Sarah's growth

- through play and experience?
- through interactions with others (friendly and unfriendly)?
- through the teacher's attention to Sarah's own concerns and needs?
- through independent choice and problem solving?

We've seen what's in a Growing Program for a child. What does it look like from a teacher's point of view? Let's follow Ms. Stein now.

The Teacher's View

When Ms. Stein arrives, she begins setting out materials for the day. She rearranges a neglected science table, adding some new magnets. As she mixes paint, she glances through the plan book to refresh her memory. She reminds Ms. Andrews that they had decided to try to get Rick and Sharon involved together at the workbench this week, and that they'd planned to work with Sarah and a few other children on a matching activity. They get the animal lotto game out of the cupboard.

After the children arrive, Ms. Stein moves to the block area, which she is supervising this morning. On an index card, she jots a few notes about the new cooperation Ellen is showing; on another she notes that Billy doesn't seem to know the difference between "longer" and "shorter." A few minutes later, she steps in to help Sarah and Alex resolve the problem of who should go to the store, then sits on the floor to build with Thomas, who is just beginning to participate in the block corner. Ms. Andrews heads for the workbench with Rick and Sharon.

Later, when the store game has run its course, Ms. Stein gathers Sarah and a few others. She plays the lotto game with them, noting which of the children are able to match the cards. She notices that Sarah can't name several of the animals and plans to play the game with her again the next day. At clean-up time, Peter keeps asking, "Where does this go, teacher?" She helps him figure the answer out for himself by looking for similar objects on the shelves.

As the children leave, Ms. Stein has a few words with several parents. She sends a note home to Chris' mother telling about the puppet show he and Al are putting on next Friday. When the children have gone, Ms. Stein and Ms. Andrews sit down to discuss two children; this is part of their weekly planning session. They talk over each child's progress, strengths, and needs and then plan some specific activities for him or her. Finally, they settle on some plans for the whole group for the following week.

YOUR GROWING PROGRAM

BY NOW YOU MAY ENVY MS. STEIN

It's true that she seems less beset by crises than the average teacher. We've left out

- the four children wailing "Teacher!" at once
- Al's bloody nose
- the spilled paint
- the unexpected visitor

We're not really trying to make Ms. Stein sound like a paragon of teaching virtue. This picture has highlighted the things she was able to do to help children grow. Can you read back over her morning and find her

- arranging the physical environment?
- planning for children?
- supervising activities?
- diagnosing difficulties?
- observing?
- supporting problem solving?

These are the things that you, too, do for your children. As your own program moves closer to *your* ideal of a Growing Program, you'll find yourself becoming more aware of how, when, and why you do these things and many others.

THINKING ABOUT CHANGE

Moving from where your program is now to where you want to be means making some changes.

The changes you're thinking about may be small (like trying a new activity) or they may be large (like revitalizing and rethinking your whole program). Or you may be about to take on your first classroom responsibilities and need a little support.

Working toward a goal, large or small, can be exciting and motivating, making us eager to try new ideas. But if you are already doing things one way, it can be hard to do them differently, even if you want to.

- We all feel more comfortable with old habits. If something works once, we tend to repeat it, even if something else might work better.
- The unknown is scary. If we try something new, it might not work. Sometimes we end up not trying at all.
- We worry about what others think of us when we make mistakes or when we try something they might disapprove of. So we play it safe.

Trying Things Out

Once you have an idea about a change you'd like to see, and some ideas about how to make the change, you will need to *try it out*. And you will need to be ready to throw out one idea and try another, if the first one doesn't work. Planning, trying, and evaluating activities can be a difficult process! It is so easy to get bogged down in everyday details, or discouraged when an idea goes awry. Whenever possible, we have provided suggestions to smooth the way, and many "Do It Yourself" activities that require you to get out there and *try*!

Putting It Together

As you try new ideas, you will find some that work well for the children, for you, and for the other adults in your room. When these ideas become part of the experience of children and staff, the Growing Program is no longer the book, it is you.

Alone or with Friends?

There are several different ways to use this book. The way (or ways) you choose will depend on what you want to accomplish.

- You may be using the book as part of a larger program, a course, or a staff development project. If so, you are in a good position to benefit from the experiences of others and to *share* yours with them. Make the most of it!
- You may be in a position where you must work alone (as many kindergarten teachers are). If so, you'll need more than the usual dose of energy and inventiveness. We've tried to give you some special suggestions in every chapter. If you can, find one other person who can be an ally. Each chapter requires that you do activities—to put into practice what you have read—and these activities are much easier to do if you have the support of a coworker. Keeping at a program is difficult when you work alone. It can become an adventure when you have someone with whom to work and share.

Making Change Easier

Some things do make progress a little easier. Try to remember them as you begin moving toward the goals you set for yourself.

1. Begin with small changes and build on them step by step. That way, you (and the children) will adjust to the differences gradually. If you like the first step you take, the next will be that much easier.
2. Work with others. Whether you are developing a new program, losing weight, or returning to school, the company of others is an invaluable source of encouragement. You share one another's triumphs and failures; you share problems and brainstorm solutions to them. In this book, we hope that you're working along with others. We've given you some suggestions for using one another as resources (for example, in observing and planning, in supervising activity centers, etc.) and for finding support if you're now working alone.
3. Use all the help you can get. Lots of people have gone through the same

process of change that you are entering. Their experiences and insights are available to you—in books, magazines, workshops, films, and exhibits. This book, too, is intended as a resource.
4. *You* decide what, when, and how you will try new ideas. No one likes change when it's imposed, especially if it involves some hard work. So take charge of the plan for your group by thinking about what your needs and your children's needs are and about how satisfied or dissatisfied you are with various aspects of your program. Use this book to help you reach your *own* goals, to get where *you* want to go.

STEPS TO YOUR GROWING PROGRAM

Like the man who wants to take a trip, to wind up where you want to go, you have to know where you're going and how you're going to get there—and you have to be prepared to overcome the obstacles encountered on the way! You need

- goals
- tools
- work.

Where to Begin

Begin with yourself. As you would with children, start where you are.

Your first job is to set your own goals. Why are you reading this book? What do you hope to get out of it? Are you looking for specific ideas to improve your program? Or did you pick up the book on impulse, because it appealed to something in you? To what?

- A vague dissatisfaction with how things are going in your room?
- A worry about a particular child?
- An irresistible urge to have a peek at every possible source of new ideas?

Whatever your reason for selecting this book, think about what it means for your goals—where you want to go with your program.

But you may be reading this book because someone chose it for you, an instructor or your supervisor. What does this tell you about your goals?

- Are you just interested in "going along with the program"—to avoid trouble or to get a grade?
- Are you willing to try but you're a little skeptical about the payoffs?
- Are you hoping for solutions to some knotty problems in your program and willing to work to find them?

Take some time to think about what *you* really want from this book, or from your program. What is it you want? How hard are you willing to work for it? Really: close the book *now*, and give these questions some thought.

DO IT YOURSELF

Take a moment to look at yourself and to look ahead. Reflect on yourself as a teacher (or future teacher) and on the classroom where you work.

What are the things you like about what you do, and about what goes on in the classroom? What are the things you'd like to change? (You don't need to know *how* they should be changed yet—just that you'd like them to be different!) If you're working with a group, take turns sharing one item from each side of the list below. It will help you know where your colleagues want to go. You may be surprised at how many people are heading in the same direction.

Save this list; we'll look back at it later.

Things I Like	*Things I'd Like to See Changed*

FORM 1-1

Are you back? Whatever you decided is up to you. It is fine if your goal is general at this point—it's the nature of goals to change and become more specific with time. If your goals are already very specific, you are a step ahead.

Whatever your personal goals, we recommend that you read the next two chapters first. "Growing Your Own: A Teaching Philosophy," will help you develop a philosophy that is consistent with who you are and what you believe. Chapter 3, "Patterns of Growth," will focus your attention on what you know about growing children, extend your knowledge of child development, and help you think about how this knowledge is incorporated into your program.

Following Chapter 3, you may either work directly through the book or take the chapters in the order of most importance for you. Are you moving into a new room? You may wish to turn first to Chapter 10, "Space and Time for Growth: The Room Arrangement and Schedule." Are parent conferences coming up soon? Try Chapter 12, "Growing Together: Parents, Children, and Staff."

Collecting Tools

Once you have chosen your goals, you will need some tools to help you reach them. Tools can be ideas, activities, guidelines, or people. Each chapter includes some tools and suggests ways to find others.

Some tools you will find in this book are:

- a basic map of healthy development to guide you in looking at your children
- ways of observing and recording children's behavior
- guidelines for doing individualized planning for children
- ways to plan and evaluate the environment you provide
- a flexible repertoire of teaching strategies that you can tailor to each child
- various ways to work with parents.

There are a lot of ideas in these chapters. You probably won't use all of them. Because your interests and needs are unique, you should select from the many suggestions in this book those which will be most helpful to you and your children.

This book can only guide you in creating your own Growing Program. *You* must prepare the ground, plant the seeds, and cultivate the crop for a rich harvest for you and your children.

2

Growing Your Own

A TEACHING PHILOSOPHY

CHALLENGE YOURSELF

You may believe
- A philosophy of education is an important part of every program.
  But can you explain clearly *your* personal philosophy, beliefs, and values?
- There are "rights" and "wrongs" in teaching children.
  But do you know the reasons behind your own "rights and wrongs," and how they affect your program?
- Teachers are professionals, with important responsibilities.
  But do you see and value yourself as a professional?

SKILLS IN THIS CHAPTER

- Developing your own teaching philosophy
- Putting your teaching philosophy to work for you

A PHILOSOPHY: THE MAP FOR YOUR TEACHING JOURNEY

In a way, teaching is like taking a journey. You start with your new class in one place in the Fall, and are somewhere quite different by Spring. There are several ways to travel. One way is to wander about from one place to another, taking in the sights, following the whim of the moment. This can be very pleasant but will probably not serve the purpose if you have a particular place to go.

Another way to take a trip is to set out with a goal in mind. You may go at a leisurely pace, pausing to explore this or that byway, but all along you are moving toward your destination. When teaching is like the second sort of trip, it is because there is a goal—there are "places" you, the teacher, want your children to go.

But, as on a real trip, problems beset the teaching journey. There is the chance of getting lost, or of not knowing quite where you meant to go in the first place. There are attractive side roads—are they shortcuts or dead ends? And there are the unexpected storms and unpredictable incidents which make you wonder why you started on the trip at all.

Of course, no trip is free of difficulties, but, as on a real journey, you will find teaching easier if you have a map. A map can show you the general direction you need to take, what turns to make, and what dead ends to avoid. For teachers, the "map" is made up of beliefs about children, ideas about appropriate goals for teaching, expectations about what teachers "ought" to do or be like. This map can be summed up as your "teaching philosophy"—the principles that guide your practice.

Of course, there can be no ready-made road map for your teaching journey. You are a unique individual, with unique children, and different ones each year. You must construct your own map, and it will be an odd one. There will be large blank spaces—areas you have not yet explored. There will be light, tentative lines and there will be dark, heavy lines, where you are confident of the way. And all these lines will move. It is a map in the making, and you are making it all the time.

Ms. Phillips is sitting at a table by the door of her classroom. She's sorting some collage materials, keeping half an eye on the children gathered around the puzzle table. More children wander in the door, coats half off in the warm spring morning. "Good morning, Jeff! Is that a new jacket?" Ms. Phillips listens as Jeff explains how his mother got him the coat, and got a lot of things for the baby. She notices that Jeff seems a little sullen when he mentions the baby, but brightens when she comments on the nice coat his mother chose for him. She plans to mention to Jeff's mother that the idea of paying him some special attention seems to be paying off, at least a little. Meanwhile, here comes Tina. She had such a bad day yesterday that Ms. Phillips is determined to see that she gets off to a good start this morning. So Ms. Phillips asks Jeff what he plans to pick from the shelf "for table time," and then turns her attention to greeting Tina.

In this anecdote, Ms. Phillips has made some choices, choices about how to spend her time, how to work with her children. For example, she has planned the morning routine of "table time" to

- match the pace of the children (a little slow first thing in the morning)
- ease them back into contact with their friends (a casual, relaxed activity requiring no leadership or followership)
- leave her relatively free (since she has no help in her kindergarten classroom) to greet and make a personal contact with each arriving child.

Ms. Phillips is putting her teaching philosophy into action. She is choosing activities that reflect her beliefs about what children need, and how she can best meet those needs.

WHY HAVE A PHILOSOPHY?

You may be asking yourself why you need a "teaching philosophy" at all. The whole idea may seem pretty far from the real life of teaching—the paint pots that must be filled, the water table to be set up, the runny nose that needs wiping.

Try thinking of it this way: your teaching philosophy (whether you are aware of it or not) is what makes these little things worth doing.

"Teaching" is a myriad of small decisions, culminating in a particular kind of school experience for the children.

- Jamie asks for more glue. Decision: give him the bottle and let him pour his own or squeeze it out for him?
- Marcie is getting frustrated with a block building that just won't stand. Decision: fix it for her, tell her she can do it, or offer a suggestion?
- Mitchel and Thomas are facing each other fiercely over the trike. Decision: direct Mitchel to let Thomas go first, ask them what the rule is about the trikes, or tell them both to go sit down for a moment and cool off?

As a teacher, you can be pulled in many directions by decisions like these, and by the hundred other details of your job. It is easy to become absorbed in the little things and to lose the map which leads to the reason for doing all this in the first place. And that reason is, of course, the children. Their growth as individuals and as "citizens of the world" is the fundamental reason for your program's existence.

The solution is to have broader goals than "just getting through the day"; you need goals to guide your actions. If you can't see where you are on the map as a whole, you can't tell which way to turn when you reach a corner.

Let's go back to the example of Jamie and the glue. Should he pour it or should you? If you believe in protecting and supporting children's growing independence, you will let Jamie pour his own glue. But if you also believe in starting where the child is, and helping him take small steps, you may decide to pour the glue yourself because Jamie can't yet. He can tell you when to stop though, and maybe the next time he can pour, with your help.

This is the kind of question we will be addressing in this book. The answer to the question—and to other questions like it—depends on you. It depends on your own teaching philosophy—the beliefs and values you've developed about children and about this particular child.

Let's look at some more specific ways a teaching philosophy can be helpful in the day-to-day life of the classroom.

- *In selecting goals for your children.* One of the problems you face in planning for a classroom is choosing what you want your program to do. You must decide what things you really think are important for children to experience and learn. You must select, out of all the possible things the children *could* do, those you want them to do. What you choose will depend on your philosophy—your beliefs about what children need. For example, if you believe in the importance of social relationships in children's growth, you will take care to plan a program which provides these. There will be activity areas where children are invited to interact with one another (like the dramatic play area, blocks, the clay table). And these areas will be *used*, not just for the half hour when you need your break from "real" teaching, but for much of the time. These activities will be the pillars of the program.
- *In choosing among the roads you can take toward a goal.* Let's say you want to plan a picnic for your group. You have chosen a picnic because it meets some of your goals: it provides a new experience for the children, and it lets them get to know their neighborhood better. Now, do you arrange the picnic with the parents and other staff, preparing the lunch, finding someone to drive it the three blocks to the park, etc., thereby effectively delivering the children to a "ready-made" party? Or does your philosophy include the belief that children learn by doing? And that children need help in developing planning skills? If so, you will let the children help you pick a spot for the picnic. *They* will plan the menu and list the things they need to prepare it. The children will pack the wagon and squabble over who is to pull it. They will be the ones to pull together to get the now-loaded monstrosity over the curbs. It will be their picnic, because that is what you have chosen it to be. Those are the "turns" you have chosen to take, guided by the map of your teaching philosophy.

Outside the classroom, too, your teaching philosophy is useful.

- *In taking in new ideas.* As your philosophy helps pick and choose among ideas for your classroom, it can also be a guide to you in perusing the tremendous number of ideas available to teachers. As you seek out new approaches, try to understand how *your* view of teaching relates to the views of others in the field. A coherent philosophy of teaching can help you select those suggestions that will really enhance the experiences you provide for children—not just the suggestions that are the "flashiest," or that come easiest to you.
- *In valuing yourself as a professional.* Have you ever said "I'm *just* a teacher"? Most of us have. While you may feel that the work you do is *really* important, you may also feel the impact of the double message society sometimes sends us as teachers. We're described as "guardians of the future," caring for the "nation's greatest resource," yet our status and pay often imply that we

DO IT YOURSELF

Take some time now to think about your own teaching philosophy. You *can* do the activity below alone, but it will be even more valuable if someone will share it with you.

Follow the instructions below *exactly*.

1. Number from 1 to 7 down the side of a piece of paper.

2. Read the following statement and then list the answers *in order of their importance to you.*

    The most important thing a child can learn is:

    - self-confidence
    - pre-reading skills
    - problem-solving ability
    - awareness of rules, respect for authority
    - sense of order
    - sharing
    - friendships with other children

    Important: *Don't talk over your choices with anyone.* This part is your own thinking. Decide what is really most important to you and write that beside number one on your paper. Select the next most important and put it beside number two, and so on.

3. When you have finished your own list, get together with from one to three other people and try to agree on a joint list. Start by trying to find an item you can *all* agree is the *most* important. You will have to give your reasons for your own selection and listen to the reasons for others'. This is where you really start to think about what you believe, and why. And the reasons others give may give you some new ideas.

    There is a lot of give and take in this exercise. It will take some talking, some persuading, and some open-mindedness to be able to reach a sound agreement on what is the most important, which is second, and so on. There isn't one "correct" ranking of the seven items. The important thing is to do some hard thinking about your own values and the reasons behind them.

    If you couldn't find anyone to do this exercise with you, at least spend some time thinking about the reasons for your choices. Try a different order . . . can you "rationalize" this one as well as your first one? Another question: do you think striving for any one of these goals means shortchanging another?

FORM 2-1

are hardly more than babysitters. A thoughtful philosophy of teaching, carefully put into practice, can help you assert your own value as a professional. You can be confident that what you do is valuable. You are not *"just"* a teacher. You are a *teacher*.

THE HIDDEN PHILOSOPHY

Everyone reading this book has some kind of teaching philosophy already. It may be more or less elaborate, depending on how much teaching you have done, and how much you have thought about your teaching. But it is there, no matter what, whether you're an experienced director or a beginning student. Some bits of your "philosophy" are conscious beliefs and values. "Each child is a person, unique in his or her own right." "Definite rules are important in helping children learn how to organize themselves." Other parts of your philosophy may not be so conscious. These form your "hidden philosophy," the ideas that are reflected in how you behave, not what you think.

> Ms. Peters, without being aware of it, consistently selects the most "realistic" of her students' pictures for display. The shapeless streaks of her less mature students seem to find the bottom of the closet until going home time.

> Mr. Fredericks frequently starts a little song as the children are cleaning up. He changes the verses to include each child's name as he circulates around the room.

Both Ms. Peters and Mr. Fredericks are putting into practice some beliefs and values, even though they may not be aware of it. Ms. Peters clearly thinks certain kinds of pictures are "good," while others are not worth showing. She may even feel she's saving her less-skilled youngsters embarrassment by not displaying their work! Mr. Fredericks acts as though he believes that each child benefits from a little special recognition of her or his own contribution to the group. His values seem to emphasize the worth of each child, although he may never have put these values into words.

Both the principles and values of which you are aware, and those which may influence your teaching without your knowing it, contribute to the "map" you use to guide your work with children. As professionals, we need to be as familiar with our own map as we can be. We need to be able to examine that "hidden philosophy" closely. We need to be able to talk about what we do and why we do it, in terms of the benefits for children, parents, and ourselves.

OUR TEACHING PHILOSOPHY

By now you will have gathered that the authors of this book are by no means neutral on the subject of children and teaching. We have strong beliefs about children, which have shaped what we have chosen to say in this book. The beliefs listed in Form 2-2 are backed up by a good deal of sound theory and research; many educators would subscribe to them, at least in theory. These beliefs are at the foundation of the approach taken in this book—you'll run into them again and again.

DO IT YOURSELF

Beliefs must be put into practice if they are to be useful, so alongside each belief below, we've given an example of an application. As you read through these ten beliefs, you might check off those with which *you* would agree. You might also think about ways in which *your* program reflects these beliefs.

BELIEFS We Believe That		APPLICATIONS A Growing Program Should Provide
1. children are curious about their world.	☐	a wealth of materials to explore and time to explore them.
2. children want to feel competent.	☐	a chance for children to overcome difficulties and meet challenges.
3. children learn through experience and play.	☐	an interesting environment with many activity centers.
4. children go through stages of development, moving from concrete to abstract thinking, from impulsive to controlled behavior.	☐	support for a child "where he or she is," and experiences on which to build a foundation for future growth.
5. each child develops at his or her own rate, and in his or her own style.	☐	an individualized curriculum in which the *child* (his or her needs and style) is the center of the learning process.
6. children learn through involvement with people who care about them.	☐	a warm but challenging environment where learning is personalized, not computerized.
7. children build a strong self-concept through many experiences of success.	☐	a chance for *all* to succeed and to know the joys of accomplishment.
8. children learn from each other—from friendship and conflict.	☐	an opportunity for children to interact freely, with teacher support in times of difficulty.
9. children need a meaningful structure to help organize experience.	☐	a predictable environment of objects and people.
10. children want to make sense out of problems and questions.	☐	encouragement of problem solving, critical thinking, and creative thinking.

FORM 2-2

GROWING YOUR OWN PHILOSOPHY

Although we have shared with you some of our beliefs about children, it is important to remember that you cannot and should not expect yourself to "buy" anyone's philosophy "as is." Teaching is still very much an art, and very much a personal one. Since a philosophy cannot be bought ready-made, you will have to "grow your own," from your experiences with children, your reading, and your contacts with other professionals.

This book is meant to be one resource in helping you to "grow your own" teaching philosophy. Here are a few other suggestions.

- *Talk.* Talk with other teachers about situations that come up in the classroom. How should Howie be handled when he gets so frightened? What other ways could be tried? What effect might these strategies have on him and on the other children? Out of these discussions will come a clearer idea of what you really value and believe.
- *Visit.* Visit other classrooms whenever you can. Go to other rooms in your own setting. Travel across town to classrooms using special programs. See a Montessori class, see a private nursery school—see every program you can. *Talk* to the teachers there. Compare what they are doing, and why, to your own program. The investment is well worth the effort. You will find some of your beliefs supported, but others will be shaken to their foundations. You will have a chance to really *think* about what you are doing.
- *Read.* Read brief articles in journals (a few are listed at the end of this chapter). Don't make it a chore—select what interests you, but then take the time to digest it. How does the author's view fit with your experience and thinking? Read books by teachers about teaching. These inside accounts are as fascinating as novels and can really raise questions about what teaching *should* be.
- *Join.* Join the local chapter of an organization such as the National Association for the Education of Young Children (NAEYC), or the Association for Childhood Education International (ACEI). Listen to what others are saying and thinking; get to know people outside your immediate circle. You will not only encounter new ideas but will find yourself part of a group that believes in the value of what you are doing.
- *Go to workshops.* Go to seminars and workshops offered in your city. Don't limit yourself to ones labeled "early-childhood education." Try the biology department's workshop on plants, or the all-day workshop for making triwall furniture, or the seminar on family crises. You will not only get ideas for specific activities, you will find your thinking stimulated as you encounter new alternatives in teaching.

And remember, in all this sampling and talking, no one else has the right answer for you. You must use your own growing philosophy as a guide to the nuggets you can really use.

PUTTING YOUR PRINCIPLES INTO PRACTICE

Your teaching philosophy grows in one crucial way that we didn't mention. It grows through use. A philosophy is like a muscle. If you put it in a cast and stop using it, it will atrophy—the cells die and the muscle slowly wastes away. Use it, and it grows; it becomes stronger and more useful. By applying your ideas every day, they will grow also. Ideas turn from slogans to strong beliefs when backed by experience. A platitude about the "value of each child" gradually turns into an inner conviction: each child really *does* have a special quality. You know it because you've seen it. And you know something about how to bring those qualities out.

But the same realities that bring substance to your ideas can also make it difficult to practice what you preach.

1. You may believe in encouraging independence in children, *but* this particular group is very immature and can't seem to handle the independence you have thrust on them.
2. You may believe in children's own art, rather than neat, teacher-directed "projects," *but* the teacher these children had before you really "wowed" the parents with the lovely napkin-holders, pencil-holders, and holder-holders the children took home each week.
3. You may believe children need limits set in a firm and calm voice, *but* you find yourself trembling with rage when a small saucy face wrinkles up its nose and says, "No! And you can't make me!"

What do you do in these cases? Since your beliefs about children and teaching are not meant to contradict the real world (which is what you are running into), you need to reexamine what you believe—and how it applies to the situation at hand. Let's look at how each of the problems above might be attacked.

1. With the immature group, you discover, in examining your philosophy, that you not only believe in independence, but you also believe in beginning "where the child is." And these children are not all ready for much independence. So you begin paying more attention to each child, discovering which ones need extra guidance and which ones already work quite well on their own. You reduce the number of activities the children can choose from and concentrate on teaching those children who need it how to manage the few that are left. You shorten the whole-group time and add small, informal story groups with the help of a high-school work-study student. And so on.
2. With the parents who still want those napkin-holders coming home, you remember that new things can be difficult to accept, and that people need to understand in a concrete way what is going on. So you begin inviting small groups of parents to your class, to observe and participate in some simple craft activities. Afterwards, you chat with the parents for a bit, talking about what the children were doing, and why you chose that particular activity. Maybe the clay is particularly important just now for the fine-motor development of a few children, and for the socialization of some new children who are just learning a bit of English. The parents will get to know you and appreciate the concern that goes into your choice of materials.
3. With your own angry reaction to the "challenging" child, you may need to do some deep searching and thinking. It is undoubtedly true that teachers are real people too. It is important not to deny the "unlovely" parts of you. Allow yourself to "start where you are," just as you do with the children.

And, just as you would try to provide a child with the support he or she needs to grow on a personal level, you need to find those supports for yourself. Talking with a more experienced teacher or just airing your worries with a friend might help. On the other hand, the reaction you have may be a sign of "unfinished business" in your own growth process, which needs to be taken seriously. This is a reality for everyone in teaching, and whether your own version of this problem is serious enough for professional counseling is an assessment you need to make for yourself.

We've looked at a teaching philosophy: what it is, what it might be, and how to "grow your own." And, in a way, that's what all the rest of this book is about—reaching a better understanding of children and of yourself as a teacher so that you can build a better Growing Program.

RESOURCES

Croft, D.J. *Be Honest with Yourself: A Self-Evaluation Handbook for Early Childhood Education Teachers.* Belmont, Calif.: Wadsworth, 1976.
> Explores the feelings that both teachers and children have during "critical incidents" of the day. Includes lots of chances to work on actual situations.

Curwin, R.L., and Fuhrmann, B.S. *Developing Your Teaching Self.* Englewood Cliffs, N.J.: Prentice-Hall, 1975.
> A humanistic approach to finding out how you really feel about yourself, your students, and your work. Contains worksheets and lively dialogues that show you how to use your strengths. Written for elementary and high school teachers but very relevant for teachers of young children.

Katz, L.G. *Talks with Teachers.* Washington, D.C.: NAEYC, 1977.
> Written by the director of the ERIC Clearinghouse for Early Childhood Education, this book is actually a collection of papers based on the author's research and experiences. She deals with pertinent questions which teachers must resolve intellectually and through their experiences. There are two major sections—teacher development and working with children; the material on teacher development includes ideas on formulating one's own teaching philosophy. The emphasis here is on the complexity of the field as we attempt to understand what the early childhood educator does.

Lay, M.Z., and Dopyera, J.E. *Becoming a Teacher of Young Children.* Lexington, Mass.: D.C. Heath, 1977.
> An unusual organization in an attempt to provide students and those in the field with the underlying concepts and materials that will enable them to become responsible, effective teachers. Through the four attributes of what the authors believe it takes to become a teacher (commitment, sensitivity, resourcefulness, and organizational abilities), they relate concepts of child growth and development, different approaches to teaching, ideas for working with children, and activities relating to specific themes. Although this is a particularly helpful resource for developing activity centers, it can contribute to your thinking as you develop or refine your own teaching philosophy.

Parker, R.K. *The Preschool in Action.* Boston: Allyn and Bacon, 1972.
> A collection of papers presented at a conference at the City University of New York dealing with "conceptualization of preschool curricula." Although difficult reading, this is an excellent representation of the major theoretical systems underlying the development of young children. The papers provide insight into the development of differing kinds of preschool curricula and give some guidelines for creating instructional materials.

Thornberg, K.R. *The Whole Teacher.* Atlanta: Humanics Ltd., 1977.
> This book explores what a teacher should know and feel before working with young children. The material will be interesting to both experienced teachers and field students as a starting point for extended thinking and discussion.

Early Childhood Magazines

These are a few of the many stimulating publications directed at teachers and teachers-to-be.

Young Children, National Association for the Education of Young Children, 1834 Connecticut Ave. N.W., Washington, D.C. 20009.

Children Today, U.S. Children's Bureau, Administration for Children, Youth and Families, Dept. of Health, Education and Welfare, Box 1182, Washington, D.C. 20013.

Learning, Pitman Learning, Inc., 530 University Ave., Palo Alto, Calif. 94301.

3

Patterns of Growth

CHILD DEVELOPMENT AND TEACHING

CHALLENGE YOURSELF

You may believe
- Children are changing all the time. But can you predict *how* they will change and *why*?
- Teachers should encourage children's development. But do you know the ingredients of healthy development?
- All children are individuals. But do you understand how they got to be that way?

SKILLS IN THIS CHAPTER

- Using developmental milestones in your work
- Becoming aware of the ingredients of healthy development
- Understanding individual differences between children
- Anticipating kinds of changes in the four growth areas

The first step in creating a Growing Program is to understand growth itself.

Here's a riddle: What do a house plant, a rabbit, a teacher, and a four-year-old child have in common?

What they have in common—and what makes them different from computers and automobiles—is their constant tendency to change, to expand, and to influence and *be* influenced by the world around them. Because living things *are* living, they grow and develop.

Your Growing Program is a living system. It's made up of individuals who are all, from the youngest to the oldest, in the process of developing and growing.

PURPOSE OF THIS CHAPTER

The *purpose* of this chapter is to help you understand that growth process in your children and yourself. We'll look at:

- the personal benefits you can get from a richer understanding of growth
- the direction of growth from infancy to adulthood
- the ingredients of growth
- the many ways of growing
- growth in the early years: what it is and how understanding it can make your program better.

Benefits for You

Your work will be both easier and more challenging if you understand what growth is and how it happens. People who have studied child development help us understand the real world in which children live and grow. If you understand that world

- you find yourself constantly fascinated by children's behavior
- you see the long-term importance of what you're doing, from block building to coloring to story telling
- you have a framework within which to place individual differences and delays in development
- you are sensitive to possible problems in development
- you can plan the details of your program in the light of solid knowledge about children
- you can chart specific directions in the program for a specific child.

PATTERNS OF GROWTH

THE DIRECTION OF GROWTH

The children you are teaching sometimes seem to be changing and growing right before your eyes. Timid, awkward Ellen becomes bright-eyed and confident; Roberto moves from halting words to a rush of sentences; Brian suddenly seems to be retreating back into clinging dependency. These rapid transformations make teaching young children a fascinating, challenging, and sometimes puzzling job.

In order to sort out these changes and understand them, you need a long-range perspective. You need to step back a bit and look at where your children have come from, and where they're going.

Continuity and Change

Think about your favorite house plant. It's probably grown a lot since you bought it. There are two rules underlying that growth. These rules are so obvious that you may never have thought about them.

- The first rule is *continuity*. The plant's basic needs—water, soil, and light—stay the same whether it's a seedling or a mature specimen. And a philodendron will never transform itself into an African violet.
- The second rule is *orderly change*. The plant *will* change, but its growth is predictable. You know that shoots will appear before leaves and buds before flowers. The plant will grow bigger, not smaller.

The growth of human beings also follows these two basic rules. Despite many changes, Henry at fourteen is the same person he was at four, with many of the same preferences and needs. The physical, intellectual, and emotional changes that have occurred have followed a predictable pattern, from simple to complex, from concrete to abstract, from impulsive to controlled.

Let's look at Jason, Claude, and Frank, three human beings of different ages, as they first wake up in the morning.

Six months. Jason opens his eyes, raises his head, and gazes around the room. He reaches for his fuzzy lamb, bangs it against the crib bars, and chews its ear. Then he puts his fist in his mouth, sucks on it for a few minutes, and begins to cry. His face reddens and his arms and legs thrash as he works himself up to a roar. Jason's mother enters the room, picks him up, sets him on the dressing table, and changes him. As she speaks, Jason calms down, smiles, and coos back to her. She carries him into the kitchen and props him in the high chair while she prepares his breakfast. As he sees his bottle, he reaches out with both hands, whimpering and finally wailing.

Four years. Claude jumps out of bed as soon as his eyes are open. He stands in the middle of the room for a few minutes, holding his teddy bear and rubbing his eyes. Then he goes to the bathroom, and a few minutes later wanders into the kitchen, where his mother is fixing breakfast. He comes up behind her and buries his face in her skirt. His mother gives him a kiss and hands him a small box of cereal. "I don't like that kind, Mom," he whines, replacing it on the counter. "Can I have cornflakes?" His mother agrees, and Claude settles down to fix his cereal, pouring milk from the pitcher on the table and giving himself a rather large helping of sugar. He makes soft racing-car noises as he weaves his spoon back and forth through the bowl. He goes to the refrigerator to get more juice, but can't handle the heavy pitcher. His mother pours it for him.

Twenty-four years. Frank groans as the alarm goes off. He rolls out of bed, mumbling as he heads for the shower. Dressed and shaved, he heads for the kitchen, where he pours himself a bowl of cornflakes and plugs in the coffee pot. As he waits for it to perk, he scans the headlines in the morning paper and turns to the entertainment section to find a good movie. He phones a friend to chat and see if she can go to the movie with him that night. She's busy. Frank is a bit disappointed but decides to ask another friend at work. He gulps his coffee, finishes his cereal and toast, and drives off to work.

Let's compare Jason, Claude, and Frank as they start their day. You may have noticed a few similarities. All three need food, human companionship, and information from the world around them.

But there are many differences, too. As we follow development from infancy into childhood and adulthood, we can see an orderly progression of changes in many areas.

For instance:

- *Physical skills:* Development moves from uncoordinated large-muscle motions to finer, more precise skills.
    - *Jason* thrashes, bangs, and chews.
    - *Claude* pours his own milk but has trouble with the pitcher.
    - *Frank* plugs in the electric coffee pot and drives a car.
- *Growth of independence:* Development moves from helplessness toward ability to manage one's own affairs.
    - *Jason* has to wait for his mother to pick him up, dress him, feed him.
    - *Claude* can do more of these things alone but still needs and wants help in some areas.
    - *Frank* showers, shaves, cooks, and works to support himself.
- *Taking in information:* Development moves from concrete, physical, or playful ways of learning about the world toward more abstract and complex knowledge.
    - *Jason* finds out about objects by putting them in his mouth.
    - *Claude* still gets information via concrete objects, but uses them in more complex pretend play.
    - *Frank* uses the printed word and the telephone to get information.
- *Communication:* Development moves from simple, nonverbal means of conveying basic needs to verbal expressions of complex ideas and emotions.
    - *Jason* has a "language" of cries, coos, and wails that his mother has to interpret.
    - *Claude* can tell his mother exactly what he likes or dislikes in simple words, though he frequently uses physical ways to communicate, too.
    - *Frank* can use language to discuss future plans, abstract ideas, and present feelings.
- *Satisfying needs:* Development moves from an urgent need for immediate satisfaction toward the ability to wait or accept substitutes.
    - *Jason* screams if his bottle isn't immediately available.
    - *Claude* whines if he doesn't get what he wants, but is able to wait a bit.

PATTERNS OF GROWTH

○ *Frank* is disappointed when things don't work out the way he wants, but can substitute other plans and create long-range goals for himself.

Let's summarize these observations. As human beings develop from infancy toward maturity, they are growing

From
- impulsive behavior
- helplessness
- learning through action
- physical communication
- immediate satisfaction

Toward
- controlled action
- independence
- learning through thought
- skillful verbal expression
- planned long-range solutions to needs

We're never finished with these tasks.

The young children you teach are just setting out on this path toward maturity. They've come a long way from the world of the infant, but they're also a long way from adult competencies.

DEVELOPMENTAL MILESTONES

There are many landmarks on this path from infancy to maturity: sitting up, walking, speaking the first word, drawing a picture, understanding concepts of size, volume, time.

Those who study children have found that they can predict fairly accurately when so-called "average" children will pass each of these and other milestones. At the end of this chapter you'll find some references which will give you this kind of information.

Uses

Knowing the approximate ages at which children can be expected to talk in sentences, or be toilet trained, or hold a pencil properly can help you in your work. You'll have some guidelines to use in deciding whether a child is significantly advanced or delayed in some or all areas of his or her growth. If so, you might want to observe him or her more closely or refer him or her for testing or other consultation. Knowing the major developmental milestones will also help you avoid a familiar trap: planning activities or routines that are either beyond the grasp of young children or so simple that the child is bored silly.

Misuses

Don't be misled by oversimplified charts, though. A statement like "a child walks at fifteen months" is a *statistical mean,* which the chart makers arrived at by averaging the ages at which hundreds of normal children began to walk—ranging, no doubt, from eight or nine months to twenty-four months. There might not be even a single child in the sample who began walking at exactly fifteen months! In

DO IT YOURSELF

Try describing the differences between an infant, a young child, and an adult. Here's one setting that should fire your imagination!

1. Picture Jason, Claude, and Frank *taking a bath*.
2. Under "Growth of independence," describe one thing that each of them might do in the bathtub to show his development in this area.
3. Do the same under "Acquiring information." To help you get started, one example is completed.

	Physical Skills	*Growth of Independence*	*Acquiring Information*
Jason (6 mos.)	Jason wiggles and splashes.		
Claude (4 yrs.)	Claude steers a boat around the tub and tries to wash his face.		
Frank (24 yrs.)	Frank adjusts the water temperature and washes himself skillfully.		

FORM 3-1

PATTERNS OF GROWTH

this and other areas of development, variations are normal and expected. Familiarize yourself with the normal *range* for each milestone rather than with a single month or year. The "average" child learns to read at six, but that "average" child is a composite of lots of children who learned at six, a good number who learned at five or seven, and a few who learned at four or eight!

Another warning: Sometimes developmental charts give the impression that children learn these skills and concepts automatically, that we can just sit back and wait for the "unfolding" to take place at four months or three years or whatever. The next section of this chapter will show how far from the truth that is, and why your work with children is so vitally important to their development.

THE INGREDIENTS OF GROWTH

We've seen what kinds of changes occur as children grow up. But what makes these changes happen at all? We're so used to watching children grow, seeing them begin to walk, talk, play, and plan, that we may never think about how this all occurs or about our part in the process.

It's not a simple matter, and even "experts" in child development often disagree about what the ingredients of development are.

One thing we do know. The course of growth is *not* wholly automatic or preprogrammed. Normal, healthy development is the result of a combination of many factors, some within the child and some in the environment. As those who are part of that daily environment, we need to understand these factors and use them to encourage healthy growth in the children we teach.

Three basic ingredients go into children's development: maturation, relationships with people, and experiences with objects. Let's look at them one at a time.

Maturation

Maturation refers to the growth of the brain, the nervous system, the muscles, and other parts of the body. Why doesn't anyone ever try to teach a four-month-old baby to walk? "He's not ready," we say. What we mean is that neither the muscles in his legs nor the pathways from his brain to those legs have grown enough to make walking possible. This process of *maturation* takes time, and it seems that there's not much we can do to hurry the process along.

In many other areas of development, too, physical maturation plays a very important part: toilet training, writing, riding a tricycle. In all these areas, the brain, the central nervous system, and the muscles must develop to a certain point before the child is capable of such achievements.

If a particular child's development lies outside the normal range, there can be many possible causes of this variation:

- Lack of opportunity to practice certain skills can slow development. Children who are *always* confined in cribs are slow to walk, for instance.
- Brain damage, malnutrition, or mental retardation can delay the maturation of the nervous system, causing significant delays in speech, motor development, etc.

- Good or bad social relationships can influence the rate at which a child matures. "Failure-to-thrive" babies are undersized, sickly children whose slow physical growth often seems to be caused by lack of love, not by lack of food.

How can you use your understanding of maturation in your work?

- Be observant in noticing children whose development is outside the normal range.

    Ms. Whitman knew that most four-year-olds are able to hop on one foot. So she was concerned when Allen seemed unable to do so in a game her group was playing. She decided to watch him outside for a few days to see if his development was delayed in other large-motor skills as well.

- Give young children time to grow rather than pushing them into tasks they're not ready for.

    Ms. Dunn has been getting pressured by some parents to introduce reading and writing skills to the three-year-olds. She was able to explain to them that the children were not yet developed enough, physically, intellectually, or emotionally, for these tasks. She showed the parents how play with the flannel board, in the dramatic play area, etc., were helping to build the concept of symbols, and how these would lead to reading. She showed them two clay figures, one made by a three-year-old, the other by a five-year-old. She pointed out the small-motor skill required by the five's work, and its importance as a foundation for writing.

- Provide a rich variety of activities through which children can practice and perfect developing skills.

    A number of the five-year-olds in Mr. Klein's group were struggling to master the use of scissors. He provided daily opportunities for those who were ready to work on this fine-motor skill. The activities ranged from simple to more difficult: cutting "fringe," cutting collage scraps, snipping tiny pieces of tissue for gluing, cutting out figures they had drawn, etc.

Relationships with Other People

Because most children do grow up surrounded by people who care about them, play with them, talk to them, we often don't pause to realize that this human interaction is essential for normal development. It's only when we meet a child who's never had these relationships that we see how devastating their absence can be—not just on social or emotional development, but on physical, cognitive, and language development as well.

What do children get out of their relationships with other people?

- At first, all their basic needs—for food, warmth, comfort—are satisfied by other people (particularly mother).
- Through the satisfaction of these needs, they develop a sense of "basic trust" which helps them explore the world with confidence.
- Much of their early information about the world comes through adults who talk to them, play with them, offer them toys and books.
- Later, by watching adults at work and play, they build up a picture of what

it is to be a man, a woman, a husband, wife, or teacher. They watch how adults solve problems and then try those skills out on their own.
- By testing their wishes and opinions against those of other children and adults, they begin to see the world less exclusively from their own perspective.

How can you use this understanding of the importance of human relationships in your work with children?

- Consciously encourage children to develop a secure attachment to one person in the classroom. Independence can only come after dependence.

    Ms. Barber found that a few children at her day-care center were very clingy early in the morning. If she let them sit on her lap, they usually went off to explore after a short cuddle.

- Rather than setting materials out and just watching, involve yourself with the children, using the materials and talking about them.

    Ms. Cantina's children developed much more creative ways of using the blocks after she spent a few mornings building with them (but on their level!) and showing by her words and actions that this was fun and important.

- Especially in full-day programs, let the children see you as a "real person" with interests and relationships and an identity besides that of teacher.

    Mr. Perez let the children who woke early from naps "hang around" as he folded sheets, made lists, and chatted with the cook.

- Use the information you have about a child's early relationships to understand his or her relationships with the staff.

    Grace had a habit of teasing her teachers. A few observations of Grace and her mother early in the morning showed the staff that Grace's mother tended to "tune out" until Grace annoyed her. By paying lots of attention to Grace when she wasn't teasing, her teachers tried to show her other ways of relating to adults.

- Provide opportunities for children to work with other children, so they can learn to deal with conflicting points of view.

    Ben had never had his opinions contradicted by his indulgent parents. But in the group block-building projects his teachers encouraged, he was forced to discuss, to share, and to compromise.

Experiences with Objects

From the first days and weeks of life, children are actively engaged in exploring the world around them. They look, suck, bang, poke, and squeeze. It drives parents and teachers to distraction sometimes, but this urge to explore is an essential ingredient of normal development. Children learn about the world by acting on it, finding out by trial and error "what will happen if..."

How does this kind of investigation contribute to healthy development?

- By discovering what effect they can have on their world, children begin to develop a sturdy sense of control, mastery, and confidence. They see themselves as people who can do things.

- Their investigations gradually build up new concepts about the world and the objects in it: hardness, softness, size and shape, number.
- Through encountering objects and situations that don't quite fit into what they already know, children are pushed to add new concepts and skills to their repertoire.

How can you use this understanding of the importance of experiences with objects in your work with children?

- Give children time to find out about things, and to master a new skill.

    It took Philip two days to figure out how to do one puzzle. Then he wanted to do it over and over. Realizing how important this feeling of mastery is, Ms. Mendez let him keep working at it rather than giving him unnecessary help, or insisting that he move on to a harder puzzle.

- Provide a daily program that is full of opportunities to learn by active investigation.

    The director of Ms. Simmons' center had given her some autumn pictures to discuss at circle time. She decided to supplement this kind of learning with walks in the woods and collections of leaves, nuts, and dried flowers for the children to sort, play with, and talk about.

- Give children a chance to learn from their mistakes and failures.

    When Charles poured so much juice into his cup that it overflowed, Ms. Quinn was tempted to take over and do it for him. But instead she showed him how to watch the level in the cup and stop before it got too high. The first few times she even marked the proper level on the cup.

- Challenge children to grow by introducing problems that are just beyond their present level of accomplishment.

    Bonnie had been building a house out of long blocks. When these ran out she said, "I can't finish it." Mr. Tanner brought over some other blocks that were half as long and asked her how she could use them. It didn't take Bonnie much time to figure out that two short blocks could do the job of one long one.

THE MANY WAYS OF GROWING

Children's growth can be looked at in two ways. One is to describe how children of a certain age are *alike*—in what ways one three-year-old is like another, for instance. We've been using that perspective so far. Another way of looking at growth is to see how three-year-old Mark is *different* from three-year-old Paula or Jimmy. That's what we want to look at now.

Although your four-year-olds have much more in common with each other than they do with a roomful of teenagers, you know that they are a collection of rugged individualists. Each one has his or her own personality and style. Even twins, while they may look alike, develop distinctive identities. A Growing Program has to be sensitive to this uniqueness. Later in this book, we'll describe some of the ways to plan activities around individual differences. But first we need to look at how and when these differences come about.

Every parent knows how early in life children begin to demonstrate their

DO IT YOURSELF

Take some time to think about how the *ingredients of development* actually contribute to children's growth. Here are several new skills that your children may have acquired. Think of a way in which each "ingredient" (maturation, relationships, and experiences) might have contributed to a child's reaching that goal.

Example: Charlie has just made a dinosaur out of clay.
- *Maturation:* He needed to acquire the necessary strength and coordination to form the clay.
- *Relationships with people:* He needed to trust an adult who could help and cheer him up if he failed.
- *Experiences with objects:* He needed to have played with clay (or similar substances) to know how to shape it, bend it, hold it. He has to have made balls, cylinders, and other shapes.

1. Felicia has just called her friend on the telephone.
   - *Maturation:* She needed to have developed the coordination required to dial the phone.
   - *Relationships with people:* She needed to have learned how to make friends and enjoy contact with them. She needs to know how to talk to people on the phone.
   - *Experiences with objects:* She has learned the proper procedure to make the phone work, *and* how to read numbers.

2. Anthony has learned to read.
   - *Maturation:*
   - *Relationships with people:*
   - *Experiences with objects:*

3. Greg has just drawn his first "person."
   - *Maturation:*
   - *Relationships with people:*
   - *Experiences with objects:*

4. Tanya and Walter have built a fort.
   - *Maturation:*
   - *Relationships with people:*
   - *Experiences with objects:*

FORM 3-2

individuality. Researchers have even observed distinct differences in cuddliness, activity level, and sleep patterns in newborn babies! Parents quickly learn that Pamela likes to be rocked to sleep, and that (unlike his brother) Alex can't stand to be bathed.

It's easy to see how these early differences can influence later ones. A child begins life with a certain kind of body build and temperament. She or he lives with a certain kind of family, which may react to her or his basic temperament positively or negatively. Because of these reactions, she or he is exposed to certain experiences and not exposed to others. The effect of *these* experiences influences the later experiences she or he chooses or doesn't choose . . . and so on.

Most of the time, these chains of events simply result in normal variations and individual differences in growth. In extreme cases, they may result in delayed or abnormal development.

Let's look at two children who are now in the same group of four-year-olds. Their teachers describe Velma and Margie as "different as night and day." How did they get to be that way?

Velma

Velma was the Madisons' first and only child. From the first week of her life she was thin, wiry, and vigorously active. The doctor described Velma as "colicky"; her bursts of energy were usually followed by fretful crying and wailing. During these fussy times, Velma's mother soothed her by walking her around, trying one thing after another to distract her.	place in family body type parent's responses
As Velma got older, she was continually "on the go," a tireless and daring explorer. Her mother let her creep all over the house and gave her a special drawer of pots and pans to play with. Still, Velma was easily frustrated and would collapse in tears when things didn't go right.	style of learning parent's responses
When Velma was three, a serious illness confined her to bed for several months. At first she was furious at the restriction on her activities, but her mother helped her channel her energy into other areas. Velma became expert at puzzles and construction toys. She tried to do them as fast as she could, one after another. When one was too hard, she would angrily push it aside and reach for another.	health parent's responses new avenues
At four, Velma entered a day-care center. She made a new friend, a child who was very different from Velma—who slowly persisted at a difficult task. Margie would stick to something until she got it right. Since Velma wanted so much to be Margie's friend, she became less inclined to jump from one thing to another.	change in environment other people motivation

Margie

Margie was the youngest of six children. She was a chubby, placid baby who seldom cried. She spent most of her time in a playpen in the living room, taking in the activities of her noisy, busy family. Margie was slow to walk and talk. Her parents weren't too concerned, though, because she was so contented and easygoing. When she did cry (which was rare), someone was always around to give her a cookie or a lollipop.	place in family body type environment family's reactions

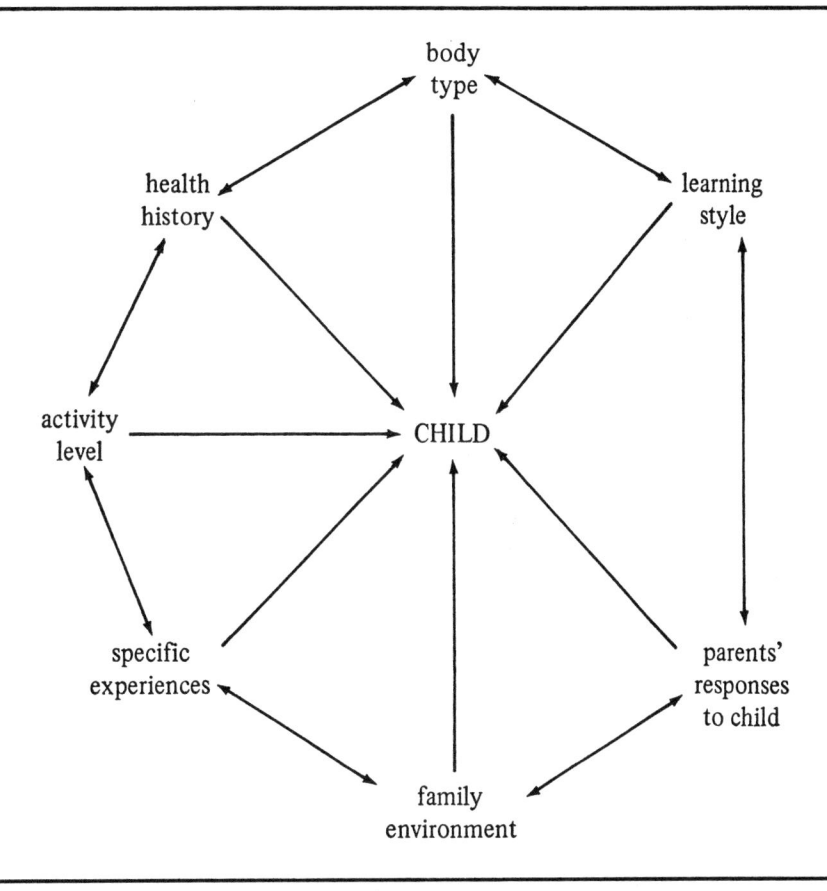

FIGURE 3-1

[Diagram showing CHILD at center with bidirectional arrows connecting to: body type, learning style, parents' responses to child, family environment, specific experiences, activity level, health history]

As she got older, Margie would get food on her own whenever she was unhappy. She turned from chubby to fat.

When Margie was three, her mother got a job and found a day-care center for Margie. Contented as always, she made a good adjustment from the start. But her teachers were concerned about her obesity and her general passivity. Margie was *too* contented.

The staff referred the family to a pediatrician for recommendations about a diet for Margie. At the center they saw to it that she munched on carrot sticks instead of cupcakes. As Margie slowly began to slim down, she seemed to become a bit more physically active. Her friendship with Velma also seemed to bring out a more vigorous streak. Even though Margie normally followed Velma's lead, she also began to start more things herself rather than wait for someone else to take the initiative. Although she remained quiet and pleasant, her motor and language skills increased considerably.

Margin notes: style of coping with stress; change in environment; reactions of others; change in environment; physical changes; learning style

At four, Velma and Margie are distinct individuals. This individuality seems to have begun at birth, with their differences in body build and activity level. But we've seen how many other factors influenced the kind of four-year-olds they became. Figure 3-1 shows some of the combinations of influences that produce the unique child you teach.

DO IT YOURSELF

Choose two children in your group who are the same age but who are very different from each other. Write three or four sentences describing each child. Then, using the categories below, write down some of the things that you know about each child. (You probably will have some blanks; that's all right.) After you have finished, go back and check the items that seem to you to have been strong influences on this child's development.

This activity will require a lot of thought about each child. You may find it easier and more interesting if you talk it over with someone else.

	Child A	*Child B*
Description		
Body build and activity level		
Health history		
Family environment (size, problems, kind of discipline, etc.)		
Child's learning style, way of reacting to stress		
Relationships with other people (adults, children)		
Other experiences		

FORM 3-3

PATTERNS OF GROWTH

In the cases of Velma and Margie, we've seen how their development was influenced by the people and experiences they met as they grew. Children certainly are individuals by the time they reach your classroom, but that doesn't mean you are powerless to affect their growth. The way you respond to them and the kinds of experiences you provide for them can be turning points in their development (like Margie's diet or Velma's friendship).

A CLOSER LOOK

Let's take a closer look at the young children you teach.

- What kind of behavior and growth can you expect in the years from two to five?
- How can you use your knowledge of development to respond to the special needs of these young children?

This section will answer those questions.

To take this "closer look," it's helpful to divide development into four growth areas:

- social-emotional development
- perceptual-motor development
- cognitive development
- language development.

Each area of development is intertwined with the others, but by looking at one area at a time, we can focus more clearly on the *kinds of growth* we see in young children. As we describe each growth area, you'll notice

- the same *direction* of development
- the same *ingredients* of development.

Of course, this brief section isn't intended to be a course in child development or a complete description of all aspects of growth in the young child. It's meant to be a *guide* and a *springboard*. In the "Resources" at the end of this chapter you'll find a number of interesting, readable books to extend this brief introduction to an important and endlessly fascinating subject. However, there are some useful guidelines here. Using your own ingenuity and the tools in the next chapter, you'll be able to use this knowledge of areas of development to understand and plan for your children, meeting them where they are and stimulating their potential for growth.

Social-Emotional Development

This growth area focuses on the child's feelings about himself or herself and relationships with others.

Infants begin life with no awareness that they are separate people. Later, many toddlers become small tyrants whose every whim must be instantly obeyed!

But gradually they begin to balance their own wishes against the rights and needs of the people they love. They become competent, caring persons in a social world.

Tasks and Goals

In the preschool years, children

- develop and maintain a sense of themselves as competent and valuable people
- begin to form attachments to adults other than parents
- continue their efforts to develop internal control of their behavior
- begin to play and work cooperatively with other children
- begin to recognize the needs and feelings of others
- express and explore their creativity.

Let's look at young children as they work on some of these tasks.

GROWING IN COMPETENCE

Everyone but Chris was ready to go outside. He stood near his cubby, trying to poke his small jacket buttons through the buttonholes.

"Here, Chris," the student teacher said kindly, putting an arm around him. "Let me help you with that."

"No!" Chris answered angrily. "I can do it myself!"

Why is Chris being so stubborn? One of the strongest forces in young children's development is their desire to do things for themselves, to make an impact on their world. At times they may go to extremes, refusing help when it's obviously needed, or saying *no* simply because an adult says *yes*. Their independence is so newly won that they're afraid of losing it, of being taken over by adults. In time, most children become able to ask for and accept help when they need it, and to work on their own when they're able.

At two, a child may
- react to adult suggestions with extreme negativism
- alternate between stubborn independence and clinging dependence.

At five, the child may
- attempt difficult projects with more realistic confidence in his or her ability
- ask other children or adults for assistance with specific tasks.

Using what you know, you may

- expect young children to have periods of negativism and "unreasonable" independence
- provide chances for children to do things on their own, while giving tactful help when needed
- watch for growing self-confidence in the children you teach.

FORMING BONDS WITH OTHER PEOPLE

Katie didn't want her mother to go. Like a barnacle, she clung to her mother's knees as Mrs. Campbell tried to back out the door. Katie's teacher carried her over to the rocker, dried her tears, and looked at a book with her until she felt better.

PATTERNS OF GROWTH

Why was Katie so upset? One of the most important tasks of the first three years of life is the formation of a secure and loving attachment to one person—usually the mother. At first, children need their mothers' actual presence to assure them that she still exists; later, they are able to keep her in mind when she's away. After this primary bond is formed, children become able to move beyond it to relationships with teachers and other children. But at times of stress they need physical comfort and support from mother or another loving caretaker.

At two, a child may
- view strangers with a suspicious eye, alternating with indiscriminate trust
- scream and sob for hours when left by mother.

At five, the child may
- form warm friendships with people outside the family
- cry for mother only when ill or upset.

Using what you know, you may

- expect some distress at separation, especially with younger children or those under some stress
- give children a chance to establish new bonds with the adults and children at the center
- support children's progress in using these attachments as a secure base from which to explore their environment.

LEARNING INTERNAL CONTROLS

Harriet and Jack reached the swing at the same time. Jack sat on it quickly.
"Give it to me!" said Harriet.
"No way!" said Jack.
Harriet grabbed Jack by the hair and began pounding him violently on the back.

Why does Harriet resort to force? We adults get angry, too, when someone frustrates or insults us. But we've learned more acceptable ways of expressing and redirecting those angry feelings and other impulses. Children hit, kick, or throw things when they don't have any other alternatives. With support from caring adults, and with growth in language and thinking skills, children become more able to tolerate frustration, accept delays, and talk about their feelings instead of *acting* them out.

At two, a child may
- hit or scream at any threat to his or her belongings or body
- be unable to deal with conflict situations without adult help.

At five, the child may
- resort to hitting only after first trying to explain, convince, cajole; or only when *very* upset
- act as a "peacemaker" in a dispute involving other children.

Using what you know, you may

- expect young children to lose control when frustrated or threatened
- support children in learning to use more socially acceptable ways of handling conflict
- watch for indications of readiness to solve conflicts independently.

Perceptual-Motor Development

This growth area focuses on the child's control over his or her body and its movements.

Infants begin life with little control over their own bodies. Their arms and legs jerk in random movements. Beginning with the larger muscles, they bring the parts of their bodies under better control. They feel competence and pleasure in using their bodies in both vigorous physical activity and finer movements like drawing and cutting. Their bodies become instruments that respond to their needs and plans.

Tasks and Goals

In the preschool years, children

- enjoy using their bodies to express their feelings and reach their goals
- begin to develop the muscular control needed for writing and drawing
- increase coordination of senses and motor apparatus
- become more competent in activities requiring balance and rhythm
- coordinate separate movements into smooth, integrated wholes
- explore the world with all their senses.

Let's look at young children as they work on some of these tasks.

INCREASING LARGE-MUSCLE SKILLS

Rainy days were always difficult in Ms. Meyer's group. Randy was typical. He'd come racing through the door, give a flying leap into the middle of the room, and hop around the table on one foot. The more his teacher tried to settle him down, the more wound up he and the others would get.

Why can't they sit still? Young children have an exuberant delight in using their bodies that we adults have largely forgotten. A baby learning to walk will practice until he or she drops from exhaustion. The children you teach are still mastering the skills of running, climbing, jumping. And they often haven't mastered the equally important skill of *inhibiting* or *controlling* these activities. Long periods of quiet leave them itchy, ready to shout and race about.

At two, a child may
- practice simple motor actions, like jumping, over and over
- become cross and fretful if required to sit quietly for more than a few minutes.

At five, the child may
- be able to remain in a group for longer periods
- use large muscles in complex, skilled games (throwing a ball, riding a bike).

Using what you know, you may

- expect young children to have a greater need for vigorous physical activity than adults
- provide frequent opportunities for children to "let off steam" outdoors or inside (with climber, mats, dancing)
- look for growth in control and in skill at physical activities.

PATTERNS OF GROWTH

LEARNING FINE-MUSCLE CONTROL

Allen was trying to build a house out of small, snap-together blocks. The pieces had to be fitted together exactly right in order for them to lock. Again and again he tried, gritting his teeth as he pushed the red and white pieces together. It just wasn't working.

Why is Allen having such a hard time? Generally, children gain control of large muscles (shoulders, trunk) before smaller ones (wrist, fingers). And there's lots of variation among children in their fine-motor skill. Even when they know what they want to do, young children often can't make their fingers do it. Whether it's printing letters or coloring inside the lines or making toothpick constructions, fine-muscle dexterity (and the concentration it requires) develops slowly in the early years.

At two, a child may
- paint with a large brush in big, up-and-down strokes
- string a few large beads and give up quickly.

At five, the child may
- draw more representational pictures
- spend longer periods working with small construction materials.

Using what you know, you may

- understand the frustration young children feel when faced with tasks that they're not ready for
- provide a variety of activities (art, construction, cooking) to develop fine-motor skills
- watch for signs of interest in more complex fine-motor tasks.

Cognitive Development

This growth area focuses on the child's thinking skills: memory, information processing, problem solving.

Infants begin life with few tools to understand the objects and events that surround them. Through countless concrete experiences of touching, tasting, and seeing, they grow in knowledge and mastery of the world. They begin to be able to use their past experience to help organize, generalize, and plan for the future.

Tasks and Goals

In the preschool years, children

- develop critical thinking, creative thinking, and problem-solving skills
- begin to understand the meaning of symbols
- explore the relationship between appearance and reality
- develop their ability to plan, follow a plan, and evaluate the results
- increase their understanding of causes and effects
- develop their awareness of similarities and differences in objects and people
- extend their awareness and knowledge of their social and natural environment.

Let's look at young children as they work on some of these tasks.

LEARNING TO SOLVE PROBLEMS

The wagon was stuck. It just wouldn't fit through the door of the "fort" Anna and Ted had made in the play yard. For several minutes, Anna shoved it and kicked it. No luck.
"I know what!" she said. "Let's get more blocks and make our fort bigger."

Why couldn't they see the problem right away? The growth of problem-solving skills is a long process. Young children are still developing a "scientific" notion of cause and effect. Anna and Ted know something is wrong, but their concrete, trial-and-error solutions depend more on "magic" (kicking the wheels) than on logical analysis. At first, they don't see that the relative sizes of the wagon and the fort's doorway are the cause of the problem. When they do, Anna comes up with a way to solve it.

At two, a child may
- give up in frustration when an obvious or "magical" solution fails
- doggedly persist with an unsuccessful solution.

At five, the child may
- actively try to figure out the cause of the problem first
- be flexible in trying out a number of solutions.

Using what you know, you may

- expect young children to be somewhat concrete and illogical in their ideas about cause and effect
- expect frustration when solutions don't work
- watch for signs of growth in ability to analyze problems and think of solutions
- create an environment where each child is challenged to solve problems that are within his or her present capacity.

UNDERSTANDING THE MEANING OF SYMBOLS

Leo held up his hand. Andre, on the tricycle, kept coming.
"Hey!" bellowed Leo, pointing at his own upraised hand. "My hand is the stop!"

What does Leo mean? Leo's beginning to understand and use a very important idea—the notion that certain things (hand signals, signs, pictures, letters) can *represent* or *symbolize* other things. Reading and writing are one product of this kind of development. The children you teach haven't gotten quite that far yet, but they are becoming aware of symbols in more concrete ways, starting with play situations. And because these symbols are concrete, children often confuse them with real "things."

At two, a child may
- "become" a daddy by putting on a necktie
- recognize his or her photograph taped to his or her cubby.

At five, the child may
- recognize his or her own written name and those of his or her friends.
- ask the teacher to write signs or labels for his or her buildings.

PATTERNS OF GROWTH

Using what you know, you may

- expect young children occasionally to confuse symbols and the things they stand for, fantasy and reality
- expect that children will need lots of concrete experiences with symbols (in dramatic play, in games, etc.) before they're ready to use them in reading or writing
- watch for increasing skill at, and interest in, using abstract signs and symbols.

SEPARATING APPEARANCES FROM REALITY

Larry glowered as he looked from his short, wide glass to Arthur's tall, narrow one. His teacher had poured the same amount of juice into each.

"No fair! He has more than me!"

"It's just the same, Larry," said his teacher. "I'll show you."

She poured Larry's juice into a glass like Arthur's.

"Well," said Larry, "*now* it's the same. It wasn't before!"

Why can't Larry understand? The world is full of things and people that keep their underlying identity even when their appearance changes. Mother is still mother with new glasses; five beans are still five beans whether they're bunched together or spread apart; and one cup of juice is the same amount whether it's in a wide glass or a narrow one. These concepts are simple for adults, but difficult for young children. To understand that things can stay the same even when they look different takes time and many experiences with objects and events.

At two, a child may
- burst into tears when he or she sees the teacher with a new haircut
- suspect that a clay figure really *can* talk

At five, the child may
- understand that masks, haircuts, etc., don't change the "real" person
- want "more" clay if he or she has a round piece and his or her friend has a long snake.

Using what you know, you may

- expect misunderstandings and fears based on a confusion between surface appearances and underlying "realities"
- create a setting in which children can extend their knowledge through active experimentation
- observe growth in children's ability to go beyond immediate appearances to see the unchanging (identity, number, quantity).

Language Development

This growth area focuses on the child's use of words to express his or her own feelings and ideas and to understand others.

Infants' cries and gurgles are their first communication with their adoring parents. Through many experiences, children begin to see that words are labels for the objects and people in their life. With their first words, they begin to discover the power language has: with words, they can make sense of their world and communicate it to other people.

Tasks and Goals

In the preschool years, children

- become more adept at using the rules of language
- develop their ability to use words to express their needs, feelings, and thoughts
- guide their thinking and action through language
- increase the size and complexity of their vocabulary
- develop interest in the meaning and sound of words.

Let's look at young children as they work on some of these tasks.

LEARNING THE RULES OF LANGUAGE

"Miss Smith!" Brendan rushed into the room excitedly. "Guess what! I goed to the circus with my daddy!"

Why do children make mistakes like this? One of the most remarkable achievements of the early years is a child's language acquisition. He or she seems to learn how to speak, not just through imitation, but by picking up the *underlying rules* of the language. "Mistakes" are often logical extensions of such rules: if "I stopped" and "I jumped," why not "I goed"? Through hearing and participating in many hours of talk, children correct these rules, learn new ones, and become competent language users.

At two, a child may
- make frequent "mistakes" in language use
- use language that is not understood except by the family.

At five, the child may
- be aware of his or her own mistakes and correct them
- use speech that, though containing some errors, can be easily understood.

Using what you know, you may

- recognize "mistakes" in children's speech as a normal part of the process of learning a language
- help children become fluent speakers by talking to them and with them rather than correcting every error
- look for signs of increasing correctness and awareness of language.

EXPRESSING FEELINGS THROUGH WORDS

Amy and Paul stood glowering at each other in front of the one red tricycle.
"*I* had it!"
"No! *I* had it first!"
"I won't ask you to my birthday."
"So what! You're dumb, anyway. I hate you!"

PATTERNS OF GROWTH

Why do they talk to each other like that? Before children learn to talk, they have no way of expressing their angry feelings except through crying and hitting. Language opens up a whole new world to them—words are powerful tools that can be used to command, to get, to shock, to hurt. There's a kind of magic in words, and young children are just beginning to try it out. It's a big step. Gradually, they learn to use words to discuss and negotiate conflicts as well as to express emotion. That's an even bigger step.

At two, a child may
- use nonverbal ways of expressing emotion
- when using language, employ simple words for feelings ("No"; "Love you").

At five, the child may
- use words to express more complex or conflicting emotions ("I'm sad and happy, too")
- use words to *solve* problems.

Using what you know, you may

- expect young children to experiment with both "good" and "bad" language
- recognize "bad" talk as a sign of progress from more physical means of communicating
- work with children on using words to solve conflicts and to express feelings.

USING WORDS TO GUIDE ACTION

The children were sitting at tables with puzzles and small toys. In the quiet, there was Henry, talking to himself.

"Here it goes—this way. No, this way. It's a big one—a big one, yes it is. Turn it around; nope. This way? Little corner, cookie corner, cookie cutter. Oops, here it goes..."

Why do children talk to themselves? Adults who expect a group of three or four-year-olds to work as quietly as their older siblings may not understand how children use language. Spoken words provide young children with a way to *comment on* and *guide* actions. You'll notice that many of them, like Henry, keep up a running monologue, especially if they're absorbed in play. It's one way they have to control and plan their activities, and to practice the language they're acquiring.

At two, a child may
- repeat words and phrases over and over as he or she falls asleep at naptime
- talk over, around, and through other children as he or she plays.

At five, the child may
- spontaneously invent rhymes and nonsense words
- talk aloud to himself or herself only when absorbed in a particularly difficult task.

Using what you know, you may

- welcome this so-called "egocentric speech" as a sign of language fluency
- set up an environment in which children's talking to themselves and each other will be an asset, not a hindrance to work.

DO IT YOURSELF

Knowing about development is only useful if you apply your knowledge—make it part of your teaching "map." So let's take a look at one developmental task, and then take an even closer look at your children.

1. Select one of the developmental tasks listed under a growth area: social-emotional (page 37), perceptual-motor (page 40), cognitive (page 41), and language development (page 44). Pick one you'd like to know more about. (If you are working with other teachers, make sure you haven't picked the same task as someone else.)

2. Using the "Resources" for this chapter, do some extra reading about that task.

3. Over the next week, watch your children with this developmental task in mind. Make notes on at least three instances when what a child was doing seemed related to growth on your developmental task.
    For example, if the task is learning internal controls (social-emotional development), you might note that Mercedes called for you when Tom took her block, rather than socking him.

4. If you are working in a group, prepare to summarize the main ideas in your reading for the others. Use your observations to illustrate some of the points.

FORM 3-4

Putting Growth Back Together

Now that we've looked at development in four separate areas, let's put it together again. For the sake of clarity, we talked about social-emotional, perceptual-motor, cognitive, and language development as if they were separate processes. They're not.

Eddie can't hammer a nail without first thinking about it; Sharon can't tell her mother she loves her without feeling emotion. Development in one area influences other areas; difficulty in one area affects others as well.

If a three-year-old can't sit through a group story time, his or her development in all four growth areas may be causing this behavior.

- *Social-emotional:* he or she may still need frequent physical contact with an adult.
- *Perceptual-motor:* he or she may be physically unready to sit still that long.
- *Cognitive:* the "plot" of the story may be too complex.
- *Language:* he or she may not grasp the vocabulary in the story.

Thinking and Feeling

In particular, cognitive and emotional development—"thinking" and "feeling"—are often spoken of as if they were separate processes, and as if they could be separated in educational settings, too. But observant teachers can come up with many examples of the influence of thinking on feeling, and of feeling on thinking.

- Danny's interest in numbers (thinking) is a reflection of his love and admiration (feeling) for his older brother.
- Emilio isn't afraid of policemen (feeling) once he finds out what they do (thinking).
- Anna's worries about her family (feeling) get in the way of her learning (thinking).
- Ursula looks through books (thinking) because then she gets to sit on Ms. Poole's lap (feeling).
- Zachary's feeling of frustration (feeling) when faced with a tough puzzle pushes him to figure out a way of doing it right (thinking).

Children learn best in an atmosphere of love and security, and they feel more secure as they acquire knowledge about, and tools to deal with, the world. A Growing Program creates a climate where each child can develop as a feeling, thinking, moving, communicating person.

RESOURCES

Almy, M. *Young Children's Thinking.* New York: Teacher's College Press, Columbia University, 1966.
   The introduction is an especially good overview of intellectual growth.

Fraiberg, S. *The Magic Years.* New York: Charles Scribner's Sons, 1968.
   Children see things differently than adults. A book about the inner world of the child, written with warmth and understanding.

Gesell, A., et al. *The First Five Years of Life: A Guide to the Study of the Pre-school Child.* New York: Harper and Row, 1940.

This classic book is an easy-to-read guide to developmental milestones.

Highberger, R., and Schramm, C. *Child Development for Day Care Workers.* Boston: Houghton Mifflin, 1976.

A practically oriented guide to the major theories of child development, with implications for day-care programs. Emphasizes the use of developmental information in understanding individual children.

Landreth, C. *Preschool Learning and Teaching.* New York: Harper and Row, 1972.

Clear, simple explanation of *why* children learn and *what* they can learn. Using guidelines like "From sensing to sorting and symbolizing," Landreth shows where children are moving and how you can help them get there.

Spock, B. *Baby and Child Care.* New York: Pocket Books, 1968.

Although written for parents of young children, this perennial favorite also presents teachers with a useful and reassuring picture of developmental milestones.

4

The Growing Child

OBSERVING AND RECORDING

CHALLENGE YOURSELF

You may believe
- Each child is different. But can you say exactly *how* Tom is different from Steve?
- Teaching should be tailored to each child's special needs. But can you describe Andy's needs, Susan's needs, Mario's needs?
- Children are learning all the time. But do you have a way to keep track of Renata's learning, Rosalie's learning, Jack's learning?

SKILLS IN THIS CHAPTER

- Using growth areas
- Using parent information
- Collecting samples of children's work
- Observing children's behavior
- Getting answers to questions about children:
  o "What's the child like?"
  o "What's wrong?"
  o "What does the child know?"
- Recording children's behavior
  o advantages of recording
  o tools for recording

USING GROWTH AREAS

Once you know what healthy development is, and how children generally develop in each area, you're ready to put that knowledge to work for you and your children.

You'll find this knowledge useful in every part of your program. But an understanding of the process of development is especially helpful in *focusing on a child*—zeroing in on where he or she is, and where he or she is going.

Children Are Alike

In some ways, as we've said, all children are alike. They're all growing in about the same direction. That's why some people talk about the "Terrible Twos" and the "Aggressive Fours." That's why we can state certain "beliefs about children" (they're curious, they learn by doing, etc.) and find that they're generally true.

Children Are Different

But children are also different from one another. Within the general framework of development children grow

- at their own rate
- in their own way
- according to their own pattern.

For example:

Arthur draws skillfully but doesn't have the language to describe his pictures.

Jenny is a "doer"—she loves to race, jump, and chatter with her friends. She couldn't care less about learning to count.

Manny worries the staff because all his skills seem to be developing more slowly than those of other four-year-olds. Yet his happy disposition endears him to everyone.

One child may be ahead of his peers in language development and social-emotional skills but may lag in other areas. Another child's development may be even, but slow.

THE GROWING CHILD

MAKING A PROFILE OF GROWTH

As teachers, we need to know where the child "is": we need a description of his or her unique pattern and style of development at one moment in time. By assessing each child's current functioning in all growth areas and comparing it to (1) the functioning of other children that age *and* (2) his or her own functioning a month or a year ago, we can gradually focus in on an *individualized picture* of that child. That picture can be called a "growth profile."

A growth profile is *your* understanding of the child's strengths and weaknesses. The profile is drawn from many different sources: the child's work, your observations in the classroom, parents' reports, and your knowledge of child development. You will probably never write down all this information in one spot. It is too complex, and it changes from one day to the next. But you can put it together in your own thinking, and *this* is a growth profile—your changing picture of the child's growth.

What good is a picture like that? It's at the core of a Growing Program, because with it you can begin to plan a program that is responsive to the unique strengths, interests, and needs of growing children. *Without it,* you run the risk of planning a rigid program aimed at some mythical "average four-year-old" that will certainly bore or frustrate many of the children you teach because the "average" four-year-old doesn't exist.

By developing such a complete picture of every child, you can help yourself

- pick up potential developmental problems—lags in speech or motor development, for instance
- individualize your program, because you understand that each child grows and learns in his or her own way
- gear activities to the special skills and interests of some children
- group children according to their need for extra help in certain skill areas
- change your program as the year progresses to accommodate to the growing capabilities of your group.

It's important to remember that the child's growth profile is constantly changing as he or she encounters new experiences. We don't want to "peg" children in September when in fact they may be very different by November. Assessing children's growth, then, is a *continuous,* ongoing process. How do we do it?

Getting a Growth Profile

Three sources of information will help you keep up to date on each child's growth profile:

1. parent information
2. samples of the child's work
3. observations of the child's behavior.

This chapter will help you use each source.

Parent Information

Children are part of a wider world that includes present and past experiences at home as well as what happens at school. Their present growth profile is built on the sum total of their interactions with people, objects, and environments. The more you know about those interactions, the better prepared you'll be to meet each child where he or she is. How can you learn more about them? One way is through the application forms completed by parents. Another is through informal contacts with the family. Both approaches are discussed briefly here, but for more thinking about how to build relationships to parents so they will feel comfortable sharing the information you need, read Chapter 12, "Growing Together: Parents, Children, and Staff."

APPLICATION FORMS

Even before a child enters your program, a well-designed application form can give you useful information about individual growth patterns. Questions about the child's past experiences (pleasant and unpleasant), skills, interests, worries—all can help you understand the child's current behavior and plan a program to take individual factors into account.

Figure 4–1 is a section of an application form sent in by the parents of a four-year-old boy. We've circled some answers that add to the teacher's knowledge of his growth profile and suggested why they might be important.

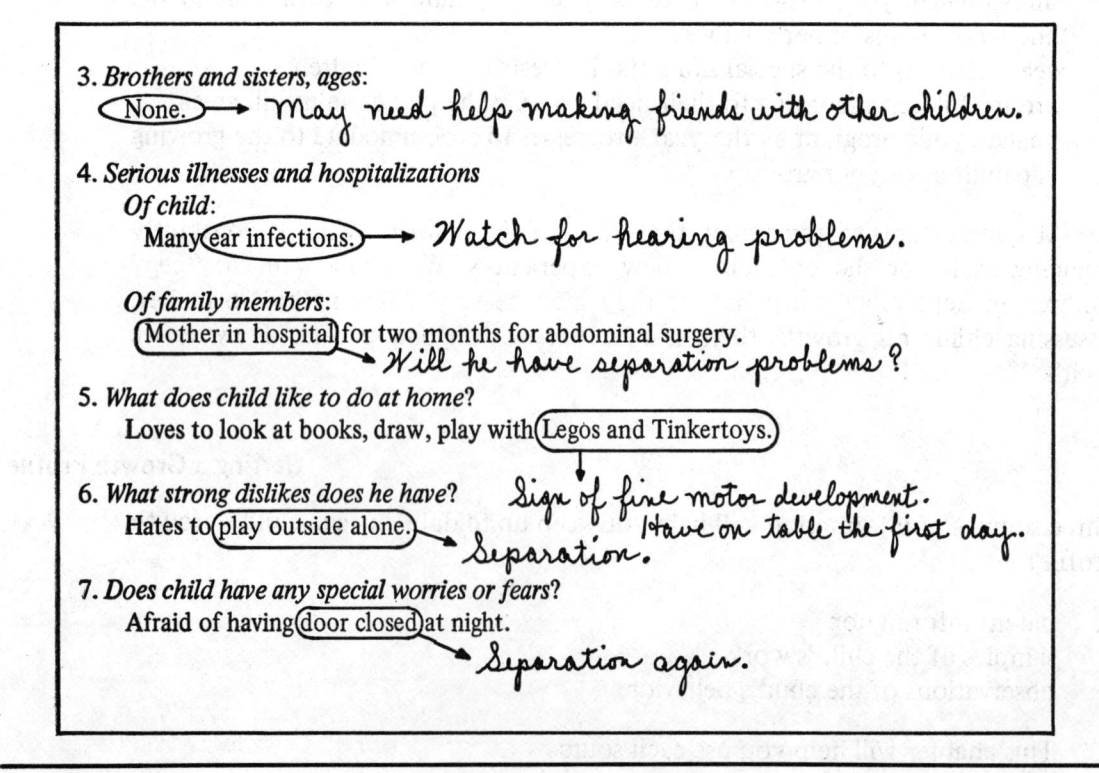

---

3. *Brothers and sisters, ages:*
   (None.) → May need help making friends with other children.

4. *Serious illnesses and hospitalizations*
   Of child:
   Many (ear infections.) → Watch for hearing problems.

   Of family members:
   (Mother in hospital) for two months for abdominal surgery.
   → Will he have separation problems?

5. *What does child like to do at home?*
   Loves to look at books, draw, play with (Legos and Tinkertoys.)
   → Sign of fine motor development.
   Have on table the first day.

6. *What strong dislikes does he have?*
   Hates to (play outside alone.) → Separation.

7. *Does child have any special worries or fears?*
   Afraid of having (door closed) at night.
   → Separation again.

FIGURE 4–1

DO IT YOURSELF

Often, the crucial information on application forms gets lost in a file drawer. We've found it helpful to summarize this information on a separate sheet or note card. This can be kept in your classroom planning file.

Student teachers: With your supervising teacher's permission, take this opportunity to familiarize yourself with background information on several children. What classroom behavior does this background information help you to understand better?

1. Look back over your children's application forms. Select two or three, perhaps those of children you've been concerned about.
2. Using the headings on the form below, summarize the information on the applications.
3. Keep the summaries available for your next discussion of these children.

Name _____ Date of birth _____

1. Special medical or physical concerns:

2. Family information
   a. Family and household members:

   b. Current family situation:

   c. Important family history:

3. Unusual developmental patterns:

4. Likes, dislikes, fears:

5. Other:

FORM 4-1

INFORMAL CONTACTS

Once the child enters the program, informal contacts with parents at the beginning or end of the day will keep you up to date on progress or difficulty at home.

> "I've noticed that Joe is reading the words on cereal boxes," his mother proudly announces.

Many developmental advances first happen in the secure atmosphere of home. Joe may not have shown any interest in reading at school, but after talking to his mother, you might plan some activities to help Joe consolidate what he's learning. On the other hand, if Joe has seemed tense and resistant to directions lately, you might look at his mother's message in a different light. Is it possible that she's pushing him into work for which he's not ready?

You might need to encourage parents to share anecdotes and information with you. Here are some things you could try:

- When the parent picks up the child, take a minute to ask a question like "How's the new baby?" and "How's Jerry getting along with her?"
- If the child is bused to the center, establish lines of communication by telephone or notes. You'll have to initiate this; often the parent won't. But you, the parents, and the child will all benefit. See pp. 234–235 for suggestions for getting started.

Application forms and parent reports provide important clues to the child's behavior. However, these are just the beginning.

Samples of the Child's Work

A folder containing samples of a child's work is a rich source of information about development. You can see

- recurring patterns
- skills
- progress and changes.

WHAT TO COLLECT

Here are some kinds of samples to collect, and just a few of the ways in which they can enrich your understanding of the child's growth profile:

Kinds of samples
- child's drawings, paintings

- stories child dictates to teacher

- child-made "books"—"Things I Like"
- sketches or photographs of block building (drawn by teachers)

Growth profile information
- feelings about self and others, fine-motor skills, use of color, growth of representation
- language development, interests, memory, fears, and pleasures
- classification skills, interests, fine-motor skills, concept formation
- inventiveness, complexity, spatial relations

DO IT YOURSELF

Here are two drawings from a child's folder, one done in September and the second in October of the following year. What obvious changes do you see, and what sort of growth do they show?

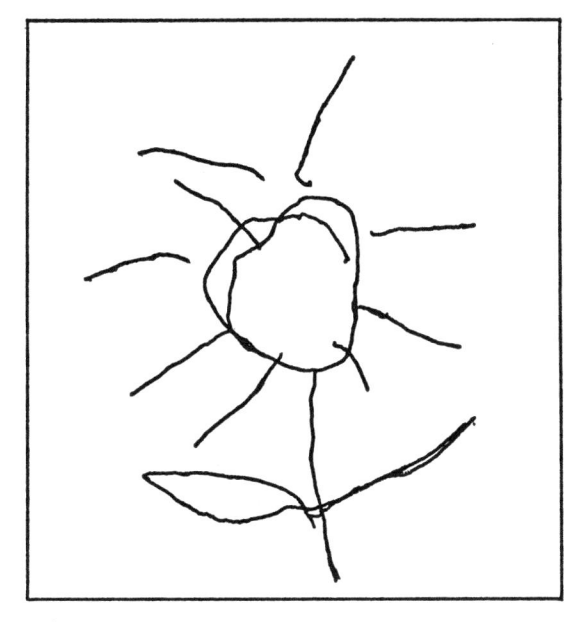

Changes: _____
_____
_____

Kind of growth
  Representation: _____
_____
_____

Detail: _____
_____

Fine-motor skills: _____
_____

Action: _____
_____
_____

FORM 4-2

- tapes of child's voice
- photographs of the child at work
- speech development, fluency, vocabulary, self-concept
- general appearance, size (relative to other children), interests, moods

HOW TO COLLECT SAMPLES

Some teachers find the following method an efficient way to collect samples:

1. Mark every work product (painting, story, collage, etc.) with child's name, date, and description if child provides one—"It's snow"; "A scary monster in the woods."
2. Don't send every item home with the child (but be sensitive to his or her desire to share his or her efforts with the family).
3. On Fridays, spend a few minutes going over the things you've saved. Select a few for each child and file them in a folder with a brief comment on the back if necessary.
4. Bring the folder to staff meetings when discussing the child.

This file of samples of children's work adds to the information obtained from parents. But it's still not enough. The most important kind of work is yet to come.

Observing and Recording Children's Behavior

Parent information and samples of the child's work are helpful, but if you want a really accurate picture of a child's growth, *first-hand observation* of behavior is absolutely essential.

HOW OBSERVING HELPS

Sometimes we can get so busy *teaching* children that we forget to really look at them.

Watch a child at play, at work, in many moods, with different people. By writing down what you see, you get a series of "snapshots" of that child. Gradually, you'll gather a tremendous amount of information about his or her particular pattern of growth. Then you can use that information to help you plan a better program for each child. Maybe he or she needs:

- special exercises for eye-hand coordination
- a story about something he or she likes
- more vigorous outdoor play
- time with one teacher
- extra help in learning to dress him- or herself
- a chance to develop early reading ability.

GUIDELINES FOR OBSERVING

1. *Get the "observing habit."* The first step in observing children is to get into the habit of stepping back and looking—*really* looking—at what's happening in your class.

THE GROWING CHILD

Let's say you're over by the easel, mixing paint. You're trying to get the cap off the jar, thinking about whether to add some white to the blue, and planning to begin clean up in about ten minutes. Stop. Take a look at the children at that easel. Really *see* them—who they are, what they're doing, how they're doing it.

Look at Charley—See him carefully wiping his brush and dabbing the paint on in small, precise spots. See him add one spot to each corner and see the smile of satisfaction on his face. See him look over at Lydia, without speaking, but eager for some recognition of his masterpiece.

Now look at Lydia. Look at her body—its tension, its determination. Look at the colors she's chosen. The vivid red, the bright yellow. (See her hand on the brush, clutching it tightly.) See the brush strokes she makes, sweeping up and down, going off the paper entirely.

What have you done? You haven't spent hours of time, and you haven't filled pages with notes (though writing it down will help). You *have* begun to get the "observing habit." The next steps will show you how to develop that habit.

2. *Use a team approach.* Observing children, and writing down what you see, is a big job. Your day is filled with many competing demands. But with two or more adults (teachers, student teachers, etc.) doing it, you can lighten the workload, and your picture of each child will be more accurate and complete.

- During activity times, have each teacher assume responsibility for observing children in a certain area (the game table, for example). Sometimes the teacher may be looking at whatever happens; at other times he or she may be focusing on one thing (which children can match colors).
- Try to spread out your observations so that you see the child in a number of settings and activities. Indoors, Joe may be awkward and uncomfortable; outside, he's active and relaxed.
- Try to get together daily—at least for a few minutes—to share notes on what you've seen.

3. *Observe often.* Because children are learning and growing all the time, they're constantly changing. Avoid pigeonholing a child ("the timid one"; "the teasing one") on the basis of observations done early in the year. By scheduling *regular* observations of *all* children during the year, you'll get a real sense of growth and progress. That's rewarding to you as well as to the children.

4. *Write it down.*

"What happened to Harry on Monday?" Ms. Williams wondered on Friday as she was writing up her reports. "Something... he was crying." Ms. Alberts, the assistant teacher, shook her head. "Was he afraid of Bert again, or was that the day he was so upset because he couldn't put the puzzle together? I can't remember, either."

We all forget things. Observing children is a big step toward planning a Growing Program, but we also need a way to *remember* and *organize* what we see.

Since watching and recording children's behavior is so important to your program, we want to make it as easy to do, and as much a part of your routine, as possible. We want the job of focusing on children's growth patterns to add to your teaching effectiveness, not detract from it.

In this chapter, index cards will give you suggestions for recording what you see. Some will refer you to the section on "Recording Children's Behavior" for more information.

5. *Have questions in mind when you observe.* Imagine that you are sitting on a hillside in the country. It's a beautiful spring day. There's a lot to see as you look around, but *what* you see will depend on whether

- you are just drinking in the sun and fresh air
- you are trying to decide if it will rain later
- you are trying to identify the wildflowers that grow on the hill.

It's the same when you're observing children's behavior. If you have a question in mind before you start observing, your "watching" will be more focused and efficient.

When teachers observe children, they're usually trying to get an answer to one or more of the following questions:

- Question 1: What is the child like? With this question, you're asking for a general impression or assessment of the child's growth pattern—what makes him or her special, where strengths and needs lie.
- Question 2: What is wrong? Here you're already concerned, and you're trying to find out if the child is showing signs of real trouble—physical, intellectual, or emotional problems that need immediate attention.
- Question 3: What does the child know? This question is usually quite specific —you're wondering about the child's ability to count, recognize his or her name, or walk a balance beam.

Each question has

- a different plan for getting answers (though all use observation), and
- different ways of recording the information you get from your observation.

HOW TO GET ANSWERS TO YOUR QUESTIONS ABOUT CHILDREN

Question 1: what is the child like?

What You Want to Know. You want to know what makes this child special. You want to find out his or her particular pattern of development. You're interested in strengths and needs, spurts and lags.

How You'll Use the Information. At the beginning of the year, this information will help you get a "feel" for the children in your group—their general level of development and special qualities. You'll plan activities on the basis of this information. Later in the year, you'll be able to look back and see where children have progressed and changed.

Plans for Getting Answers. There are two ways of recording children's behavior: anecdotal records and brief jottings. We'll look at each in turn.

1. *Anecdotal records:* one way of observing a child is to watch him or her in action, while you write down as much as possible of what he or she does and says, as well as *how* he or she does and says it. Write down the unexpected as well as the expected, the conflicts as well as the cooperation. Remember, your goal is to gather useful information, *not* to disapprove, judge, or moralize. On the other hand, dry, skimpy language doesn't convey the feeling of the child's behavior. Use expressive, descriptive words whenever possible.

THE GROWING CHILD

Here are three sets of written observation notes about the same child. Which one gives you the fullest picture without judging or moralizing?

1. Tony runs into the room. He puts his jacket away and pushes Jill down. Then he sits under the table.

2. Tony tears into the room with a fierce expression. He quickly shoves his jacket into his cubby and glares around. Jill is standing with her arms around Ms. Loftus. Tony shoves her down, looks quickly at Ms. Loftus, and crawls over to hide under the table, head down.

3. Tony is having another bad morning. He disrupts the group by tearing into the room noisily. Without bothering to hang his jacket up properly, he pushes little Jill over. Then he tries to avoid punishment by hiding under the table.

Observation 1 is objective, all right, but the notes don't contain enough detail to give a vivid picture of Tony's behavior. Observation 3 is more detailed, but the teacher's irritation with Tony shows up in her choice of words: "disrupts the group...tries to avoid punishment." This is going beyond description into blaming. Observation 2 is a good written description, capturing the quality of Tony's behavior but steering clear of judgments.

Teacher's objection: "I can't be writing down everything my children do and say; I'm too busy *teaching*."

A reply: Of course you can't. But how about writing in brief snatches? You can learn a lot about a child by focusing on him or her for three minutes or even one minute! Try it at "slower" times of the day—early morning or late afternoon; when children are drinking juice or settling down for naps. You'll find it pays off in increased understanding of their behavior and that will help you teach better.

One teacher is often able to take notes at the playground. Here's a record she made of Manuel's behavior the first week of school. See what kind of information this record gives you about Manuel's development in the four growth areas, and about his individual "style."

Manuel runs over to David, who is riding a trike. "Bang! Dead!" he shouts, pointing his finger. David ignores him and rides off. Manuel wanders over to the sandbox. He gets busy making cakes by packing sand firmly into pans of different sizes. He makes a row of cakes, lining them up from smallest to largest. Without speaking, he holds one out and offers it to Julie.

When Manuel's teacher reads over these observation notes, she can extract a great deal of information that might otherwise have slipped away in the morning's bustle.

- *Language development.* It sounds as though Manuel's language is limited to one-word phrases, although you'd need more data to confirm this. He seems to use gesture (pointing; holding the "cake" out) to supplement and replace language.
- *Social-emotional development.* The notes show the close relationships between different areas of development. Manuel's problems with language seem to be getting in the way of his social relationships. Without words, it's hard for Manuel to establish relationships with other children, except by pretend fighting (which gets rejected). He does keep trying, though; the observation

DO IT YOURSELF

Practice making anecdotal records of children's behavior.
1. Find a "partner" who can observe at the same time you can. (A staff member from another class? Your supervisor?)
2. Schedule two five-minute time periods, when you and your partner can both observe the same child.
3. Compare your written observations.
   What things did you notice that your partner missed?

   What did your partner see that you missed?

   What did you learn from this observation about observing?

   About the child?

4. If you are working with a group, save this worksheet to share with others.

FORM 4-3

shows that Manuel is eager to have a friend. The teacher can capitalize on this desire.
- *Intellectual development.* Again, the growth areas are linked. Manuel's sand play shows that he can concentrate on a plan and carry it out. When he lines up the pans, he shows us that he can order things from smaller to larger. But is this activity Manuel's choice, or is it a kind of retreat from other areas where he's not as competent? More observation will be needed to answer this question.

2. *Brief notes.* Here's another plan you'll want to use sometimes, when you don't have time to write full anecdotal records.

During your teaching day, something a child does or says will often attract your interest and attention. It may strike you because it's:

> Index cards are great for anecdotal notes and quick jottings. If you keep them handy, you'll get into the habit of using them.
> For more information on using index cards, see the section on "Recording Children's Behavior."

- part of a pattern of typical behavior for that child

> Andy spent half an hour crying in the corner again.
> Date: 10/24

- a sign of growth

> Ellen just painted her first picture (a mommy)!
> Date: 11/3

- a sign of difficulty

> Fred went into a rage over possession of a doll, and violently attacked Brad.
> Date: 11/5

Brief jottings, made "on the spot," can later be expanded when you have more time. But it's better to write a few words than to write nothing. Of course, there's no sense in writing down *everything* that happens—if Judy eats lunch every day, you don't need to make a record of it! But even *brief* jottings of unusual

DO IT YOURSELF

Make some plans to answer the question "What is she like?" for one child.
 Begin by recalling two things you saw that child do in the last few days. Record them below.

Child's name _____

   1. _____
      _____
      _____

   2. _____
      _____
      _____

Now, thinking about each, decide whether you think it is

- part of a typical pattern
- a sign of growth
- a sign of difficulty.

Make a note beside the anecdote.
Now plan to do some actual observing of this child over three or four days. Take both anecdotal records and short jottings.

Anecdotal records (three-five minutes of writing)
  Planned day(s): _____
  Time: _____
  During what activity: _____

Jottings
  Planned day(s): _____
  Times: _____
  During what activities: _____

If you try this on several successive days, you'll find your skills increasing.
 Look back over the observations you have made, searching for further signs of *patterns, growth,* or *difficulties.* Are your hunches in step two confirmed? Or do your observations suggest new directions of growth or concern?

FORM 4-4

THE GROWING CHILD

behavior or signs of change can add up over the months to a very useful profile of a child's growth.

Question 2: what is wrong?

What You Want to Know. You'll want to be especially alert to signs of potential trouble. Hearing loss, vision problems, speech defects, emotional disturbances, and developmental delays may need expert consultation, and the sooner you spot them the better. Routine screening will help you identify some problems, but your daily observations will also turn up certain behaviors that may be signs of trouble.

How You'll Use the Information. If your observations reveal evidence that a child may have a serious problem, you may want to refer him or her for medical or psychological evaluation. If referral doesn't seem necessary, you should discuss the problem in staff meetings, make special plans for the child, and continue your observations.

Plans for Getting Answers.

1. *Watch for "signs of trouble."* Observe *all* the children for potential problems, particularly at the beginning of the year. You will probably feel uneasy about certain children (teachers' intuitions are remarkably good). Pay special attention to those children.

What to watch for
- A child who can't form relationships with children or adults
- A child who hits frequently without reason
- A child who worries or panics at changes in routine or at mild criticism
- A child who clings to anyone available
- A child who can't stand any attempt at control or restraint
- A child who shows no emotion
- A child who has violent temper tantrums
- A child who can't or won't communicate
- A child who can't see similarities or differences
- A child who can't follow simple directions
- A child who is unusually clumsy in large- or fine-motor skills.

Most of the time, you'll spot these trouble signs during the daily routine—perhaps particularly at stressful times of day. You'll see:

- Shawn, who screams in rage when anyone approaches his primitive block building.
- Duffy, who sobs alone in his cubby when rejected by a friend.
- Barbara, who stumbles over everything and complains of headaches and dizziness.

At other times, you might want to set up a game or activity to check up on something.

- Use a "Simon Says" type of game to check on children's ability to follow one, two, and three-step directions.
- Use a lotto game to screen children's abilities to identify similarities.
- Use building toys and table games (like snap-together blocks) to give you information about how well fine-motor skills have developed.

> Use index cards to record signs of trouble—noting when and in what setting it happened.
>
> If you've set up an activity as a way of screening children, use checksheets to keep track. For more information on checksheets, see the section on "Recording Children's Behavior."

2. *Do follow-up observations.* If you note one or more signs of trouble in a child, you'll want to watch that child carefully. Don't jump to conclusions about the cause of the problem behavior; there can be *many* possible explanations, and only careful observation (or expert consultation) will reveal the cause.

Here's an example:

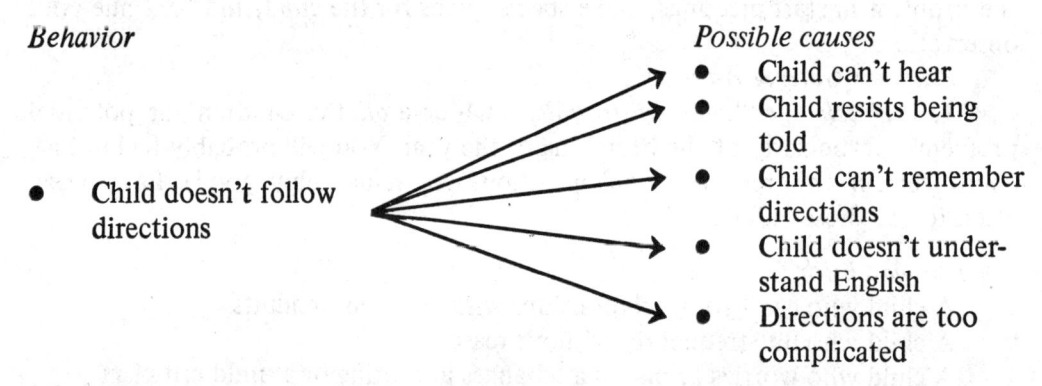

Behavior
- Child doesn't follow directions

Possible causes
- Child can't hear
- Child resists being told
- Child can't remember directions
- Child doesn't understand English
- Directions are too complicated

To find out more about problem behavior, try writing anecdotal records at the time of day when the behavior often occurs. If Tom's tantrums usually come at clean-up time, make a point of observing him then.

Record what happens

- before
- during
- after

the behavior you are worried about.

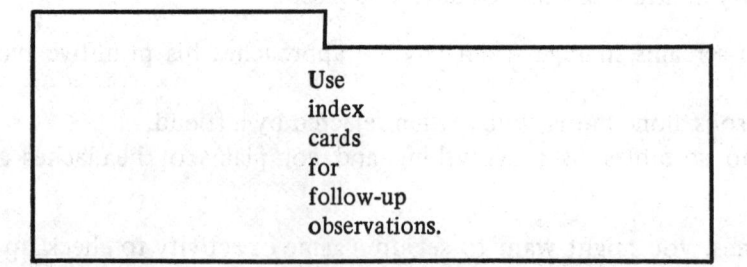

> Use index cards for follow-up observations.

You will need to be especially alert to catch the important "before" events. Since the trouble hasn't started yet, the event that actually sets it off may go unnoticed.

Keeping a Perspective. Remember, young children are always growing. That means that a problem that's here today may be gone tomorrow. As teachers, it's important for us not to label a child as "having a problem," but to consider it as one part of a changing person.

DO IT YOURSELF

1. Select one child in your classroom about whom you are concerned.
2. Plan to observe this child three or four times. Settings should include free time, regular routines, and a structured activity. Record your observations below.

Date _____ Setting _____
Notes:

Date _____ Setting _____
Notes:

Date _____ Setting _____
Notes:

Date _____ Setting _____
Notes:

FORM 4-5

3. Try to answer the following questions.
   - What patterns did you see?

   - What worried you most? Why?

   - What strengths did you see?

   - If you do see a problem, what information do you need to get next? How?

If you are working with a group, you can save this part of the exercise for "class time," and then you can find a partner to read over your observations and help draw conclusions.

FORM 4-5 (Continued)

THE GROWING CHILD

Question 3: what does the child know?

What You Want to Know. Sometimes you have very specific questions in mind when you observe children—you want to find out whether a child has acquired certain skills, concepts, and behaviors.

- Can five-year-old Tyrone cut with scissors?
- Does three-year-old Allan know the difference between *big* and *little*?
- Who is ready to begin work on letter recognition?

In general, specific questions about what children know are more likely to be asked by kindergarten teachers who are beginning to be concerned with teaching specific skills. However, many skill areas are of concern even to teachers of 3's. For example, you will want to keep an eye on:

- language development
  - names of common objects
  - verbalizing requests
  - following simple directions
- concept development
  - size relationships (bigger, smaller; taller, shorter; same)
  - colors
  - sorting (what things could go together)
  - numbers (beginning with one-to-one correspondence)
  - same and different

Remember: if you notice a lag in one child's understanding of some idea (relative to other children that age) you *don't* have to leap in with a regimen of prepared "remedial" activities! For example, you can work on size relationships in the block corner, with cookies that are getting smaller and smaller as the child nibbles, or with the height of the children themselves.

How You'll Use the Information. Answers to specific questions about what children can do can be helpful to you in planning your day-to-day program, and in assessing the effectiveness of your teaching. If Yolanda already knows how to match shapes, you don't need to include her in the small group you're working with; if Mark isn't sure of names of body parts, you'll plan some special games to reinforce his learning.

At this point you may be wondering if there is a magical list of questions you need to answer for each child. Answer them all, and you will have the key to that child's life, growth, and problems! Well, obviously, no such list exists. The key is to let the things you want children to learn dictate the questions you ask. As the year goes on, repeated observations will turn up many signs of progress—by June, amazingly, everyone can zip a jacket!

Plans for Getting Answers. To find out about a certain skill, it's very inefficient to watch and record *everything* the child does. You'll find out more by watching him or her doing *a specific thing* (cutting with scissors, choosing some colored paper) with your question firmly in mind.

Lots of commercial games and diagnostic tests are designed to get specific information about a child's skills and knowledge. But with a little ingenuity, you can get *most* of the same information by watching the child working with materials that are already in the room.

1. *Using what's out.* You'll usually be able to think of several ways to answer a question about a child's abilities. Most of these ways require only the ordinary materials and routines of the day.

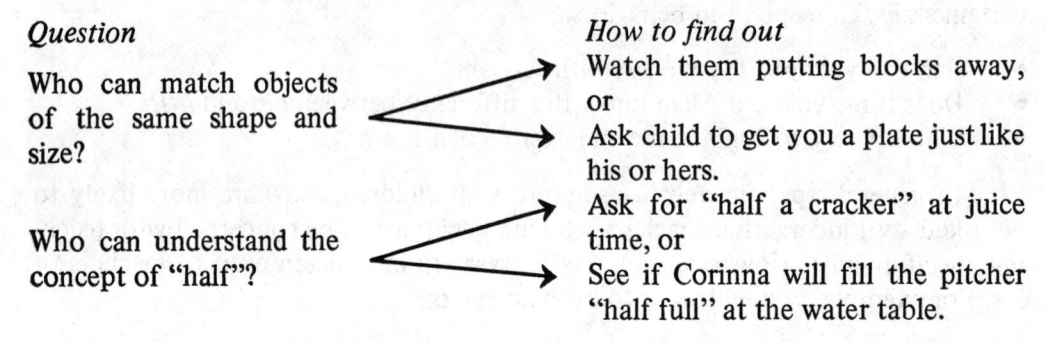

Question

Who can match objects of the same shape and size?

Who can understand the concept of "half"?

How to find out

Watch them putting blocks away, or

Ask child to get you a plate just like his or hers.

Ask for "half a cracker" at juice time, or

See if Corinna will fill the pitcher "half full" at the water table.

2. *Setting up a special activity.* Sometimes you may need to set up an activity designed to answer specific questions. Again, it does not have to be an elaborate diagnostic test—look in your closet or go next door and borrow something.

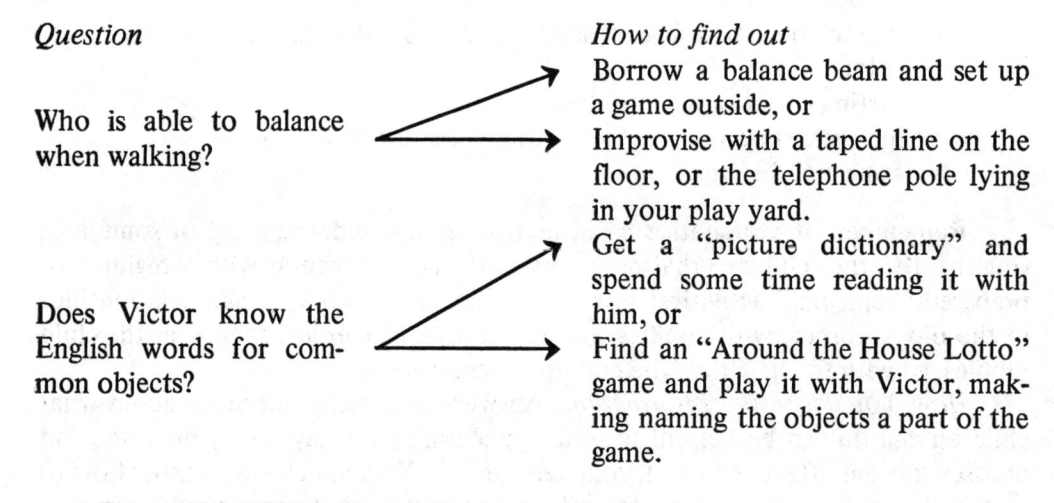

Question

Who is able to balance when walking?

Does Victor know the English words for common objects?

How to find out

Borrow a balance beam and set up a game outside, or

Improvise with a taped line on the floor, or the telephone pole lying in your play yard.

Get a "picture dictionary" and spend some time reading it with him, or

Find an "Around the House Lotto" game and play it with Victor, making naming the objects a part of the game.

These kinds of activities can be used with

- one child
- a small group or
- the whole group

depending on what question you're trying to answer.

> If your question applies to *most* of the group, checksheets are the best way of keeping track.
> Index-card notes are better if you're working with one or two children. See "Recording Children's Behavior" for more information.

In the "Resources" section at the end of this chapter, you will find some suggested readings for a more comprehensive discussion of diagnostic teaching.

DO IT YOURSELF

Make some plans to answer the question "What does he or she know?" for one child. Think of *two* specific questions about the child's skill or knowledge. Then, for each question, think of *two* ways you could find an answer.

1. _____

   _____

   ⟨ _____

   or

   _____ ⟩

2. _____

   _____

   ⟨ _____

   or

   _____ ⟩

Select one of the alternatives for each question, and plan to carry out the activity. (*Student teachers:* Your supervising teacher will want to help you choose the activity and plan for its execution.)

Plan: What day: _____ Time: _____

Activity: _____

Materials needed: _____

FORM 4-6

RECORDING CHILDREN'S BEHAVIOR

Throughout this chapter, we've stressed the importance of *writing down* what you see, and we've given you some hints about how to record your observations. In this section, you'll find additional suggestions for recording your observations in a practical and efficient form.

Advantages of recording

Written observations have several advantages:

- *In the short run*
  - they will help you *focus* your observations
  - they will help you remember specific behaviors and incidents to use as a basis for staff discussions about children
- *In the long run*
  - they will give evidence of growth and of areas of difficulty in your children
  - they will give you evidence of your own teaching accomplishments

Tools for recording

1. *Index cards.* The key to easy recording is having lots of index cards. They're great for several reasons:

- they're the right size for jotting quick notes
- they're less noticeable than a big clipboard to children
- they're easy to file.

Have cards (or pads of dime-store scratch paper) available at all times, in all places. Stack cards on top of shelves, stick in pants pocket, put in pocket of smock. Remember to have lots of pencils around!

OBSERVATION DATA

Child: _____ Date: _____

Area of the room: _____ Observer: _____

_____ Time of the day: _____

What I saw: (Fill in "on the spot" whenever you can) _____

_____

_____

_____

What it might mean: (Fill in later, over coffee) _____

_____

_____

_____

FIGURE 4-2

THE GROWING CHILD

Use cards for:

- writing anecdotal records while watching one child
- writing quick jottings about unexpected happenings, new skills, patterns of behavior:

    "Tom was able to identify block shapes—square, rectangle, triangle."
    "Molly doesn't seem able to hop on one foot."

If you can, it would be helpful to have the index cards dittoed, as shown in Figure 4-2.

2. *Checksheets.* When you're working with a *group* of children on an activity, it's hard to use individual index cards. Sometimes you want a way to keep records of which children have participated in a certain activity, demonstrated certain skills, etc.

The easiest way to record this information is to have a lot of 8½" X 11" sheets dittoed with an alphabetical list of the children. (See Figure 4-3).

Activity or skill: _Animal Lotto_ Date: _1/4_

NAME	PARTICIPATED	COMMENTS
Anne	✓	Hated it! *Why?*
Barb		
Chris	✓	Didn't recognize animals... liked being in group.
Danny		
Greg		
Homer		
Katy		
Luke	✓	Quick and skillful in matching.
Mary		
Megan	✓	Wanted to keep all the cards for herself... knew all the animals.
Ned		
Pete		
Sam		

FIGURE 4-3

Keep some of these lists in each activity area, even outdoors if possible.

- These are quick to fill out during or just after an activity.
- They're good for evaluating an activity and deciding which children to group for special instruction.
- Some comments can be transferred to individual file cards if they're especially significant.

3. *File boxes.* To keep information where it's easily available and well-organized, you need a file box for each child (or one big file box with dividers). Your index card notes will go here. See Figure 4-4.

Using dividers labeled for each growth area (social-emotional, perceptual-motor, cognitive, language) will help you organize each child's file cards. You'll be able to see at a glance whether you've been ignoring that child's behavior in one area, and whether there are lags or spurts in other areas. Besides organizing by growth areas, you may want to include other categories in which to file observations: routines (e.g., child's behavior at meals, naps), or transitions. You will also need a "general" section in the back for observations that don't emphasize any of these categories.

- Date the cards and keep them in order throughout the year.
- Whenever possible, note at the top of the card the growth area your observation emphasized.

4. *Folders.* Besides the file for index cards, you'll also need a *folder* for each child. This should contain:

- application form with parent information
- reports of physical and other examinations

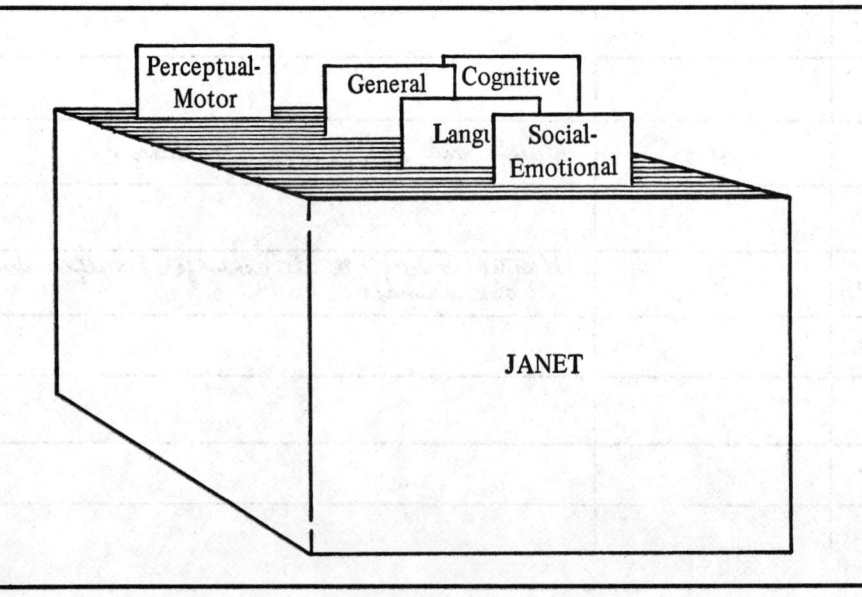

FIGURE 4-4

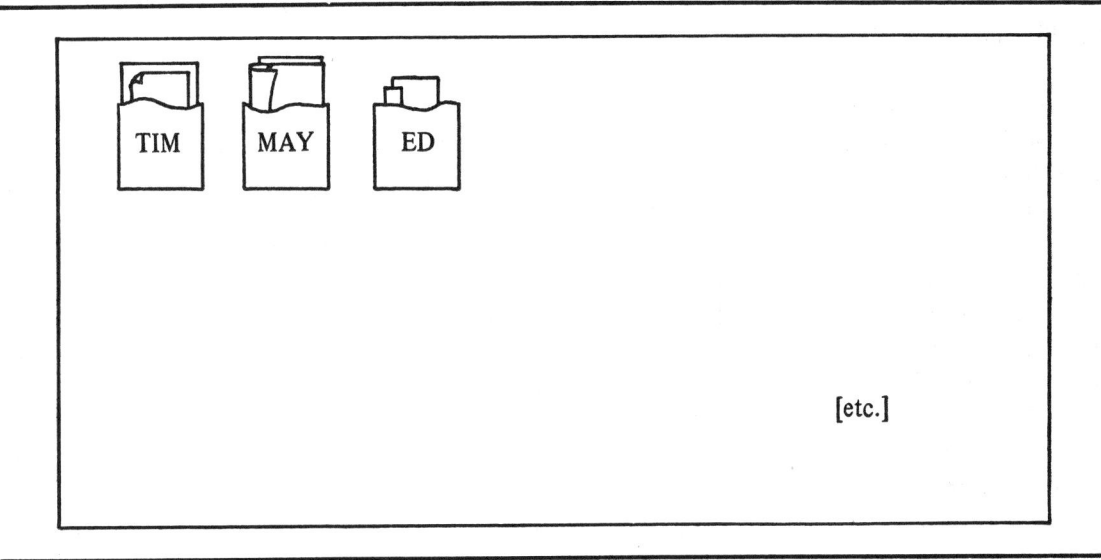

[Figure 4-5: Wall pocket chart with pockets labeled TIM, MAY, ED, [etc.]]

FIGURE 4-5

- samples of child's work
- summaries of staff discussion of child (every two-three weeks) and plans made for him or her (see Chapter 6).
- reports of conferences with parents (see Chapter 12).

5. *Wall pocket chart.* Another device some teachers like is a wall pocket chart made of oaktag. It has a pocket for each child's cards, where they could be left before filing. (See Figure 4-5.) The pockets could also contain individual plans for each child—games to play, special activities, etc.

(Warning: Children's privacy needs to be protected. Don't use this unless you're sure people won't be wandering in and reading your notes. *Always* keep notes and records in a safe, private place.)

Stumbling blocks

Once it's underway, a systematic approach to observing and recording children's behavior should be very helpful in charting each child's growth, so you can plan more effectively.

But . . . if you've never used a system like this before, you may run into some problems. Maybe we can help with them.

Problem
- "The children interrupt me when I'm taking notes and ask what I'm doing."
- "It takes too long!"

Possible solution
- Tell them you're "writing" or doing "teacher's work." The novelty will wear off.
- Don't get overwhelmed. Start slowly, let's say by writing one brief note a day, until you get the hang of it.

DO IT YOURSELF

Getting Underway with Observing and Recording

We've covered a lot of ground here, from identifying growth areas to observing and recording. The chart below should help you put it together. If you read it from left to right, you'll be following a teacher's decision-making process.

First the teacher focuses on one or more growth areas. With that focus, he or she asks a question about a child, chooses a way to get an answer, and finds a way to record it.

We've left some sections of the chart blank; check your understanding of the observation process by filling them in. There is seldom one "right" answer; part of being a good teacher is knowing lots of ways to accomplish the same purpose.

If you're working with others, fill in the chart independently and then compare notes. At the end of the chart are four blank rows. You may use these to plan observations of some children in your class.

Student teachers: Consult with your supervising teacher about which children to observe.

My Question	*Growth Area*	*One Way to Get an Answer*	*How to Record and File*
Larry's brand new in school. I wonder what he's like.	All	Watch him during routines—how he reacts to change, how he copes with problems, how he uses his body, materials, other people.	Write down everything that happens in five minutes. File in "General" section. Follow up as needed.
Which children can count objects up to five?	Cognitive	⟨?⟩	Checklist.
Why does Don bite people?	Social-Emotional	Have teachers record all biting for two or three days, including what the setting was, what happened before/after the incident.	⟨?⟩
Is there something the matter with Ellen's vision?	Perceptual-Motor	⟨?⟩	⟨?⟩
(Your own children)			

FORM 4-7

My Question	Growth Area	One Way to Get an Answer	How to Record and File

FORM 4-7 (Continued)

SAMPLE APPLICATION FORM

Dear Parent:

So that we may better understand your child and thus work with him or her more effectively, we are asking you to share your knowledge with us. If yours is an adopted child, please answer the questions for which you have information. We consider all information confidential. Thank you for your help.

Name of Child _____
                    (first)   (middle)   (last)

Sex _____ Birth date _____ Present address _____

Name by which child
wishes to be called _____ Phone _____ (home)
                                           _____ (work)

Family

1. Father: Age _____ Education _____ Occupation _____
   Mother: Age _____ Education _____ Occupation _____
   If parents are not living together, with whom is the child living? _____

2. Names and birth dates of all other children in family (list in order of birth, from oldest to youngest). Check if not living with family.
   _____   _____
   _____   _____
   _____   _____

3. Is either parent away for long periods? _____
   If so, for approximately how long? _____

4. If parents take trips, who cares for this child (i.e., a relative, a friend, a sitter, etc.)?
   _____

5. Anyone other than mother or father regularly living in the home:
   _____   _____

FORM 4-8

Developmental History

1. Developmental milestones:

   Please give age if known

Sat alone	_____
Stood alone	_____
Walked	_____
Said words	_____
Said sentences	_____
Toilet trained:	
bowels	_____
dry day and night	_____

2. As a baby was your child (circle the ones that best describe him/her):

   happy   cross   active   placid
   high-strung   even-tempered   colicky

3. Past illnesses and physical condition:

   List any accidents, operations, or hospitalizations (use back of page if more space is needed):

       Situation   *Date*   *Explanation*

4. Are there any special medical conditions to be watched for in school at the present time? Elimination problems, hay fever, asthma, sinus, allergies, ear infections, other? Please explain.

FORM 4-8 (Continued)

Social Experiences

1. Has your child previously attended play group, nursery school, or day care?
   a. Name of center _____
   b. Length of time attended (hours a day, days a week, etc.):
      _____
   c. Child's feelings about previous experiences away from home:
      _____

2. Does your child have regular responsibilities in the home? Please list.

Personal Background

1. Can your child care for his/her own toilet habits? _____

2. What terms does he/she use for toileting at home?
   Urination _____ Defecation _____

3. Does your child have strong likes and dislikes in food (please be specific)?

4. What special interests does your child have—favorite games, toys, activities? How does your child like to spend time at home?

5. What special dislikes or "pet peeves" does your child have?

6. We all know any child can occasionally have problems. What behavior problems, difficulties, worries, or fears do you think your child's teacher should be aware of?

7. Is there anything else you could tell us about your child (past experiences, future experiences, future concerns, etc.) which would aid his/her teacher in understanding how he/she thinks and behaves? Please be as extensive as possible; the more we know about your child, the more we can teach and help him/her. Please call for an appointment if you would like to discuss these matters in person.

FORM 4-8 (Continued)

EMERGENCY INFORMATION CARD

In case of illness at school, indicate the following to be called:

If parents cannot be reached _____ _____
(phone)

Physician _____ _____
(phone)

Hospital _____

Name of person(s) who will pick up your child if other than yourself:

_____

_____

_____

Date _____ Signed _____
(parent)

FORM 4-9

- "I feel guilty just standing around watching the children—shouldn't I be *doing* something?"

- " 'Team approach,' my foot! I'm the only teacher in this group."

- You *are* doing something. The few minutes you spend standing back and watching will pay off. You'll understand your children better and will use the rest of your time much more effectively.

- You might ask your director to come in and observe a child once in a while, to get another opinion. Rely on slow times of day, more checklists, and "quickie" comments. The more you know about your children, the better you can handle your solo role.

A FINAL WORD

A plan like the one we've described *must* be flexible. You should feel free to adapt it to your own style, your own environment—as long as you keep certain "basics" in mind:

- teamwork
- attention to all areas of development
- fitting the strategy of observing to the reason for observing
- on-the-spot recording where possible
- easy availability of cards and checklists.

Once you've begun to use this plan, we think you'll start to see immediate results:

- more understanding of your children's growth, and (like the children as *they* grow)
- a feeling of *competence* and *control* as a teacher.

RESOURCES

Cartwright, C.A., and Cartwright, G.P. *Developing Observation Skills.* New York: McGraw-Hill, 1974.
> Describes how to use tallies and checklists (including many sample forms) as well as anecdotal records. Geared to the busy classroom teacher.

Cohen, D., and Stern, V. *Observing and Recording the Behavior of Young Children.* New York: Teacher's College Press, Columbia University, 1958.
> The "must have" basic book, concentrating on developing skill at writing anecdotal records.

Hartley, R.E., Frank, L.K., and Goldenson, R.M. *Understanding Children's Play.* New York: Columbia University Press, 1952.
> Excellent, detailed observations of children painting, building, dancing, fighting. At the end of the book is a complete guide for doing observations.

Medinnus, G.R. *Child Study and Observation Guide.* New York: John Wiley and Sons, 1976.
> Emphasizes a wide range of methods for observing and covers the areas of behavior and development that serve as reference points for observing children. The many examples make the book particularly useful.

Mowbray, J.K., and Salisbury, H.H. *Diagnosing Individual Needs for Early Childhood Education.* Columbus, Ohio: Charles E. Merrill, 1975.
> Stresses importance of pre-entrance records and interviews; gives sample forms. Many ideas on how to record, keep, and interpret information from observation of children.

Raskin, L.M., Taylor, W.J., and Kerckhoff, B.G. "The Teacher as Observer for Assessment: A Guideline," *Young Children,* 30 (July 1975), 339-344.
> Good, specific guidelines in looking for behavior patterns that could be signs of trouble. Avoids hasty diagnosis.

5

Directions for Growth

GOALS, OBJECTIVES, AND PLANS

CHALLENGE YOURSELF

You may believe
- It is important to teachers to know where they—and the children—are going. But do you have goals for your children? And can you translate these into objectives and plans?
- Each child is an individual. But do you have different goals for different children? And do you really plan activities for individual needs?
- The proof of the pudding is in the eating—or, the proof of an activity is in the results. But do you have a way to tell whether an activity has reached its objective?

SKILLS IN THIS CHAPTER

- Selecting goals
- Designing objectives
- Using goals and objectives to guide activity planning

While some people observe children for the sheer fascination of watching their behavior, most teachers are more practical. You need to be able to *use* your observations in ways that will result in benefits for you and the children.

This chapter and the next will help you realize those benefits. In this chapter, we'll offer some suggestions about how your observations of children can be used as the basis for formulating *goals, objectives,* and *plans* for those children. Then in the next chapter, we'll talk about how staff can work together to create an individualized program.

From Watching to Helping

Now that you've become more skilled at watching children, how can you use what you see? The process goes something like this:

1.	You see a child doing something.	For example... Jeremy has told his mother that he has no friends at school, and you have noticed that he spends a lot of time alone.
2.	You use that information to set a general goal (for this child or the group), or to see if an earlier goal is still appropriate.	You decide that you want Jeremy to develop better relationships with other children.
3.	You get more specific, defining the goal in terms of one or more objectives—steps on the way to the goal.	You'd like to see Jeremy work with one other child on a joint project— Patrick would be a good partner. He's a rather quiet child himself.
4.	For each objective, many plans (activities, teacher behaviors) are possible. Usually, you'll pick one or two that will help the child reach the objectives and the goal.	See if Jeremy is interested in running the snack bar with Patrick; you could also give him the job of caring for the rabbit with Susan.
5.	Once you've got a plan, the next step is to put it into action.	You ask Jeremy and Patrick to run the classroom "snack bar" together. They both seem to like the idea.
6.	Now you return to observing, to see if what you planned is really making a difference, and to set some new goals and objectives ... and so on.	You see that other children are attracted to Jeremy's project and that his friendships are branching out. But you also see that he's getting a little bossy.

DIRECTIONS FOR GROWTH

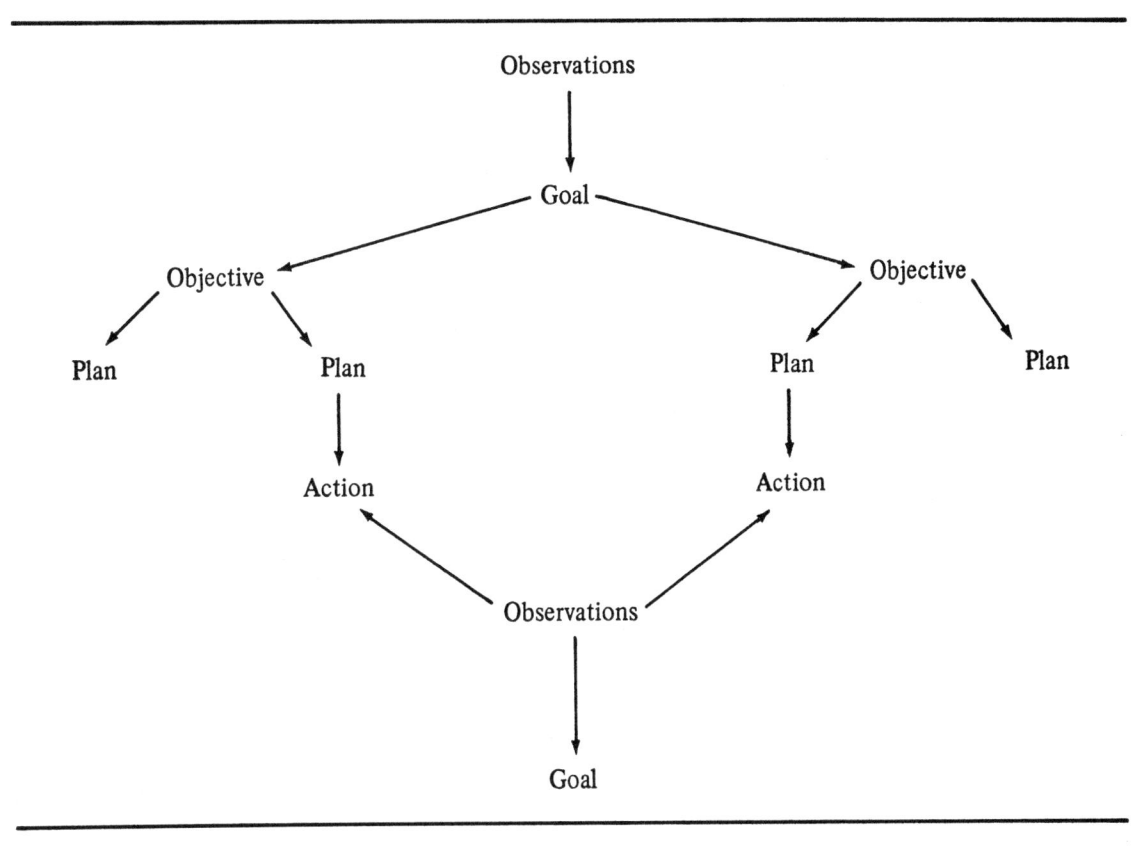

```
                        Observations
                             ↓
                            Goal
                          ↙      ↘
                  Objective        Objective
                  ↙      ↘         ↙      ↘
              Plan      Plan    Plan      Plan
                         ↓       ↓
                       Action  Action
                          ↖    ↗
                       Observations
                             ↓
                            Goal
```

FIGURE 5-1

So the observation of children—your children—is closely tied to every step of the teaching process in a Growing Program. The tools of teaching—goals, objectives, and plans—grow out of careful observation, and their success is evaluated by more observation.

It all fits together as shown in Figure 5-1.

Let's take a closer look at goals, objectives, and plans.

GOALS

What Is a Goal?

A goal is a general statement of what you want for the children in your program. For example, you might want your children:

- to recognize the feelings and needs of others
- to develop the ability to plan, and to follow a plan
- to increase their ability to use more complex language
- to begin to develop control of hand and finger movements.

What Are Goals Based On?

Goals don't appear out of the blue. In the last three chapters we have provided a foundation for developing your own set of goals for your children. These goals should be based on three things:

1. Your own beliefs, values, and philosophy of teaching (see Chapter 2). If you place a high value on creativity, for example, your goals for children will reflect this priority.
2. Knowledge of how children develop (see Chapter 3). The more you know about patterns of child development in the four growth areas, the more realistic your goals will be—you won't expect a group of three-year-olds to sit silently for long periods of time!
3. Knowledge of individual children (see Chapter 4). Your own observations, parent information, and the child's work will help you tailor your goals to individual strengths and needs.

Why Are Goals Necessary?

Goals are essential to your program. It's easy to get caught up in trivia—Paul's toilet accidents or Ms. Arnetti's complaints about the lunches. Goals give you, the staff, something to *move toward,* some larger framework into which you put your day-to-day activities. Every center should have a written list of goals. If you don't have such a list, you might want to look back at Chapter 3, which lists "Tasks and Goals" for each growth area. This list will get you started, and then you can add your own emphases to this basic set of goals.

Once you've developed such a list, don't file it away to gather dust. Post it in each classroom, send it home to parents, discuss it, and update it at staff meetings. With your goals public and visible, you'll have a better sense of where you're going and why.

Why Are Goals Not Enough?

Useful as they are, goals alone won't accomplish much. Let's take an example from the goals listed above. *Goal for children:* "To recognize the feelings and needs of others." This is certainly an important and worthwhile thing to want, but the goal by itself doesn't give you:

- any plans for actually helping children *learn* to "recognize the feelings and needs of others"
  - will they just grow into it?
  - will you lecture?
  - will you plan some games?
- any way of finding out whether and when children have reached that goal
  - how will you know?
  - how will they act?
  - what will they say?

That's why you need objectives.

DO IT YOURSELF

Here are some things you might observe in your classroom. Beside each, write one general *goal* that seems appropriate for that child or group. If you can, discuss your answers with another teacher.

Possible goal for child

1. Marcia has been crying every morning when her mother leaves.   To become comfortable and secure in the group.

2. Charlie teases other children when they make mistakes.

3. Peter and Billy hide under the table every day at story time.

4. Anita has admired Sarah's skill on the indoor climber.

5. Lauren gave up in frustration after spending only a few minutes on a project.

6. The children leave boots and mittens all over the hall.

7. Jesse seldom speaks except in a whisper.

FORM 5-1

OBJECTIVES

What Is an Objective?

Teachers often say to each other: "You know what I'd like to see? I'd like to see Paula really get her hands into that clay and play with it."

"What you'd like to see" is an objective.

An *objective* is a statement, *not* of a general goal ("I wish Ed were more generous"), but of what you would like to see the child doing.

1. "I wish Ed were more generous" = Goal
2. "I'd like to see Ed give someone an extra car or bit of clay" = Objective

What's the Advantage of Developing Objectives for Children?

There are a number of advantages:

1. You have something specific to aim for. It would be a lot easier to think of activities to achieve the objective you've developed for Ed than to achieve the general goal. And specific objectives *will* add up to your goal in the long run.
2. You *know* if you're succeeding. Everyone needs a sense of accomplishment. But if the goals for your children are always broad and vague ("I want the children to feel good about themselves"), it's hard to tell how much progress you and the children are making. There's nothing wrong with broad goals in the long run, but in the *short run,* a series of specific objectives ("I'd like to see Ellen show other children her work products and talk about them") gives you a sense of the child's progress in relation to the goal.
3. You have a way of recording and talking about the child's progress. Instead of telling her parents "Ellen's been doing really well this year," you'll be able to say "Ellen's made progress in a lot of areas. In September, she avoided talking to the other children in the art area. Lately she's been showing her drawings to them. We're hoping that soon she'll feel comfortable talking about her work, too. . . ."
4. You can involve children in planning their own program. This usually happens in one of two ways. Often children point out something specific they want to do, like "I want to paint tomorrow." This is a self-created objective which you can help the child reach. This is the first, and simplest, kind of objective setting with children.

    Sometimes children want to master a new skill. This will require more of your help, and more planning. The child's goal may be beyond his or her immediate achievement, like "I want to play basketball." You can help set more realistic objectives and provide the setting in which they can be reached. For example, for the child who wants to play basketball, you could bring in a ball, and work with bouncing it, throwing it, catching it, and tossing it through a low hoop.

Objectives: Steps to the Goal

For every general goal that you've established, you'll have many specific objectives —steps that mark children's visible progress on the way to the goal. Some objectives will be appropriate for all children; others will apply to one particular child. As the year goes on, and a child gets closer to the goal, your objectives for him or her will change.

Here's an example. *Goal for children:* "To recognize the feelings and needs of others." At the beginning of the year, Carlo showed no awareness of the feelings of others. He would literally walk over another child without showing any sign of concern at his or her screams of outrage. A series of objectives emerged from Carlo's teachers' observations of him. Notice how the objectives changed as the year went on.

Objective 1: "I'd like to see Carlo turn and notice another child's distress."
Objective 2: "I'd like to see Carlo ask the teacher about another child's distress."
Objective 3: "I'd like to hear Carlo describe how he thinks another child is feeling."
Objective 4: "I'd like to see Carlo attempt to help a child who is hurt or unhappy."

Sequencing Objectives

Carlo's teachers didn't expect him to change overnight. They knew that changes in behavior come slowly, bit by bit. So they thought carefully about the steps that led to "recognizing the feelings and needs of others." They thought about what should come first in this process. Obviously, Carlo was not going to help another child unless he first noticed that the child needed help. So the sequence began at that point, with helping Carlo *see* what was going on in the room. After that was accomplished, they planned the next steps: helping him *ask* for information, then having him describe the situation, and (building on all these earlier learnings) finally having him *help* another child.

Here's another example of *sequencing* a series of objectives in order to help children reach a goal. Ms. Andrews wants to share her interest in embroidery and "creative stitchery" with some of her kindergarten children. But she realizes that many specific skills and techniques will have to go into the finished product. She analyzes those skills and thinks about which ones provide the foundation for the others. She comes up with this sequence.

The children who are interested in this activity will need to learn to:
1. Thread a large needle
2. Develop skill in manipulating the needle in and out of cloth (freehand)
3. Follow a line with one stitch
4. Thread a smaller needle
5. Practice one or more additional stitches
6. Plan a design

7. Transfer the design to cloth
8. Follow the design.

While Ms. Andrews has developed this general sequence before she starts working with the class, her observations may cause her to adjust the sequence for some children. She may find, for example, that several children don't have the coordination to work with the floppy burlap. So she inserts another step: developing the ability to "sew" through punched holes on a card. Of course, each step could be broken down into even smaller ones. Threading a needle is a skill that's composed of several "sub-skills."

How do you decide when to stop in the process of breaking down a goal into specific objectives? As always, the needs and abilities of the children should guide you in your planning. With some children (e.g., a very distractible child or a child with mental or physical handicaps), you may need to separate each task into small, defined pieces, and teach those pieces step by step. Other children learn best when the thread, the needle, and the cloth are simply placed in front of them. They'll figure it out on their own.

Kinds of Objectives

It's helpful to think of two kinds of objectives: *process* objectives and *behavioral* objectives. Both *process* and *behavioral* objectives are specific descriptions of what you'd like to see in the classroom. Both are sequenced to reach a goal. But in other ways they are different.

Process Objectives

Lately, Connie has been spending most of her free time alone looking at books. You have two goals for Connie: you want her to have more experience with art materials and you want her to interact with other children. So you formulate this objective: "I'd like to see Connie experiment at the collage table today." This is a *process objective*. A process objective describes an encounter or a meeting between a child and a material, a child and an adult, or a child and another child. You're interested in seeing Connie become involved with a variety of materials and with other children. At this point, the end *product* or behavior isn't as important as the *process* of involvement. Connie may end up

- collaborating with another child
- combining collage materials with clay to make a sculpture
- dictating a story to go with her collage.

Neither you nor Connie knows ahead of time what the endpoint will be. Process objectives are especially appropriate in guiding children's free experimentation with new materials and concepts.

If your program reflects strong beliefs in children's curiosity and in the importance of free exploration of materials, then process objectives will be an important part of your planning. Here are some examples of process objectives:

DIRECTIONS FOR GROWTH

Goal
To work cooperatively

To develop fluency in language

To explore concepts of weight

Process objective
You'd like to see Rico and Fred work in the block area together.

You'd like to see Darlene spend time with Ms. Peters in the puppet corner.

You'd like to see Willy work at the balance scale, experimenting freely with a variety of materials.

Behavioral Objectives

There are also times when you have something more definite in mind. You'd like to see a piece of specific learning result from the child's experiences in the classroom. A *behavioral objective* is a description of that learning. It describes the precise way in which the child will demonstrate what he or she has learned.

Besides wanting Connie to become involved with art materials, you may also want her to learn the names of simple geometric shapes—a piece of knowledge which, your observation shows, she's lacking right now. So you formulate this *behavioral objective:* "When presented with a set of three geometric shapes, Connie will be able to point to and name the shapes" (circle, square, triangle).

Behavioral objectives are most appropriate for screening for certain developmental problems, teaching specific skills or concepts, and for checking on whether children have acquired them.

Here are some examples of behavioral objectives.

Goal
To develop fine-motor coordination

To follow directions

To increase English fluency

Behavioral objective
You'd like to see Albert string at least four large beads.

You'd like to see several children follow this two-step direction without a mistake: "Get a pencil from the table and put it in the basket."

You'd like to see Jimmy name the eating utensils at lunch.

WRITING BEHAVIORAL OBJECTIVES

Behavioral objectives have to be precise to be useful. In writing them, it's important to specify

- *what* behavior will be demonstrated
- under what circumstance (spontaneously? when asked?)
- using what materials (special equipment? objects in room?)
- to what criterion (perfectly? with one mistake?)

The resources at the end of this chapter will help you sharpen your skills in writing effective objectives.

DO IT YOURSELF

1. Some of the following are *goals* (G), some are *process objectives* (P), and some are *behavioral objectives* (B). Label each statement G, P, or B.

    ___ (a) Steve will be able to make a plan and carry it out.

    ___ (b) Michelle will be able to express feelings more appropriately.

    ___ (c) Junior will be able to select objects by color (red, blue, and yellow) from a set of small objects.

    ___ (d) Marcellus will decrease interruptions in group meetings to three or less.

    ___ (e) Anna will go to circle by herself, without being asked, at least three times in one week.

    ___ (f) Harold will spend some time at the workbench with Phil and Irene.

    ___ (g) Joseph will show increased self-reliance.

    ___ (h) Edward will use the materials in the science area.

2. Write the three statements you identified as *goals* above in the space below.

    For each goal, invent two objectives—a process objective and a behavioral objective—which could help lead a child to that goal.

    (a) _____ (a) i. Process Objective:
    _____   ii. Behavioral Objective:
    _____

    (b) _____ (b) i. Process Objective:
    _____   ii. Behavioral Objective:
    _____

    (c) _____ (c) i. Process Objective:
    _____   ii. Behavioral Objective:
    _____

Answer to Question 1	
Goals:	a,b,g
Process objectives:	f,h
Behavioral objectives:	c,d,e

FORM 5-2

3. Take some time to apply the practice of using goals and objectives in planning for your own children. In the space below, list three children in your class. For each child, list one general goal. Then list one process objective and one behavioral objective related to that goal. Make sure the objective is within the reach of the child's ability.

Child	Goal	Objective
	To...	Process: Behavioral:
	To...	Process: Behavioral:
	To...	Process: Behavioral:

Reminder: The objectives you set should be:

- specific
- descriptive of either the process or the behavioral product that you'd like to see
- reasonable (in terms of where the child is right now).

FORM 5-2 (Continued)

Can't Objectives Be Misused?

Sure they can—like any other tool. To use objectives properly, keep the following points in mind:

- You should individualize objectives whenever possible, and fit them to the needs of the child rather than to some rigidly prescribed curriculum. Let your objectives grow out of the children's current interests. If Marcus is already working doggedly at writing his name, let that be the focus of the objectives and plans you evolve instead of imposing something entirely new. Also, use your observations of the child to determine *where he or she is* and use that information to decide how far it's reasonable to expect him or her to progress.

    You've seen Marta spending every morning huddled in her cubby. You have formulated a goal for Marta—to play with other children. It would be *unreasonable* to set this objective to help reach the goal: "I'd like to see Marta play happily with the other children all morning." This is a *reasonable* objective: "I'd like to see Marta leave her cubby briefly at least once a morning with the teacher's help to watch what other children are doing."

- You should be prepared for, and sensitive to, *unexpected* signs that a child has reached an objective.

    After two days of color lotto, Eddie shows his ability to match colors by painting a red streak down Pat's red shirt. (You might need to do some quick planning in the social area!)

WHAT NEXT?

Goals were not enough by themselves. Neither are goals and objectives enough in themselves. One more step is needed, and that's the step into *action*.

PLANS

Since an objective only tells you where you are headed, once you have chosen your objectives you still must decide how to reach them. For example, one of the objectives in the exercise on page 90 is:

Behavioral objective: When asked, Junior will be able to select objects by color (red, blue, and yellow) from a set of small objects.

If you were to leave a note to a substitute teacher with just this objective, she still would not know exactly what to do with Junior.

An objective tells you where to go, not what to do. To get from an objective on paper to a real result, you must have a *plan*.

A Plan = *what* will happen, *when*, *who* will do it, and *how* to check its success.

The *"what"* part of the plan may be an activity (e.g., a game), a sequence of activities, an experience (e.g., a trip), or a teacher's intervention (e.g., reassuring the child).

DIRECTIONS FOR GROWTH

Here's the same objective we used above, this time with a *plan*.

Objective
Junior will be able to select objects by color (red, blue, and yellow) from a set of small objects.

Plan
Activity: Play "Simon says—color" with Junior, Maurice, Teddy, and any other children who want to. Have Junior use a blue card for two days.
Who: Ms. Simpson.
When: In quiet time (8:00–8:30 A.M.).
Check: When it seems like Junior is catching on to blue, check it by asking him to pick the blue block from four or five of different colors.

You may have noticed:

- This particular plan is only one step toward the objective. More planning will be needed for the next steps.
- Any one of several other plans could do as well as this one. There is almost always more than one way to skin an objective.

Here's another example, showing how several plans may be made for one objective. Only the *what* of the plan is given here. We have left out the *who, when,* and *where* details.

Let's look at Carlo again. The first objective his teachers developed was: "I'd like to see Carlo turn and notice another child's distress." To help Carlo reach this objective, they made many plans:

Plan 1: Check Carlo's hearing to make sure his lack of awareness doesn't have a physical cause.
Plan 2: Talk to Carlo about what other children are doing: "Oh, Sandy's sad—she's crying."
Plan 3: Praise Carlo if he seems to be watching other children: "Carlo, you really noticed that Peter was unhappy. Did you see his tears?"
Plan 4: Play some group games that focus on listening and observation skills.
Plan 5: Read a book about feelings.
Plan 6: Be sure to comfort Carlo when *he* is distressed and comment on what you're doing: "I saw you crying, so I came right over to sit with you and help you feel better."

When Plans Don't Work

What do you do when plans don't work?
But that's silly. Given all the care you have invested in selecting goals, objectives, and plans for each child, success is guaranteed, right?
Wrong.
If there is one thing you can count on, it is that plans can, and often will, go wrong. In the real world of the classroom many things can prevent a plan from going into operation—illness, unexpected schedule changes, and so on.

DO IT YOURSELF

Practice thinking about planning for individual children.

1. Complete the following by making up one objective (either process or behavioral) and one activity.

Goal	Objective	Activity
Steve will be able to make a simple plan and carry it out.		

2. Complete the following for one or more of your own children using the goals and objectives you created on page 91.

Goal	Objective	Activity

FORM 5-3

DO IT YOURSELF

Take a few moments to get some mileage out of one of your less-than-perfectly-successful experiences with your class. If you are part of a team, you can do it together.

1. Recall a recent activity you planned, for one child or a group, which "fell flat" in some way. Keeping the activity in mind, list as many reasons as you can think of why it might have gone wrong.

    Activity

    Reasons

2. Now think about how you might set up the same activity the next time. What would you do to lessen the chances that the same problems will occur?

    New plans

FORM 5-4

Even if the plan does get carried out, it may not have the desired result. Maybe Junior doesn't *like* to play "Simon says"! Maybe the excitement of the group is too distracting for him.

In that case, congratulations! You now know more about Junior and how to plan for him than you did before. Having to go back to the drawing board for another plan does *not* mean that you are a terrible teacher. It means you are responding to the realities of your students and classroom. Hurrah for you!

To help yourself on your trip back to the drawing board, pause to ask *why* the first plan went astray.

- Does it make unreasonable demands on staff schedule?
- Do the staff members involved know how to do what they are meant to do?
- Does the activity make demands which the child can't meet?
- Are there other disturbing or distracting factors affecting the child?
- Is the *objective* appropriate for the child or does it need to be simpler, harder, or just different?

Plans in Perspective

There are many different kinds of plans, and many different ways to make and record them. Plans may be made for individuals, or for small or large groups.

However, the best planning in the world is useless unless it is:

- related to "real life"
- carried out!

The next chapter is about one approach that can help you be sure your plans: are based on what the staff knows about the child, *can* be carried out, and *will* be carrried out. This approach is called *staffing*.

RESOURCES

Hogden, L., et al. *School before Six: A Diagnostic Approach.* St. Louis, Mo.: Cemrel, Inc., 1974. 2 vol.
>   Emphasizes the importance of assessing both the needs and strengths of a child before planning activities. Includes useful planning sheets.

Mowbray, J.K., and Salisbury, H.H. *Diagnosing Individual Needs for Early Childhood Education.* Columbus, Ohio: Charles E. Merrill, 1975.
>   Organized under "physical," "emotional," "social," and "mental" development, guidelines are provided to help you move from identifying the individual child's level of development to planning experiences that will help him or her move ahead.

Thomas, J.I. *Learning Centers: Opening Up the Classroom.* Boston: Holbrook Press, 1975.
>   Discusses the distinction between "behavioral" and "expressive" (or process) objectives. Also contains a rich variety of suggestions for activity areas. Although geared to elementary schools, it will fire your imagination.

6

Setting Directions for Growth

PUTTING GOALS, OBJECTIVES, AND PLANS TO WORK

CHALLENGE YOURSELF

You may believe
- Individualized planning is basic to a good program. But do you really plan for each child?
- Teachers should consider individual children's strengths and needs. But have you scheduled times to discuss those strengths and needs?
- Teamwork is important. But do you work as a team to evaluate and plan for each child?

SKILLS IN THIS CHAPTER

- Individualizing your program through staffing, the process of team planning.
- Implementing and evaluating the individualized plans you've made.

SETTING DIRECTIONS FOR INDIVIDUAL GROWTH THROUGH STAFFING

The last four chapters have given you some basic tools to use in creating a Growing Program. You've thought about your teaching philosophy, considered the process of development in young children, observed and recorded that development, and recognized the place of goals, objectives, and plans in your program.

Now you'll get a chance to put all those tools to work. There's a great deal of talk about "individualized education." What does that mean? We think that a truly individualized program begins by assessing each child's development—both strengths and needs—and goes on to plan for that child, as a unique person. As much as you may want to "individualize," you won't do it if your advance planning is always for the whole group:

- a field trip for Monday
- some interesting nature projects
- a new song to teach.

These things are important, and some of your staff meeting time should be spent on them each week. Chapter 11, "The Growing Staff," deals with this kind of planning. But you need to set up a system for discussing, evaluating, and planning for each child in your group *as an individual.*

We have a name for this process of individualized planning: "staffing" a child. We call it "staffing" because it's a process that uses the combined resources and insights of your whole staff to develop the best possible program for each child. If your "staff" is one person—you—then you'll still need to do this important thinking and planning. Perhaps you can confer with another teacher or an outside consultant from time to time.

All this may sound very formal and difficult. But you've probably begun to do it already. "Staffing" is just a more organized, purposeful version of talking about children. We all do that!

TALKING ABOUT CHILDREN

Everyone loves to talk about children. They're fun, they're frustrating, they're constantly surprising. Parents regale you with Tim's latest funny saying or Leroy's accomplishments on the piano; teachers have a never-ending supply of anecdotes about the time Randy poured all the glue into the rice pudding or the day Sheila dressed up like an aardvark. Most of us could go on for days.

This kind of chatting is fun. But the discussions, while interesting, may be

SETTING DIRECTIONS FOR GROWTH

aimless and unproductive. When we are working, we need to be able to *shift the focus* of our talk about children...

- from Mary's "cute" sayings
- to analyzing the reason for them: could she be trying to get attention by imitating her baby sister?

- from Bob's irritating mannerisms
- to examining the cause of our annoyance and doing something about it

- from Amy's total—and funny—confusion about colors
- to making some specific plans to help her in this area

We can turn the time we used to spend just "chatting about" children into time spent "staffing" children.

"Staffing" is a process by which those responsible for the children and the program discuss each child's past progress and present needs, to set goals and objectives, and to plan activities to further the child's growth. This process applies whether there is one teacher in the room or four.

These regular staff discussions provide a way to use your observations of one child, and your knowledge of goals and objectives, to plan a truly *individualized* program for him or her. And that's what a Growing Program is all about.

Steps in staffing:
1. *Getting ready* for staffing.
2. *Sharing information* about the child.
3. *Summarizing child's progress* in growth areas since last discussion.
4. *Defining child's needs and strengths,* and teacher's questions about child.
5. *Setting objectives and planning activities* for child in terms of those needs.

Results of staffing:
- *problems* identified and *goals* set
- *steps* and *plans* decided upon
- a *written record* of problems, plans, and goals.

The form of the written record is up to you, the people using it. A sample form is used in this chapter. Yours should contain *at least* as much information as this one.

IF YOU'RE ALONE

Although the descriptions we've given of each step are for a group, the main ideas also apply to teachers working alone. You need to plan regular "meetings with yourself" at which you follow the five steps in evaluating and planning for the children you teach. But do try to bring someone else in on the process if at all possible: a director, a supervisor, a student teacher, a consultant.

Step 1: Getting Ready for Staffing

Your "staffings" will run much more smoothly if you plan ahead. Here are a few points you and your fellow teachers should clear up at the start.

1. *Time and place for staffing.* Everyone has a busy schedule, and planning is often the last thing on it. Your meeting will be more likely to happen if you have scheduled a time and place and if everyone knows when it will be over. Other pressing demands are easier to put off if you know you will soon be free to get back to them.

    Once you have set a time, stick to it. Starting on time will help you finish on time, and both help you fit planning into your busy day.

    Sometimes it is hard to get together though. If you need a little encouragement, try a small bribe for yourselves—coffee and donuts?

2. *Notes during staffing.* The work you do in staffing is only as good as your follow-through. Good record forms both help you plan well and make follow-through easier. We have included the forms we like as examples, but feel free to invent your own. You may be one of those people who hates forms. But planning gets wasted if you don't keep a record of what you decided to do. Adapt, streamline, simplify—make the suggested forms fit your own style—but *do* write things down.

3. *Jobs and roles during staffing.* Any meeting (whether two people or 100) goes better if people know what's expected of them.

    When three or more people are involved, some teachers find it helpful to have one person be responsible for presenting the observations about the child, with others adding more information, raising questions, etc. Another person can act as "manager," summarizing the discussion, jotting down comments, and filling in the staffing form. These jobs will rotate each time you meet.

4. *Ground rules for discussion*
    - Don't cut people off. When a staff member is presenting information about a child, others should not jump in with opinions and suggestions. *Questions* to draw out more information are helpful, though.
    - Once information has been thoroughly shared, have one person *summarize* what's been said. Only then proceed to planning.
    - In planning activities, use a "brainstorming approach." Encourage *lots* of suggestions—seemingly far-fetched schemes sometimes turn out to make good sense!
    - Stick to the point. Try to avoid long-winded anecdotes of praise and blame (of child, parents, other teachers). Instead, think in terms of *problems to be solved.*

Now you're ready to begin. As we discuss each step in the child-staffing process, let's make it real by following the discussion of an actual child, four-year-old Ronnie.

The dialogue may sound a little too good to be true. That's because it's missing all the little side comments, jokes, and interruptions found in most real meetings. It has been stripped to the bones, to emphasize the main points.

We'll assume that the staff members have already gone through step one,

SETTING DIRECTIONS FOR GROWTH

getting ready for staffing. It's early in the year: Melissa, the head teacher, Sam, the assistant teacher, and Alice, the student teacher, are seated around the table drinking coffee at the end of the day. Today Sam is responsible for "managing" the discussion.

Step 2: Sharing Information

Excerpts from Discussion of Ronnie

Sam: Let me tell you about some incidents I've observed in the last few weeks. Yesterday I watched Ronnie for a few minutes when he first arrived. I could hear him coming —roaring and jumping as if he wanted to make sure everyone knew he was here! He almost knocked over Andy. Then he marched around shouting "I'm the strongest guy!"

Alice: Did you know he has two older brothers? No wonder he wants to be strong!

Sam: No, I didn't. That may explain a lot. My notes show a lot of times when he seems to be annoying other children or the teacher—grabbing books, knocking over buildings, poking people at nap time—and enjoying their reaction.

Melissa: I've seen that, too. At music time yesterday he suddenly hit Ella with a cymbal. Then he looked at me, grinned, and hid under the piano bench.

Sam: There's another side to Ronnie, though. When we worked at the workbench together, he was relaxed, cheerful, cooperative, and really skillful in using tools. Did you see the boat he made?

Melissa: I did—it was great. But his mother ignored it when she picked him up.

Alice: What activities does he like? I've noticed he loves water play.

Sam: He does. Actually, he's been enjoying all the activity areas. He can do all but the very hardest puzzles we've had out this week.

Melissa: I know he's capable, but there *are* a few things that concern me about his intellectual development, Sam. He doesn't seem to know colors at all.

Sam: I hadn't noticed.

Melissa: He was totally lost in the color game we played the other day. I did wonder if he might be color blind.

The staff continue discussing Ronnie.

What's Going on in Step 2

Sam is sharing the information he has collected about Ronnie. His observations are being supplemented by the other teachers, helping to build a more complete picture of Ronnie's behavior. This is the time when contradictory views of a child can surface, raising questions that lead to a fuller understanding. In our example, Melissa points out some areas in which Ronnie may not be as capable as Sam had thought, or in which he may have a physical problem.

Purpose
- Share information about the child gathered since last discussion so staff will know what he or she has been doing—progress, problems, etc.

Resources
- Written observations.
- Incidents recalled by staff.

- Checklists of activities participated in.
- Parent conferences or informal discussion.
- Information from referrals, if any (hearing test, psychological evaluation, etc.).

Checkpoints
- Does everyone get a chance to contribute?
- Do you have enough information to use as basis for discussion? (If not, get more!)
- Are you staying away from opinions and suggestions till all the information has been shared?
- Are you being objective—avoiding blame and praise, *describing* rather than *moralizing*?

Step 3: Summarizing Child's Progress

Discussion of Ronnie, Continued

After more discussion . . .

Sam:	It sounds like we're about ready to write a summary now. Where should we start?
Melissa:	Let's start with areas in which Ronnie's progressed. He's able to leave his mother at the door without crying now and he's very comfortable with *one* adult—like you at the workbench, Sam. We have mentioned that Ronnie has real problems adapting to routines like lunch and naptime—it's hard for him to leave the other kids alone. He gets *so* tired at nap, but he keeps himself awake so he'll be noticed.
Sam:	(groaning) I notice him. . . . I think we should also mention that he enjoys using materials and is really good at puzzles. He enjoys the challenge and keeps working at them till he figures them out.
Melissa:	Slow down, Sam—I'm writing . . . Okay. I'm also going to note that he has trouble identifying colors. Language skills?
Alice:	Well, we said he certainly talks well for his age, but he seems to use language to bully and impress other kids, not to communicate in a friendly way.

What's Going on in Step 3

This is the point at which it seems that most of the important observations have been shared, and it's almost time to move on to planning. Taking a few minutes to summarize helps crystallize the important points, gives you a written record of major observations, and lets everyone know planning is about to begin. Your life will be a lot easier if someone in the group takes responsibility for moving the meeting along, as Sam did here. You can take turns being "chairperson," making sure the meeting doesn't get bogged down in one phase or another.

Purpose
- To use information about the child to write a summary of "how he or she has been doing" since the last discussion, including where appropriate:
    ○ progress and difficulty in each growth area (social-emotional, perceptual-motor, cognitive, and language)
    ○ special interests, events of note at home or school.

SETTING DIRECTIONS FOR GROWTH

Resources
- Information shared in step two.
- Summary sheet.

Checkpoints
- Is the summary *balanced* (attention to all growth areas) and *accurate*?
- Is the summary based on specific observations and information?
- If teachers have conflicting opinions about the child's progress, are they discussed and noted?

Step 4: Defining Questions about Child; Child's Needs and Strengths

Discussion of Ronnie, Continued

After the summary was finished ...

Sam:	Well, let's move on to *questions* we have about Ronnie. What do we want to find out in the next month or so?
Alice:	I think we'd all like to know why he's so rough with the other kids. Could we concentrate on that question for now?
Melissa:	Good, but let's put it a little more broadly. I think we really want to know why Ronnie continually tries to provoke people—adults *and* children. You know, what does he *gain* from that? Can we put it that way?
Alice:	I'd go along with that.
Sam:	OK. Strengths?
Alice:	I'd say his ability to solve puzzles is a real strength—it shows concentration and problem-solving skills, too. *And* his liking for adult companionship.
Sam:	What about his needs? I'd put *attention* at the top of the list. What else?
Melissa:	He really needs *limits,* too—a sense of how far he can go. Sometimes when he looks at me I can almost hear him saying, "Are you going to stop me?" There are a couple of other things that are a bit less important right now. He certainly needs help with identifying colors, and we have to check out the possibility that he's color blind.
Sam:	Any other ideas, Alice? No? Then, let's get started doing objectives and plans for Ronnie.

What's Going on in Step 4

Again, Sam keeps the meeting moving when he suggests going on to questions. Why bother with questions? Deciding what you most need to understand about a child is the key to really getting to know him. Think of what you *don't* know—what are the greatest puzzles this child presents? Then, as a team, you can be alert to clues that may lead you to an answer.

Purpose
- To use the summary of child's progress to:
  - define *questions* about the child for which teachers want answers
  - describe the child's most important *needs and strengths*

Resources
- Information shared in first part of discussion.
- Summary of child's progress.
- Summary sheet.

Checkpoints
- Are questions and needs stated *objectively*? (Without blaming or criticizing—*not* "what he needs is a good talking to!")
- Are you sufficiently aware of the child's *strengths*?

Step 5: Setting Objectives and Planning Activities

Discussion of Ronnie, Continued

Melissa: It sounds to me as if we've set a goal for ourselves, as well as some for Ronnie.
Alice: What's that?
Melissa: Well, we want to find out what's causing Ronnie's provoking behavior. What can we do to get some answers?
Sam: We can observe him—oh—and how about giving his mother a call?
Melissa: OK, I guess I'd better do that. I can call this afternoon. I can suggest that he get his eyes checked, too.
Sam: About observing... I'm supposed to supervise the workbench this week...
Alice: How about if I take over for you first thing every morning for a bit?
Sam: That would be great. Five minutes is all I need to write some good notes. Early morning's a hard time for him, too. Maybe I can get a feel for what sets him off.
Melissa: So much for our plans for ourselves. What about some goals for Ronnie?
Alice: We really want him to work cooperatively with other people, without all this teasing, don't we?
Melissa: That would be great eventually! Let's think of a few smaller objectives to start him off. Since he works so well with adults, why not begin by aiming for his completing a cooperative project with an adult.
Sam: More woodworking? Or maybe just a walk to the store...
Alice: How about taking him out in the hall for a story? No—I know! How about using his interest in puzzles? He could do puzzles with one of us.
Melissa: That would help satisfy his need for attention. What if I helped him *make* a puzzle?

Discussion continues, setting more objectives and making more plans.

What's Going on in Step 5

Here the thorough work earlier in the staffing is beginning to pay off. Since everyone understands—and agrees!—about what needs to get done, each new idea seems to build on someone else's, and a plan can take shape pretty rapidly. The spirit of cooperation makes it easy for everyone to speak up. There's another message here, too. Follow through! If you decide someone should call a parent, who will it be? and when? Without a plan, it may never happen!

Purpose
- To *set objectives* and make *specific plans* which will:
  - help teachers get answers to questions about the child
  - help the child use his or her strengths and meet his or her needs while moving toward appropriate goals

Sample Summary Sheet for Ronnie

SUMMARY SHEET

Child's Name ___Ronnie___   Date ___10/9___

General Summary (progress and difficulty in growth areas; specific events at home or school; interests):

Ronnie has trouble in relationships with teachers and children, because of his teasing, provoking, sometimes aggressive behavior.

He has difficulty adapting to routines (e.g., lunch and nap). He seems to bother other children in order to get attention.

Ronnie is able to separate from his mother now and enjoys the company of one adult.

He enjoys using many materials and is very good at puzzles, showing persistence and problem-solving ability.

He is not able to name colors.

While his vocabulary and grammar are advanced for his age, he uses words to boss or impress children, instead of talking *with* them.

Questions:
1. What does Ronnie gain from provoking other people?
2. Could he be color blind?

Strengths:
1. Concentration and problem-solving ability.
2. Enjoyment of adult companionship.

Needs:
1. Attention.
2. Limits.
3. More work on colors.

FIGURE 6-1

Resources
- Summary sheet listing questions, strengths, and needs of child.
- Resource books of activities.
- Creativity and experience of staff.
- Blank target sheet.

Checkpoints
- Are you helping yourself succeed by setting specific objectives, as well as general goals?
- Are you using "brainstorming" to make plans for child? Staff should think of *many* plans before choosing one.
- Are your plans *specific, workable* in your program, and *reasonable* in terms of *this* child's growth pattern?
- Are you helping yourself put the plans into action by:
  ○ assigning responsibility to specific teacher(s)?
  ○ giving that teacher assistance in fitting the new job into his or her workload?

Step 6: Ending the Staffing

Have you ever sat in a meeting that dragged on and on, where no one seemed to know how to bring it to a close? Or have you left meetings feeling vaguely dissatisfied and disgruntled?

We don't want that to happen. Your first staffing will not be perfect, but if yours is really a *Growing Program,* each discussion should be better than the last. How can you make that happen?

Here's a way that many groups have found helpful, especially when they're just beginning to work together. After you've finished making plans for the children you've discussed, have each teacher stop and think a minute, and then complete these two sentences:

- One thing that helped get things done today was _____. ("Ben's good notes"; "Rosalie's way of bringing us back to the point.")
- One thing that made it hard to get things done today was _____. ("Our digressions"; "Carol's being late"–*not* personal gibes like "Alan's big mouth"!)

Then take just a moment to read them out. You don't need to get into a discussion of these comments; they will give the staff something to think about before the next meeting. Rosalie will know she was appreciated. And maybe Carol will be on time next week.

A FINAL WORD: USING YOUR PLANS

Your lovely plans are no good if they're gathering dust in a drawer.

- Keep a notebook with individual target sheets and weekly group plans where it's *handy.* Get into the habit of looking through it first thing in the morning so you won't forget what you planned to do.

Sample Target Sheet for Ronnie

[T] = for teacher
[C] = for child

TARGET SHEET

Child's Name _____Ronnie_____   Date _____10/9_____

Goal	Objective(s)	Plan(s)	Who	When
[T] To find out more about the reasons for Ronnie's provoking behavior	Watch Ronnie's behavior in school.	Observe R. for first 5–10 min. each morning.	Sam	All week
	Get information about what's happening at home. Check out the possibility that R. is color blind.	Telephone R.'s mother to discuss situation.	Melissa	Friday
[C] To become more able to work cooperatively with others	We'd like to see R. work at a project with an adult.	Puzzle-making project with teacher.	Melissa	Wednesday
	We'd like to see R. share something of his with other children.	Have R. show finished puzzle to other children and work it with them.	Melissa	Thursday
[C] To learn colors	We'd like to see R. learn to match identical primary colors and find out if he *can* learn them!	Play game with R. using color chips—teacher name color as they're matched.	Alice	Monday
		At lunch, informally ask children to find something in room the same color as their shirt, dress, etc. NOTE: If more observation suggests color blindness, drop the activities until we get a vision report.	Sam	Lunchtime—Mon., Tues., Wed.

FIGURE 6-2

DO IT YOURSELF

Make plans to get together with the rest of your teaching team to try out the "staffing" plan we've suggested. Use the blank summary sheet and target sheet on the next pages to record your discussion of a child. At first, you might want to limit yourself to one goal, objective, and plan. Practice thinking in specifics, and monitoring your staffing to make sure you don't miss a step.

Student teachers: If you can't arrange to work with this approach in a staffing, try it with another student who works in your classroom—or do it alone if necessary. And remember, you must be able to back up your summary with specifics, especially if you have to report to someone else!

IF YOU ARE ALONE

Use these forms as a guide in doing your private staffing.

FORM 6-1

SUMMARY SHEET

Child's Name _____ Date _____

General Summary (progress and difficulty in growth areas; specific events at home or school; interests):

Questions:

Strengths:

Needs:

FORM 6–1 (Continued)

[T] = for teacher
[C] = for child

TARGET SHEET

Child's Name _____   Date _____

Goal	Objective(s)	Plan(s)	Who	When

FORM 6-2

SETTING DIRECTIONS FOR GROWTH

- Use individual plans as a basis for planning activities for the whole class. The puzzle-making project may be aimed at Ronnie, but others will learn from it, too. You may end up with every child making his or her own puzzle. Even though the activity is the same, your goals will be different for each child. Patsy's puzzle may be helpful in improving her fine-motor skills; Jeremy may expand his vocabulary in telling you about it; Mason's self-concept may get a badly needed boost. See Chapter 7, "Places for Growth: Activity Areas" for more on matching the activity to the child.
- Be honest in evaluating the success or failure of plans. No one's perfect—and you can always try again.
- *Follow up* at your next staffing. Which plans really got implemented and which got sidetracked? What were the problems? Successes? What next?

RESOURCES

Decker, C.A., and Decker, J.R. *Planning and Administering Early Childhood Programs.* Columbus, Ohio: Charles E. Merrill, 1976.

Provides some thoughtful discussion of the planning and administering of all types of programs for young children. It focuses on curricular as well as noncurricular administrative decisions that are involved with an effective program. It is helpful in offering the reader a variety of alternatives for making decisions as well as suggesting many adaptations to enhance logical problem solving.

Hasling, J. *Group Discussion and Decision Making.* New York: Thomas Y. Crowell, 1975.

Discusses decision-making barriers to communication, finding solutions, and structuring group discussion. Not written as a guide for teachers but could be helpful in improving your group planning sessions.

7

Places for Growth

ACTIVITY AREAS

CHALLENGE YOURSELF

You may believe
- Children need to learn to work independently. But are your activity areas set up to foster this kind of independence?
- Children have different styles of work and play. But do your activity areas invite children to express their individuality?
- Activity areas need planning and supervision. But do you know why you have the areas you do and why you have left out others?

SKILLS IN THIS CHAPTER

- Setting up and evaluating activity areas
- Selecting activity areas
- Maximizing learning in each area
- Supervising activity areas

HOW CHILDREN LEARN

Children are learning *all the time, from everything they do*. They learn by watching, listening, doing, making mistakes, fixing mistakes, playing, arguing.

Sarah is learning in all these ways.

Sarah pauses in the doorway to watch Molly and Kay putting on a puppet show in a theater the teacher has just set up. She goes to the shelf and gets a furry tiger puppet. "Growl!" she calls. "I'm gonna eat you up!" "You get out of here, you stinker!" shouts Molly. "Kay and me are *friends*." Sarah sucks her thumb a minute and then takes her puppet over to a corner. She tries to make its head move, but it keeps flopping over. Finally she gets her fingers in the right position and sings a growly song as the puppet bobs its head in rhythm. After a while she carries the puppet over to the block area and begins to make a cave for the tiger out of some large hollow blocks. "He's hungry," Sarah says to herself. She dashes over to the dramatic play corner and gathers up some dishes and cups. Crawling into the cave, she joins the tiger for "lunch."

A lot of important learning is going on here. Sarah uses the information she gets from watching her friends to figure out what those puppets are for. Her fierce approach to the other girls is rejected, so she learns something about social interaction, too. The challenge of mastering the puppet gives her a chance to solve a problem on her own and to practice small-motor skills. She goes on to organize her own play with the tiger, incorporating materials from around the room.

Since children are learning and growing all the time, you'll want to be sure they learn valuable and helpful things in your group. As a teacher you can provide *places* and *resources* that will encourage children's growth by taking advantage of their natural tendency to explore and investigate.

Places for learning = Activity Areas

Resources for learning = Activities and Materials

This chapter will help you create places for learning—activity areas—which fit with your goals for children and your understanding of how they grow. Chapter 9 will focus on materials and activities.

ACTIVITY AREAS AND PLAY: HARNESSING NATURAL ENERGY

Watch some children when they're not in school. They wiggle, move, poke in the dirt with sticks, and chat with their friends. They ask a lot of questions. *They're learning.* And they're doing it without being forced and without direct instruction.

Activity areas take advantage of this "natural energy" behind growth.

Activity areas give children a chance to learn in the ways that are easiest and most natural to them:

- through exploration

    Larry pours water from a big container to a small one. "It won't fit!" he announces.

- through real-life problem solving

    How can Annette and Marcia fix their building so it won't crash down again?

- through socialization

    "Look at my snake!" Ellen shows Peter. "I'm going to make a longer one," Peter announces, comparing his to Ellen's.

An Activity Area Is

An activity area is part of the classroom, set up so children can choose to work with different kinds of materials and topics. In a classroom arranged this way, children are seldom all doing the same thing at the same time, nor are they told exactly what to do with the materials provided.

Here are a few activity areas in operation:

- a block area

    Ms. Davis has arranged one corner of her room as a block activity area. Today, Ed and Joanne have made a road out of long blocks. When they ran out, they found two shorter blocks would fit the same space. Now they are getting cars and a gas pump for the "turnpike." Ms. Davis brings over some play money for the "gas-station man" to give his customers.

- an art area

    Today a table in the art area is set up with long paper strips and paste. Megan nervously watches Brian and Josh smearing the paste and dips a tentative finger into the dish. Brian is lost in the pleasure of sliding the paste around on the paper; after a while, he begins making "sandwiches" of paper strips. Josh suddenly discovers that a strip becomes a circle if you stick the ends together. Seeing this, Ms. Alda shows him how to make a paper chain, and soon all the children, even Megan, are constructing chains.

- a planting table

    As a preparation for spring, Ms. Branche has introduced a planting table into the science corner. When some of the children begin to explore the area they find several spades, a watering can, a table filled with potting soil, and a shelf beside the table with packets of flower seeds, twigs, bulbs, and some clay pots filled with small plants. After Sandy and Carol plant many different seeds, they ask Ms. Branche to come over to help them. She suggests that they make a chart with the names of what they have planted.

Not Just a Frill

Although most teachers of young children have activity areas in their classrooms, some still think of these areas as "frills," as places to keep children busy and amused until it's time for *real* learning—at formal, sit-down lessons for the whole group.

These teachers look at what children are doing in activity areas and think, "They're just playing." A closer look might tell a different story.

Psychologists tell us that play is much more than a time waster or a way to burn off excess energy. Play is the child's "work"—one of the ways he or she becomes a competent participant in the social and physical worlds. Through play a child can:

- Make sense out of objects in his or her world, developing concepts and sorting out ideas. Through hours of "playing" with blocks, a child learns which are light, which heavy; which long, which short; which balance or fit together.
- Learn to use symbols, and to think of what "might be." A block becomes a road, play dough is a hamburger, and these "play" symbols will help create an understanding of the symbols used in reading.
- Master worries and prepare for the future—to discover and understand him- or herself, his or her feelings and ideas. It's easy for a child to be brave about scary animals when his or her hand controls the tiger puppet, and maybe it'll help the child be less afraid of imaginary tigers in the dark.
- Organize many kinds of experience. Planning and executing a game of "gas station" requires many intellectual and social skills: independence, imagination, problem solving, memory, and integration of experiences with family and peers.

Because play is so important, free-play time, or the "activity period," is the heart of the day for young children. At this time, children may explore one or more activity areas, work with materials by themselves or with other children, work in a small group with the teacher, or even work with the teacher alone.

The Teacher's Job

If play is such a rich source of learning we might ask what teachers are meant to be doing while children are playing? Does it mean that you never challenge a child

- to tell a story
- to make a book
- to count
- to figure out how many cookies are left?

No.

Does it mean that you do not guide and plan for children's learning? That you have no responsibility for what children learn?

No.

There is a great difference between unsupervised play in an unplanned environment, and play that occurs in a well-thought-out room, with the support, challenges, and limits provided by skilled and caring staff.

This is your role: to provide the environment and experiences that enrich and extend the child's learning and living. In this book we touch on many of the ways in which teachers do that. One way is by planning activity areas. Let's look at these now.

What Activity Areas Can Do

The workbench "theme" in the 4's this month is musical instruments. Juanita started it all by making a guitar like her father's. Soon everyone wanted guitars, so a generous supply of rubber bands (for "strings") was added to the workbench, along with pictures of guitars and other instruments. Ms. Tees invited various friends and parents to visit the class with their instruments, and soon children were manufacturing drums, cymbals, and even a bass fiddle!

What might Ms. Tees, the teacher in this example, have been trying to do? Certainly much more than "just" keeping the children amused! She is

- building on the children's interests (the music)
- helping them set challenges for themselves, and meet them (how could you make a drum?)
- introducing them to adult interests

Ms. Tees might also be using this opportunity to work toward goals for individual children. For example, she might be:

- helping Geoff spend time with other children
- giving Jeanie a chance to exercise her planning skills
- helping Tisha to an experience of success
- expanding Lieu's English vocabulary

You can see that activity areas can have many uses. Let's step back a bit from Ms. Tees's class and consider these possible uses more broadly.

Exploration

Provide a rich physical and social environment to explore.

> In planning her room, Ms. Eden has made sure to include both social, active areas, like the block corner, and quiet areas, like the book corner; both challenging areas, like a table game area, and soothing areas, like the listening corner. Within each area she selected a range of materials that are varied but go together. In the outdoor play area she has a first-aid kit and rope (hoses!) to go with the firemen's hats; in the game area there are familiar puzzles, but without the frames.

Imagination

Provide materials that adapt themselves to the uses of the child's mind rather than limit it.

> One of Ms. Ina's first moves when she took over her new 5's classroom in September was to stash the stack of partly used coloring books left over from the previous teacher's reign. She replaced them with an inviting supply of paper of various colors and sizes—including some 10 by 4 inch scraps from a paper-supply house that became "cartoon" strips!

Independence

Encourage children to be independent in making choices about what to do, and in doing it.

> Ms. Clark works to help her 4-year-old children be aware of the choices they have, and of what things they want to do. She asks each child at circle time what she plans to do before the child is dismissed:
> "Marnie, what are you planning to do this morning?"
> She helps children think ahead:
> "Fred's using the tape recorder now. Do you want to put your name up for it next?"
> She helps children think of alternatives:
> "It looks like that road (in the block area) is going to run into Sophie's house. How else could you build it?"

Individuality

Provide a wide range of activities to fit the needs of each child.

> Ms. Stakey noticed the ways in which different children used the areas in her room:
> Sean, a reflective child, can often be seen sitting on the big chair in the book area, dreaming over a picture book, or working with crayons, drawing his latest "story."
> Letitia, a methodical child, retires to the game table when she has enough of the bustle and confusion of more active areas. Here *she* is in control, as she assembles a familiar puzzle or builds a neat symmetrical construction with plastic squares.
> Jane, a vigorous child, can usually be seen at the heart of the current dramatic play activity, building a "car," dressing a wound, or even rearranging all the furniture!

Interests

Reflect the interests of the children, modifying the focus of an area to build on ideas they have introduced.

> Jamie returned from a trip full of stories about a big bridge he had crossed. He soon set to work building one, and some of the other 5's joined in. Ms. Dunn brought a few pictures of bridges to circle the next day, and they talked about how they looked, how they might be held up, etc. The pictures went into the block area, and the next day she was pleased to note that someone was experimenting with the art of ramp building. Soon snapshots of the children's own bridges were being added to the picture wall.

Individualization

Take advantage of the opportunities activity areas offer for individual work with children.

> Mr. Tasch looks for moments, however brief, when he can support the growth of each individual child. Sometimes he asks questions to help the child put his or her thoughts into words:
> "Looks like there's quite a fight going on there (among the dolls). Why are they so mad?"
> Sometimes he stimulates thinking, or helps the child out of a tight spot.
> "What would happen if you tried that block over there?"
> Sometimes he takes advantage of moments when he can just be with a child, and those can be the most pleasant of all.

Basic Activity Areas

In the last section we talked about some of the uses of activity areas, and we implied that small changes are going on all the time. But these changes go on within a fairly stable framework. Just as you don't rearrange your whole house every week, you don't need to—and shouldn't—be adding new activity areas all the time! Certain areas are "basics" in most programs. These areas continue throughout the year—the "changes" are modifications on the basic theme. The basic areas are the ones that give the most mileage. They are the ones children seem to come back to time and time again, and where the most learning goes on.

The very basics
- book corner
- art area
- block area
- dramatic-play area
- puzzle and table-activity area
- outdoor area

The next most basic
- water/sand tables
- listening area
- science corner
- movement/music area
- writing and/or math area

Why are these areas so important? Taken together, they seem flexible enough to accommodate the widest possible range of interests and goals. The books can always be changed or the dressing clothes replaced, leading to new encounters and new learning.

These areas are basic also because of what children can learn in them. Their flexibility allows preschool children to learn math concepts, language skills, social understanding, and motor skills in the course of activities that are part of the child's play.

Here are a few examples of things children can learn in one area. Let's use the *block area.* In the block area, children can learn

- math concepts
  - practical size relationships (two of these will make one of those long ones)
  - shape relationships (filling in spaces to make a "floor"; using two triangles to make a rectangle)
- science concepts
  - balance (maybe it won't tip if I put this one here)
- social studies
  - building cities, towns, farms, airports
- motor control
  - placement of blocks
  - learning not to accidentally bump buildings

- pre-reading skills
  - use of symbols (this is a stoplight, and this is a lamp post)
  - written signs ("Make one that says 'Stop!', and one that's '35 miles an hour'")

We organized these examples according to traditional curriculum areas, but we might also have listed them by growth area. You can probably think of many more things children might learn in a rich and varied block area, which would stimulate *cognitive, language, social,* and *perceptual-motor* growth.

Imagination, Thinking, and "The Right Answers"

Children grow and learn from many different kinds of experiences.

Imagining
- Through play, Matina masters the separation from her mother by repeatedly "leaving" her baby in the dramatic play area.
- Christen sits in the block corner thinking for a bit, then sets to work building the airport she visited last week.

Discovering
- Marvin picks up a battery and one of the bulbs in a small display, and sets himself the job of getting the bulb to light.
- Leo picks up one of the math workguides (for the advanced kindergarteners) and sets about trying to fill the outlines with Cuisenaire rods.

Finding the right answer
- Three-year-old Sophie works diligently at matching sets of color strips on a tray—red with red, blue with blue, etc.
- Marsha, tongue sticking out, carefully copies letters from a printing guide.

Matina, Christen, Marvin, Leo, and Sophie are all learning. But the activities they are learning from involve each of them in different ways.

Imagining
- Matina and Christen are guiding the play—setting its "goals," and deciding how to go about reaching them. This kind of play draws on the whole child. It allows children to "work on" things that they need to explore, whether feelings (Matina) or ideas (Christen), which you cannot anticipate. You can't know before Matina comes in that her mother's trip is on her mind, and how she needs to cope with it. What you *can* do is have activity areas available which invite the *whole* child (art, blocks, dramatic play).

Discovering
- Marvin and Leo are trying to find a route to a goal. The goal is set by the activity, not the child. But there are different ways of reaching each goal. The child's problem-solving ability is brought into play. If I try this, or this . . . what will happen? The child practices focusing and directing his thinking, trying and discarding solutions.

DO IT YOURSELF

Can you fill in the missing pieces?

If you have...	What might children learn in each growth area?
A water table with plastic containers of various sizes (1/4 cup, 1/2 cup, 1 cup, 1 pint, etc.)	cognitive language social perceptual-motor
An art area with collage materials, easel and paint, crayons and paper	cognitive language social perceptual-motor
A block area with a large number of unit blocks, and two small fire trucks	cognitive language social perceptual-motor
A workbench with a collection of light-weight tools, styrofoam, glue, box filled with bottle caps	cognitive language social perceptual-motor
A clay table with clay, 2 rolling pins, a set of cookie cutters, and a cookie sheet	cognitive language social perceptual-motor

FORM 7-1

Finding the right answer
- Sophie and Marsha are working with activities which each have one, and *only* one, right answer. Both the goal of the activity and the way it must be done are set. The child puts very little of "herself"—her fantasies, ideas, or thinking—into these projects. Their advantage, though, is in teaching very specific skills or bits of knowledge. Children (especially older fives) often like to learn skills they see as part of "growing up," and they enjoy the neatness and orderliness of the activity.

Some activity areas seem to foster one kind of learning experience more than others.

Imagination	• block area
	• dramatic play
	• art area
Discovery	• puzzle and table games of many sorts
	• science area (if it has been planned to provoke thought)

In most preschool classrooms there is no one area that is full of "right answer" experiences. And, in fact, there are often overlaps among the others. The main point is to keep a *balance*.

- Are there really plenty of opportunities in your classroom for "whole child" experiences?

    "Mrs. B., I'm going to be a *captain* today! I'm going to make a ship, and it won't sink!"

- Do children encounter challenges to their minds?

    Barry struggles with the problem of making a tiny bulb light, using a "problem box" with batteries, bulbs, and wire.

- Do you have a few opportunities for the experience of learning the *right* answer to a problem?

Just one more note about "right answer" experiences: there is a danger here, and it lies in wait, not for the child, but for the teacher.

These activities are *easy*. They are easy to set up, simple to supervise, and don't make much of a mess. For some teachers these activities have become *the* program, and this doesn't leave much room for the *child's* ideas, worries, choice.

The solution, of course, is a balance, one which will allow children to test themselves against "right answer" tasks at times, in the context of a classroom which provides richly for imaginative and problem-solving activities.

Evolution and the Preschool Program

Darwin pointed out that living things change over the generations, as they try and succeed or fail. So do preschool programs. Activity areas, in particular, are seldom the same from one "generation" (that is, week) to the next.

Tammy trotted off to the art area, as usual, after circle time. She headed for the smocks.

Halfway there, she paused. On the table were an orange, a lemon, and an apple. "Hey, Ms. Stout," she called. There was also paper, and a cloth in a tray, with blue paint all in it! What *is* all this? Then Tammy spied a chart on the wall—it showed a series of pictures: half an orange in the paint, then on the paper . . . "Hey Jeanie, come here! Something new!" Before long Ms. Stout joined the two girls.

Like Ms. Stout's art area, basic activity areas change all the time. In fact, part of what makes them "basic" is the fact that each is so flexible. By using this flexibility you keep your program lively and interesting. If you *don't* use it, you'll find the play in one area after another becoming repetitive and limited. And you'll hear more and more . . . "But what can I *do*?"

When you modify an activity area, it's usually part of a larger plan. You may want to:

- pick up on an interest shown by a child, or a group of children

    Mr. Morris supplied some "campers" in the outdoor area with a sheet for a tent, and some cardboard tube "logs."

- extend a topic or skill you have introduced

    The "fours" had a series of "color" tables in their science area. One week everything was blue, the next week red, and so on. (The teacher might supply the first item, with the children adding more as the week goes on.)

- provide for one child's needs

    Josh's new baby sister was really "getting on his nerves," as he put it. Ms. Wiley added some books about new babies to the book corner and made a point of reading a few with Josh.

Setting up Activity Area

Let's look at a group of four-year-olds in January. They already have a number of activity areas—an art area (easels, clay, crayon and collage materials, special projects), a table-game area, a dramatic-play area, a block area, etc. But Barbara, the teacher, feels that the group is getting into a rut. She's considering either creating a new activity area or changing an old area in some way.

Lots of ideas occur to her. How about

- a science area with magnets?
- a print shop with rubber letters and paper?
- an indoor sandbox?
- puppets and a puppet theater?
- a cozy music corner with records?
- a grocery store to replace the house corner?

How can Barbara decide? She needs to think about the following considerations:

- time of year (simpler activity areas and fewer materials early in year)
- children's interests and needs (individual and group)

- group versus individual involvement
- kinds of learning she would like to take place
- physical space
- balance with other areas in room (quiet/noisy; exploratory/problem solving; hard/soft; familiar/new)
- length of the school day
- amount of supervision and instruction required in the area.

Here is how Barbara thinks about the problem.

By January, Barbara feels the children could use a bit more complexity and challenge. She doesn't have room to set up a large new center, but the class is running well enough that she has more time to spend in one activity area. She's noticed that some of the children are becoming interested in numbers, that the quality of dramatic play has deteriorated in recent weeks, that some of the boys are avoiding the house corner, and that activities in each area could be extended in many ways. She decided on the grocery-store area as being best suited to her own plans and the children's interests and needs.

Now that Barbara has an idea of what she wants, she can begin to think about how she will set up this new or expanded area. How will she supervise it? Should it be available to the children all the time? She, and you, should consider the following.

Steps in Setting up an Activity Area

1. *Prepare children as necessary beforehand.* Barbara wanted her class to be involved in planning the "store" area. She began by asking them about their own trips to the store—what they saw, what they bought, how it was paid for. The class took a trip to the local supermarket, where they were taken "behind the scenes." Everyone was enthusiastic about starting a store in the house corner. With Barbara's help they made lists and drew pictures.
2. *Have materials available.* Again Barbara wanted to involve the children. They made play money, asked parents for empty cans and boxes, and painted a large refrigerator carton to serve as the "store." Materials on shelves were rearranged to provide a place for all this extra equipment.
3. *Clarify rules about use of area.* Barbara had a few unexpected problems here. The first day, *everyone* wanted to "play store"—and be the storekeeper! Tears and fights ensued. Barbara helped the children decide how many could play in the area and made a list of turns for storekeeper. Next time she and the children will set up the rules ahead of time. She might try some of these ideas:
    - Have a certain number of necklaces hanging near the grocery-store area. Each child who decides to play there takes a necklace. When there are no necklaces left, the area is filled.
    - "Roles" for the day could be established at group time. Children could decide with Barbara who would fill those roles for a designated period of time.
    - Children could help establish all the rules that they believed were important. These could then be posted, perhaps in picture form, in the grocery store area—"Rules of the Store."
    - As a last resort, if children could not follow the rules then the area

would have to be closed temporarily. A "Store Closed" sign would appear for a few days.
4. *Keep area attractive and interesting.* After a while the "groceries" began to look shabby and the "money" began to get dirty and torn. Since the children were still interested, Barbara replaced the worn-out materials and introduced a few new ones—a cash register and a grocer's apron. These additions kept the dramatic play going for several weeks more.

Supervising Activity Areas

We have covered a lot of ground in this chapter, ideas about choosing an activity area, setting it up, and preparing children to use it.

And yet your job has just begun. The next step is to help children use the area in a productive, constructive, and safe way. This help is called "supervision." In planning an activity area, you have created a "structure" for children to learn from. Yet, by nature, what is used will also tend to get misused, and used up. Without your supervision the "structure" of activity areas will begin to disintegrate.

- books find their way to the wrong shelves, jumbled in with trucks and people
- dress-up clothes get torn; spoons lost
- puzzle pieces disappear.

Children's experiences are also less pleasurable, and less productive, without your support.

- Martha's sculpture keeps getting knocked over by two rambunctious "truck drivers" using the collage table as a highway
- Eric gives up his snap-together car project in frustration
- Hiram feels his monumental block building goes unappreciated

Your help in maintaining order, soothing social friction, and offering suggestions is necessary in every area. Here are a few general suggestions.

Supervision Checklist

This checklist will help ensure that you are doing all you can.

- Allow children to explore new materials without jumping in too fast. It might be a good idea to introduce new materials or a new area at a time when your group is gathered together. Allow them to look closely, touch, ask questions, etc.
- See that materials are respected, treated, and stored properly. Establish and discuss rules of usage with the children. Code storage areas with picture symbols so that children can see where things belong.
- Protect children's right to work without interference from others. Clearly establish and code activity areas that are limited to one, two, or more

children, such as a listening area or water table. Have a variety of such groupings in your classroom.
- Keep children's safety in mind by limiting the number of children for some activities. Some areas (such as an indoor climber) may only be available to children when an adult can supervise closely.
- Keep the "big picture" in mind. When working with one child or in one area, keep one eye and one ear on the rest of the room, ready to forestall any emerging crises. It helps to avoid working with your back to the room. Keep your face to the large group, so a glance every minute or two can keep you in tune with the class.

Getting Enough to Go Around

You'll probably find supervision easier if a team of teachers and assistants have the primary responsibility for specific areas in the room for given blocks of time. Although this is certainly the ideal, it is most unlikely that you will ever have enough staff to carefully supervise and involve an adult in every area that you want to have available. You may want to consider some of the following techniques for smooth classroom operation:

- *Group some areas together.* Incorporate the planting table into the science corner, or the art area and a special spring display table.
- *Close an area.* Consider temporarily closing an area that is too difficult to operate without close adult supervision (the workbench). You may want to have this area open for only certain periods of the day. A regular schedule lets the children know what to expect.
- *Limit your audience.* If you have decided that two children would profit from working with a particular language game, then invite just those two to try it out in the game area. Sometimes you may want to work with only two to five children at a time. You can set up the cooking area so that each group cooks, eats its product at a nearby table, washes the dishes, and sets the table for the next group. Then others can take their turn.
- *Set up self-help guides.* Provide children with visual guides for activities.
  - Arrows lead a child from the "listening post," where he has heard a story, to the library corner, where he will find that same story on the "Book-of-the-Week" display shelf.
  - Hanging shoe pockets in the math area have different math games in each pocket. A felt number pasted on the front of each pocket goes from number 1, the easiest game, to number 5, the most difficult. An adult or a friend is always available if there is a problem.
  - A picture suggests that two children should try the large horseshoe magnet with a variety of objects in an accompanying shoe box lab.

Observing in Activity Areas

When children are working in an activity area, you have a great chance to see what they're really like.

Step back a bit and look at what's going on.

You might want to ask:

DO IT YOURSELF

1. Are you and your children getting the most out of your activity areas? Take some time to look carefully at your classroom. Then see which of the following statements apply to your use of activity areas:

	In my class...	Yes	No
GENERAL USE OF ACTIVITY AREAS	1. Children have large, comfortable blocks of free-choice time in activity areas.	☐	☐
	2. Children work independently in activity areas.	☐	☐
	3. Children spend a good part of the time working with materials that don't have "right answers."	☐	☐
	4. Children have a chance to work individually with the teacher in activity areas.	☐	☐
	5. At some point in the day, the teacher observes and records what children are doing in activity areas.	☐	☐

Circle the "No" answer that you would most like to change to a "Yes." What are some things you could do to meet your goal?

_____
_____
_____
_____

2. Now list your activity areas here:

_____   _____
_____   _____
_____   _____
_____   _____
_____   _____
_____   _____
_____   _____
_____   _____

FORM 7-2

In the space below, write in the name of the activity area in your classroom which best fits each statement:

	Pluses	*Minuses*
PLUSES AND MINUSES IN SPECIFIC ACTIVITY AREAS	+ Children use this area constantly when it's available. _____	− Children don't use this area much. _____
	+ Children find and put away materials by themselves. _____	− Children tend to get out of control here. _____
	+ New things have recently been added to this area. _____	− Children are constantly asking for help here. _____
	+ I work with individual children in this area. _____	− I spend too much time supervising this area. _____

Area I'm most dissatisfied with: _____

Why: _____
_____
_____
_____
_____
_____
_____

What needs to be done to improve it:

☐ adding new area: what? _____

FORM 7-2 (Continued)

☐ revamping
present
area .... ☐ new materials
☐ better rules
☐ more teacher input
☐ more input from children

Immediate plans:

_____
_____
_____
_____
_____
_____
_____
_____
_____
_____
_____
_____
_____
_____
_____
_____
_____
_____
_____
_____

FORM 7-2 (Continued)

DO IT YOURSELF

Here is an example of some picture "instructions" that might be used for older preschool children. These are for making lemonade. This chart should be posted as a reminder for children who have made lemonade before, not for those who are just starting out.

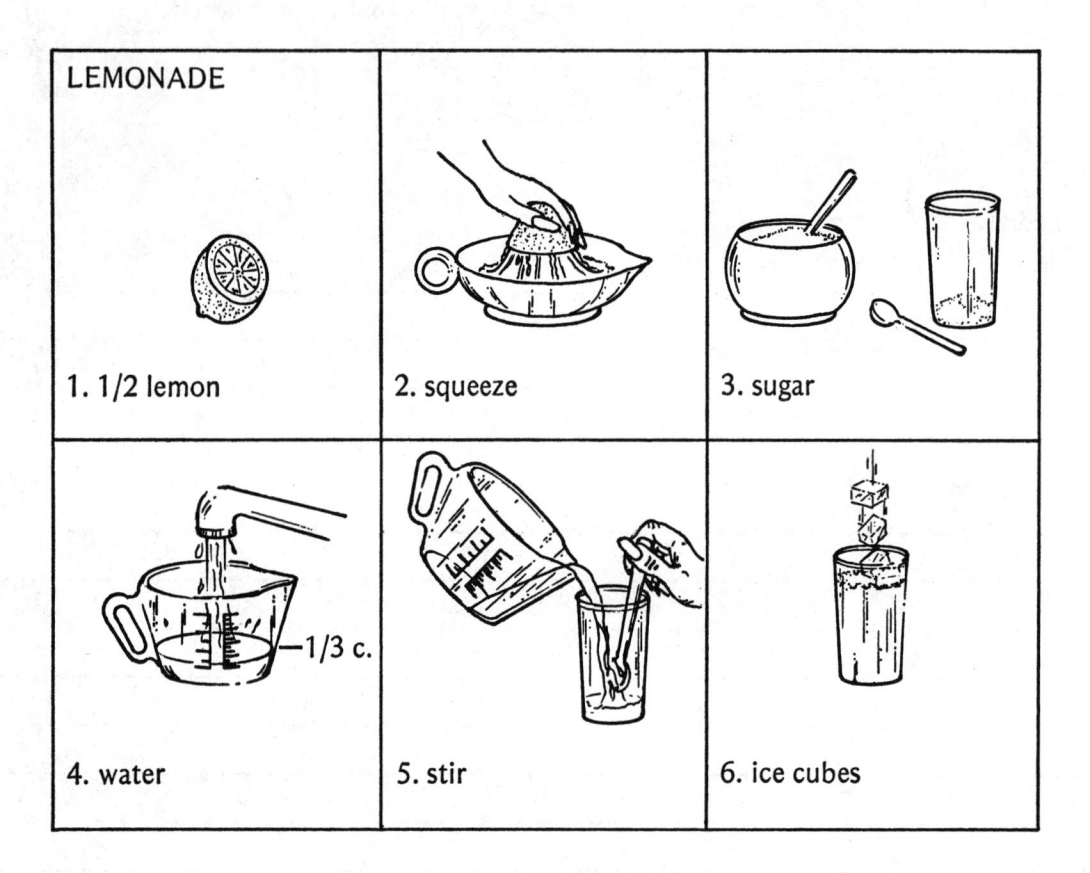

LEMONADE		
1. 1/2 lemon	2. squeeze	3. sugar
4. water	5. stir	6. ice cubes

FIGURE 7-1

Pick one of these activities (or one of your own) and sketch out some picture instructions. Then have a friend try to follow them. Ask him or her to see how many mistakes he or she can make, following your directions!

Then revise, make a chart, and try it with your children!

- making play dough
- using stencils and paint to make designs
- using the phonograph

FORM 7-3

- What are children doing with the materials in the activity center? Are they bored, involved, creative, destructive, timid? Lots of individual differences here! Write them down.

> Have checksheets and index cards handy so you won't forget what you see.
> For more information on using checksheets and index cards, see the section on "Observing and Recording Children's Behavior" (pp. 70–73).

- What are children learning from the materials and each other? Are they learning what you expected? other things? good things?
- What needs to be added or changed to make the area a better place to learn?
  - new materials?
  - rules about use of area?
  - teacher input?

Here's what Ms. Loftus saw when she watched her four-year-olds at the water table:

Andrew and Chrissie were blowing bubbles with plastic straws. They giggled as the bubbles rose over the top of the cups they were using and ran down the sides back into the water. After a while four more children arrived, bringing dishes to wash. "He's in my way!" complained Andrew. Someone got the idea of using paper towels as "washcloths." Before Ms. Loftus knew what was happening, the tubs were full of disintegrating paper towels. A few dolls had been added by other children who wandered by. Everyone was having a wonderful time.

This observation showed Ms. Loftus a number of things. Although the water area was enjoyed by the children, she decided it needed some changes.

- She limited the number of children at the water table to three at a time.
- She limited the number of things the children could use at one time.
- She added some sponges and washcloths to the supply of water-play materials.
- She worked with Andrew and Chrissie the next day, blowing bubbles, popping them, talking about their size and color.

RESOURCES

Almy, M. *Early Childhood Play.* New York: Selected Academic Readings, 1968.
   This collection of articles by leading educators, researchers, and theorists will convince you of the importance of play in a child's development.

Fleming, B.M., and Hamilton, D.S. *Resources for Creative Teaching in Early Childhood Education.* New York: Harcourt Brace Jovanovich, 1977.
   A unique resource book that integrates curriculum ideas and learning opportunities for every subject and part of the day. Although ideas are grouped under several general head-

ings, they emphasize that children can learn a concept through experiences in many different and well-equipped environments.

Hill, D.M. *Mud, Sand, and Water.* Washington, D.C.: NAEYC, 1977.

A delightful exploration, through words and photographs, of children using mud, sand, and water in settings other than a classroom. By providing encouragement, flexible materials, and periods of uninterrupted time, through the creation of a living and learning environment, children are free to explore and use the materials in many ways.

Lay, M.Z., and Dopyera, J.E. *Becoming a Teacher of Young Children.* Lexington, Mass.: D.C. Heath, 1977.

An unusual book providing students and those in the field with concepts and materials that will help make the most of classroom time.

Sargent, B. *The Integrated Day in an American School.* Boston: National Association of Independent Schools, 1970.

Written by an experienced and innovative teacher, this book is useful for its many ideas for organizing activity areas around children's interests. The author's frank evaluations of the success or failure of various activities are refreshing.

Schickedanz, J.A., York, M.A., Stewart, I.S., and White, D. *Strategies for Teaching Young Children.* Englewood Cliffs, N.J.: Prentice-Hall, 1977.

This is more than a book of collected activities. It presents activities that are ordered by areas and levels of difficulty, with a clear relationship made between the activity and the child's specific level of development. This is very usable and is filled with numerous additional suggestions, variations, and photographs to highlight the many well-developed activities.

8

Resources for Growth

ACTIVITIES AND MATERIALS

CHALLENGE YOURSELF

You may believe
- Activities should benefit children. But do you select activities according to your children's needs and interests?
- Children learn by active involvement. But do you provide activities and materials that encourage children to try out their own ideas?
- The best materials are sometimes free. But have you developed a system for getting, storing, and using these free materials?

SKILLS IN THIS CHAPTER

- Choosing activities
- Getting the most out of the materials you have
- Getting more materials

THINGS FOR LEARNING: ACTIVITIES AND MATERIALS

You may feel that the last thing in the world you need is some more information about activities and materials for your classroom. The "education business" is bulging at the seams with books of activities, overeager toy salesmen, exhibits of teaching materials, and catalogs listing literally thousands of things to do with children.

At first, it seems nice to have so much choice. But after a while, you may begin to see a few problems:

- Many of the resource books give you ideas for hundreds of "fun things to do with children." What they *don't* give you is help in
  - individualizing activities (Will it work for Ben?)
  - sequencing and connecting activities (How does this number game build on what you did last week?)
  - getting the most mileage out of what you've already got (How can you use those tin cans left over from juice time?)
- Many materials are too complicated, demanding an excessive amount of time to prepare and supervise.
- Many of the materials on the market simply cost too much.

We'd like to suggest a different way of thinking about activities and materials —one that's more realistic and more in tune with how children actually learn best.

ACTIVITIES

Sometimes being poor can make you a better teacher. We know that children learn best by doing. One way of "doing" is to "fool around" with things in many different ways, making and solving problems. This kind of "doing" doesn't need an elaborate, teacher-created set of fancy materials or activities. As a matter of fact, those things would probably do more to *hinder* learning than to *help* it.

What you *do* need are the "basic ingredients" of learning: the children, some materials, and an idea about what you want to do with them.

Out of these basic ingredients you *and* the children can create an infinite number of "things to do" (*activities*). These activities may be:

- planned by the children or planned by you
- simple or elaborate
- short-term or long-term

- preplanned or "instant teaching"
- open-ended or structured.

Purpose of Activities

What should activities do? They should *not* just

- please parents
- make teachers feel clever
- keep children occupied and out of trouble.

The *main purpose* of activities is to help children learn and grow in their own special way. That's why the *starting point* of an activity always has to be

- the *goals* and *objectives* you've set for the children
- the *interests* and experiences of the children
- the *materials* you have.

In other words,

$$\text{Goals} + \text{Interests} + \text{Materials} \rightarrow \text{Activities}$$

By keeping this equation in mind as you plan activities, you'll make certain that your activities are more than "fun things for children to do." You'll be giving activities an important place in your Growing Program.

Helping You Choose Activities

The problem in selecting activities is that there's so much choice. "Activity books" fill the shelves of bookstores; you could probably have five new activities every day for a year and still not run out. What you need is some help in deciding which activity will best contribute to *this* child's growth at *this* time. This is where the "equation" can be helpful. By considering every part of the equation, you'll make sure your activities add up to growth.

$$\boxed{\text{Goals}} + \text{Interests} + \text{Materials} \rightarrow \text{Activities}$$

Beginning with Goals

If you are observing, thinking, and talking about the children in your classroom, you are probably also beginning to formulate goals and objectives:

- for one child

    The staff would like to see Ronda talk to other children more readily.
- for a small group

    Ms. Palmer wants these four children to learn to read their names.
- for the whole group

    Over the course of the year, the staff wants this group to become more able to talk about their feelings.

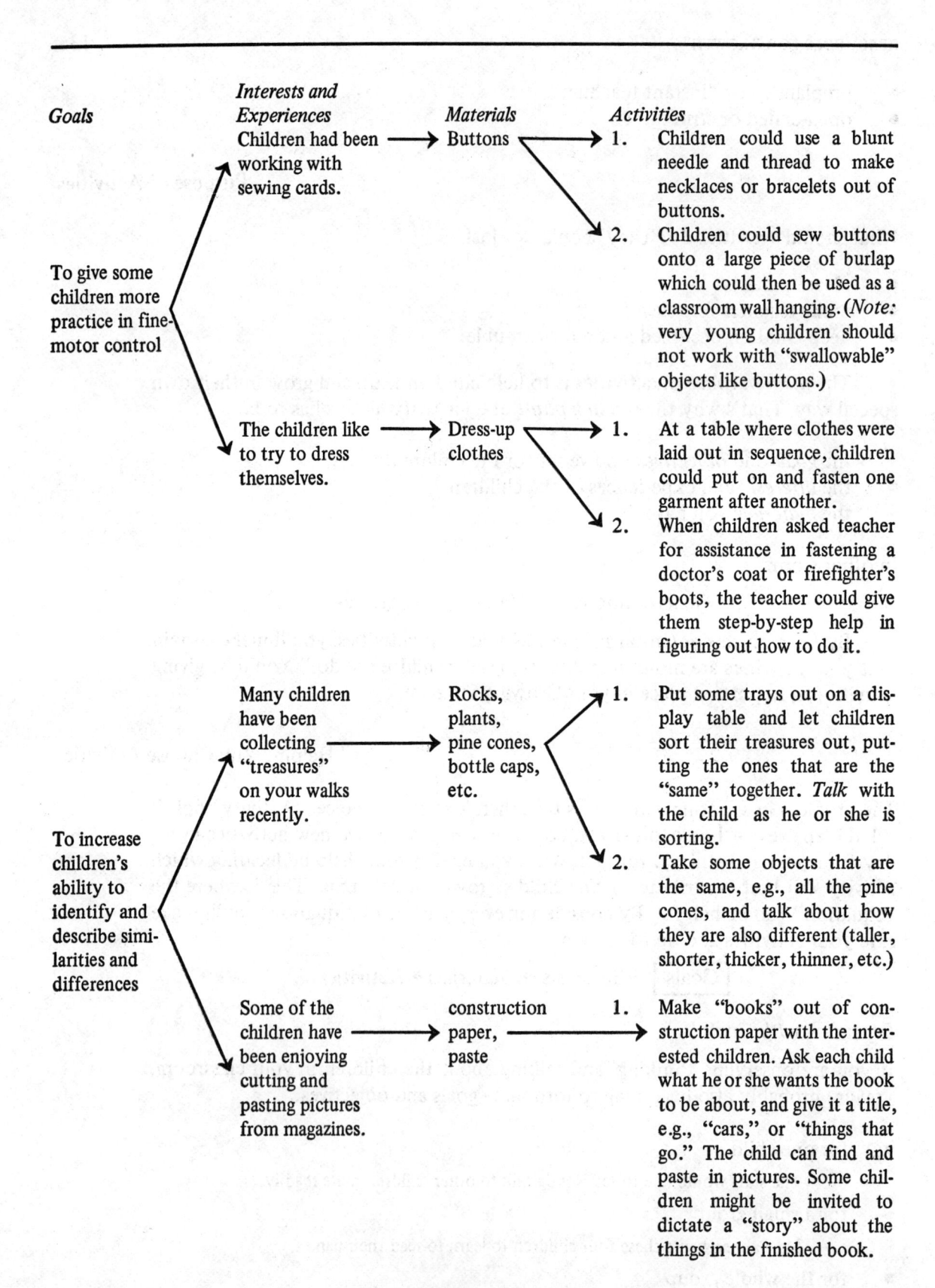

Goals	Interests and Experiences	Materials	Activities
To give some children more practice in fine-motor control	Children had been working with sewing cards.	Buttons	1. Children could use a blunt needle and thread to make necklaces or bracelets out of buttons. 2. Children could sew buttons onto a large piece of burlap which could then be used as a classroom wall hanging. (*Note:* very young children should not work with "swallowable" objects like buttons.)
	The children like to try to dress themselves.	Dress-up clothes	1. At a table where clothes were laid out in sequence, children could put on and fasten one garment after another. 2. When children asked teacher for assistance in fastening a doctor's coat or firefighter's boots, the teacher could give them step-by-step help in figuring out how to do it.
To increase children's ability to identify and describe similarities and differences	Many children have been collecting "treasures" on your walks recently.	Rocks, plants, pine cones, bottle caps, etc.	1. Put some trays out on a display table and let children sort their treasures out, putting the ones that are the "same" together. *Talk* with the child as he or she is sorting. 2. Take some objects that are the same, e.g., all the pine cones, and talk about how they are also different (taller, shorter, thicker, thinner, etc.)
	Some of the children have been enjoying cutting and pasting pictures from magazines.	construction paper, paste	1. Make "books" out of construction paper with the interested children. Ask each child what he or she wants the book to be about, and give it a title, e.g., "cars," or "things that go." The child can find and paste in pictures. Some children might be invited to dictate a "story" about the things in the finished book.

FIGURE 8-1

RESOURCES FOR GROWTH

Both goals and objectives guide your program. For convenience, in this chapter we have used "goals" as a shorthand to refer to both. Once you have one or more goals in mind, you might think next about your children's:

Interests and Experiences

- present

    Ms. Jackson's group loves to play doctor.

- or past

    Ms. Plotkin's group has just finished an art project about Spring.

- or by group

    All the children in one group love to dance.

Usually a teacher has certain materials on hand when he or she's trying to choose an activity.

Sometimes the "materials" you begin with will be concrete objects:

- blocks
- clay
- measuring cups.

At other times the routines of the day will be your "materials":

- storytime
- music
- lunch.

Materials

Think about the materials you have available, keeping in mind the goal you've selected and the interests of your children. Which materials would lend themselves to meeting that goal? Which seem most in tune with the children's (or the particular child's) interests? How could you use those materials to help reach the goals you have?

When you have answered these questions, you have described the *activity* you have chosen.

Of course, you can probably think of more than one activity to do the job for any one goal. And it's a good idea to have more than one activity in mind, in case the first doesn't interest the children, or you need to reinforce what they are learning.

Let's look at this planning process in action. In Figure 8-1 we've given two goals and shown how each can lead to a variety of activities, depending on the children's interests and the materials available.

Other Places to Begin

Although your goals for children are always the basis of activity planning, sometimes you may begin your planning at another place in the equation. You can begin with *interests:*

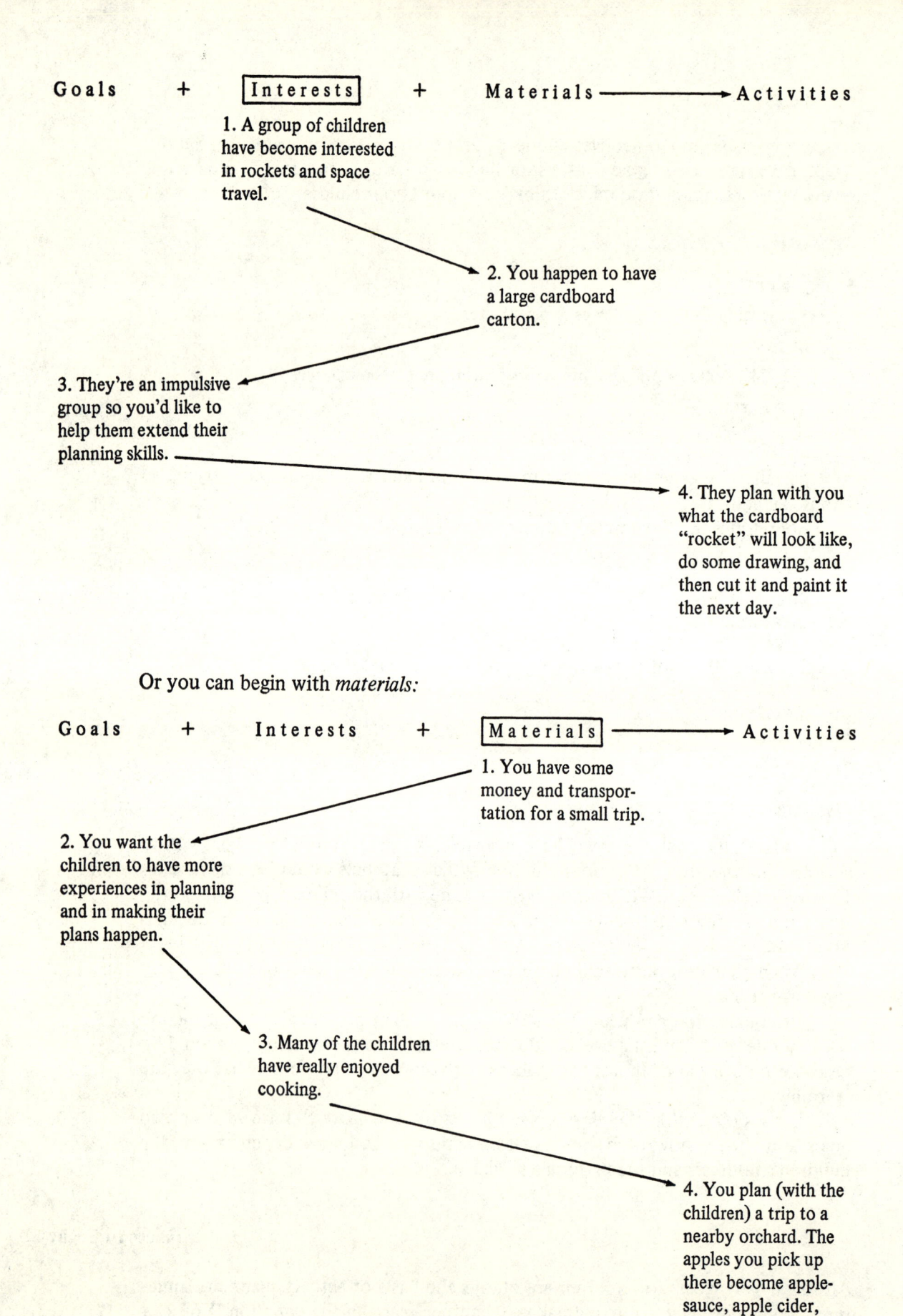

Goals + |Interests| + Materials ⟶ Activities

1. A group of children have become interested in rockets and space travel.

2. You happen to have a large cardboard carton.

3. They're an impulsive group so you'd like to help them extend their planning skills.

4. They plan with you what the cardboard "rocket" will look like, do some drawing, and then cut it and paint it the next day.

Or you can begin with *materials*:

Goals + Interests + |Materials| ⟶ Activities

1. You have some money and transportation for a small trip.

2. You want the children to have more experiences in planning and in making their plans happen.

3. Many of the children have really enjoyed cooking.

4. You plan (with the children) a trip to a nearby orchard. The apples you pick up there become applesauce, apple cider, baked apples and apple fritters.

Or you can begin with an *activity*. Usually this happens when you get hold of one of those ubiquitous activity books or see an activity in another class or at a workshop. Something looks like so much fun that you can't wait to try it.

Stop! Before you plunge in, ask yourself whether this activity fits in with

- the way children learn by active involvement
- specific goals you have for the group or individual children
- other things you and the children have been doing
- materials you have or can get.

If your answer is "Yes," then go ahead.

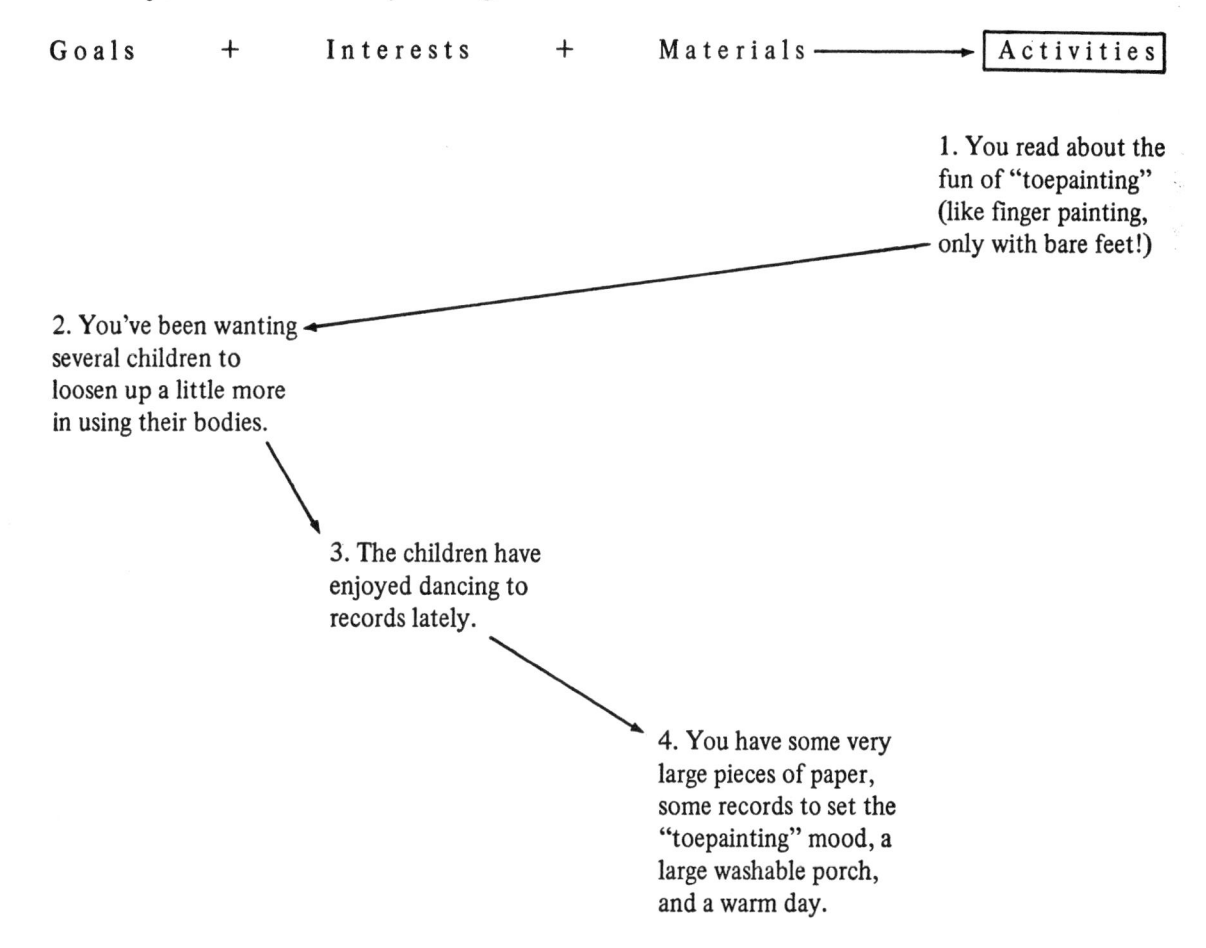

Goals + Interests + Materials ⟶ Activities

1. You read about the fun of "toepainting" (like finger painting, only with bare feet!)

2. You've been wanting several children to loosen up a little more in using their bodies.

3. The children have enjoyed dancing to records lately.

4. You have some very large pieces of paper, some records to set the "toepainting" mood, a large washable porch, and a warm day.

Evaluating and Keeping Activities

It's easy to forget just what you did with the laundry starch last year, or how that counting game went. A system for recording and filing activities will help you remember, and will be a resource for other teachers.

As with new recipes, it's usually a good idea to try an activity once before making a permanent record of it. To determine whether the activity was successful, you might ask yourself these questions:

- Did it seem to help the child reach the goal you'd set?
- Did the child or children enjoy it and ask to do it again?

DO IT YOURSELF

Now try out your ability to use the "planning equation."

1. Follow the sample on page 136, and begin with two goals or objectives you have in mind—for an individual, a few children, or the entire class. Then move on to interests, materials, and activities. See what you can come up with!
2. If you are working with a group, exchange your worksheet with a partner for suggestions—either for additional ideas or for ways to improve the activities.
3. Select one of the activities you have designed, plan it, and go do it! *Student teachers:* before doing an activity, you will need to show your worksheet to your teacher. If there is an activity you might try, perhaps he or she will help you plan in more detail.

Goals	Interests and experiences	Materials	Activities
	1.		1.
			2.
	2.		1.
			2.
	1.		1.
			2.
	2.		1.
			2.

FORM 8-1

RESOURCES FOR GROWTH

- Was it reasonably easy to set up, supervise, and clean up (or, if it *was* complicated, was it worth it)?

If it was successful, write it down.

File cards and a file box will keep your activities organized. Below is a format to use for the file cards. File according to activity area (art, blocks, table games, water play, etc.). Most activities can contribute to development in more than one growth area, and you can note that on your card. For example, while all songs help develop musical "sense" (e.g., rhythm), some also contribute to language skills (e.g., naming body parts), social skills (e.g., songs about feelings), and cognitive skills (e.g., singing directions, then doing them).

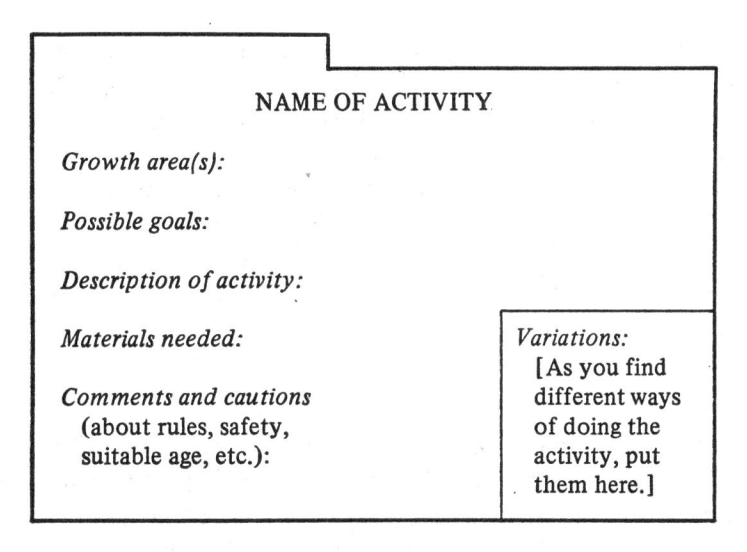

```
┌─────────────────────────────────────────────┐
│              NAME OF ACTIVITY               │
│                                             │
│   Growth area(s):                           │
│                                             │
│   Possible goals:                           │
│                                             │
│   Description of activity:                  │
│                                             │
│   Materials needed:      ┌────────────────┐ │
│                          │ Variations:    │ │
│   Comments and cautions  │ [As you find   │ │
│     (about rules, safety,│ different ways │ │
│     suitable age, etc.): │ of doing the   │ │
│                          │ activity, put  │ │
│                          │ them here.]    │ │
└──────────────────────────┴────────────────┘─┘
```

MATERIALS: INGREDIENTS FOR LEARNING

In the first part of this chapter we talked about selecting (and inventing!) activities that are right for your children. In Chapter 6, we described the activity areas which are the machinery to get the Growing Program going. However, just like a car needs gas, activities and activity areas can't get far without materials. Children need "things" to do activities *with,* and these things must be interesting and attractive.

This is where some of you throw up your hands and say—"*Don't* tell me about all the fancy equipment I need! I don't have any money!" or, "I don't use half the stuff I have in the closet already!"

Relax. We are not going to tell you all the things you "have" to have, but can't afford. We are not going to stuff your closet even fuller with games which somehow never get used. We *are* going to help you get the most out of what you already have.

Of course, sometimes you do need more materials. Here the trick is to find ways of getting materials that are free, inexpensive, or (if you have to spend money) of good quality. But let's begin by looking at what you already have.

Getting the Most Out of What You've Got

You probably already have "the basics"—the standard set of equipment that is found in most centers.

- toy stove
- blocks
- boxes of crayons
- easels
- rhythm instruments
- rubber farm animals
- and so on.

If you think about it, there's a very good reason why these materials *are* "the basics" and are found in so many schools. They let children learn the way they learn best—by exploring and doing. They invite creativity and imagination by suggesting many possibilities.

What can you do with a *block,* for example? Get your mind in gear and think of all the possibilities for this basic material. You could, for instance, build with it, measure with it, float it, wash it, dry it, trace around it, weigh it, make music with it, balance on it, use it as a plate, a boat, a car, a telephone, a bed, and on, and on, and on....

Getting the "Teaching Habit"

When you were thinking about that block just now, you were getting the "teaching habit." The teaching habit is free, and it's the most important resource you have in planning things for children to do in your class. It's the habit of constantly looking at the basic ingredients—the materials *and* the children *and* your goals for them—and thinking "What can we do right now to help these children grow?"

Let's look at a few basic materials and see what activities we can imagine that would extend the learning possibilities they offer.

- *the water table/water play*
  - free exploration
  - pouring with various size containers, strainers, sifters, measuring cups, funnels
  - squeezing with sponges, squirt bottles, rubber tubing
  - experiments with floating and sinking objects
  - washing dishes or doll clothes
  - "painting" the fence with water
  - hosing off cars and trucks
  - bubble blowing
  - watering flowers
  - make-believe play with plastic people, animals, boats, and cars
- *the sand table*
  - free exploration with a variety of objects
  - pouring and sifting

RESOURCES FOR GROWTH

- hand or foot prints
- sand tea party
- make-believe play with toy cars and people
- creating a sand village
- rivers and lakes
- measuring sand
- sand castle and towers
- filling the sand table or large basins with wood chips or sawdust (these are fun for a change)

- *collections of small objects (e.g., buttons)*
  - free exploration
  - sorting by color
  - sorting by shape
  - guess how many buttons
  - see how many ways you can sort
  - match the button to the card
  - find the smallest button, the largest button
  - weigh the buttons
  - sew buttons on cloth
  - collect all the buttons with two holes, then with four holes
  - make a button collage
  - use as counters for board games

More Ways to Get the Most

How can you get even more mileage out of these basic materials?

1. *Keep some materials back* until later in the year, a rainy day, etc.

    Ms. Bremer started the year with only simple blocks in the block area. As the children became skilled at building with these basic pieces, she gradually added accessories—trees, animals, more complex block shapes. In this way she kept up the children's interest and matched the materials to their growth.

2. *Rearrange and recombine* old materials in new ways.

    The children seemed to be getting tired of playing at the water table until Ms. Asta brought over some doll clothes to wash. This started an enthusiastic new game which lasted a week.

3. *Use the same material in different ways.*

    After the children had been painting at the easel for some weeks, Ms. Oldman created a floor easel out of a cut-down box and let them paint there. On a nice day she tacked easel paper to a fence outside.

Getting More

Even the most ingenious teacher would like more materials. In thinking about what to add to your collection of basics, you'll need to consider both *what to get* and *how to get it.*

DO IT YOURSELF

Do you have the "teaching habit?" Think of at least three different ways to use each of the common materials in the chart below.

Material	Possible activities
a box of crayons	
colored beads	
a favorite story	
construction paper	
clay	
wood scraps	

If you are working in a group:

1. Do this activity at your meeting in smaller groups (three-four people). One person can be the recorder for the ideas your group comes up with.
2. Allow each small group to share its ideas with everyone else.
3. If you have time, pick a few activities and think about some of the goals they could help meet.

FORM 8-2

RESOURCES FOR GROWTH

What to Get

In deciding what you need, keep the following points in mind:

1. *Level of development.* Materials that are great for kindergarteners may be a disaster with a roomful of three-year-olds—and vice versa. Even within the same age group, you'll find a wide range of development. If your classroom has a mixture of ages, you will be especially concerned about offering a range of materials within each activity area, so that the needs of each child can be met. A three-year-old and a five-year-old may both like to cook, but you won't be showing a three-year-old a recipe card for play dough saying "Call me if you need me." Figure 8-2 compares other materials that might be chosen for younger and older children and explains why there should be differences in your choices.
2. *Number of children.* In ordering quantities, you'll also want to be sure that there are enough materials so that children can play together cooperatively. One snazzy red fire engine will only invite fights. It might be better to invest in three or four smaller ones, or in a stack of inexpensive firefighters' hats.

Activity Area	3-Year-Olds What	3-Year-Olds Why	5-Year-Olds What	5-Year-Olds Why
block corner	limited number of basic shapes	buildings are simple, and they are just starting to learn about size relations	greater numbers of sizes and shapes	have had more experience with a variety of shapes and more complex structures
workbench	lightweight hammers, glue, large nails, pieces of soft wood or styrofoam	just beginning to develop coordination for use of simple tools under close supervision; process still far more important than product	variety of tools, assorted nails, wood, spools, screws, old broken toys, etc.	exhibit greater coordination and interest in creating useful objects, "inventions," etc.
puzzles	simple puzzles with only 4-6 large pieces	beginning to use small muscles skillfully; beginning to learn to see size-shape relationships	more difficult puzzles, including jigsaw	more advanced fine-motor skills; able to envision more complex interrelationships in size, shape, and color
clay table	large balls of clay	interested only in the free exploration and sensory experiences of the clay itself	clay, assortment of tools, use of kiln, paints, or glazes	interested and skillful in shaping the clay; growing desire to create "real" things and save them

FIGURE 8-2

3. *Goals of your program.* Before you decide to get any new material, especially if it's expensive, look at your list of goals for children and ask yourself what this material would add. If your answer is "Nothing," don't get it. If one of your goals is to encourage creative use of art materials, a stack of color-by-numbers books would be a bad investment. Fifty pounds of clay would be better. Some other examples of some of your goals might be:
    - to develop large-muscle skills: some sort of climber or riding toys.
    - to increase sensitivity to color: some unusual shades of paint to use at the easel, sample paint chips.
    - to develop small muscles: puzzles, chalk and a chalk board, clay, beads for stringing.
    - to become fluent in language use: puppets, tape recorder, language games which encourage conversation, toy telephones.
4. *Need for variety of materials.* Look at what you've already got. Do you have a balance of:
    - materials that stimulate growth in all growth areas?
        - *social-emotional*—hats, "tickets," hole punch, doctor's kit
        - *perceptual-motor*—puzzles, dressing boards, obstacle course, large rubber balls
        - *cognitive*—balance scale, dominoes, found materials for classification
        - *language*—books, flannel board, listening post, records, games, puppets
    - challenging and relaxing materials?

○ *Challenging*	○ *Relaxing*
new puzzles	floppy dolls
lotto games	clay
erector set	quiet records

    - open-ended and structured materials?

○ *Open-ended*	○ *Structured*
water table	pattern cards
paints	classification games
collage materials	tangrams
blocks	alphabet cards

Freebies—the Beautiful Junk!

Once you've decided what you need, you have to find a way to get it. One way is the "freebie" method.

Few things are more satisfying than getting something for nothing. Here are some likely sources of free (or at least very inexpensive) materials:

1. *You—the staff.*
    - Think of the things you throw out at home—styrofoam meat trays, juice cans, cake-mix boxes. "Beautiful junk" is essential for creative art activities—you never know what a five-year-old will make out of an egg carton.

        Set aside a special bag at home and toss all these things in; when it's full, bring it to school.

- Get together with other teachers and *make* materials to use in your group. Have you tried creating
  - a sorting game with egg cartons and buttons?
  - lotto games with cardboard and magazine pictures?
  - a puppet theater out of a refrigerator carton?
  - a color-matching game with paint-sample cards?

  These materials would eat up a large chunk of your budget if purchased at an educational supply store. You can create their low-cost equivalents —and probably have a good time doing it.

2. *Parents.* Parents are often delighted to improve their child's program by donating materials.
   - They throw out egg cartons, too! Early in the year, send home a list of "beautiful junk" that you'll always welcome. And don't forget to express warm appreciation when parents *do* remember to send it in.
   - Many parents work at jobs where they have access to surplus or free materials. Often a casual chat (or a question on your application form) will reveal that
     - Eddie's father can get stacks of computer print-out paper, and it's great for drawing.
     - Marie's grandmother, a dressmaker, will let you have fabric scraps and empty spools of thread.
     - Ted's mother works at an appliance store where they throw out all sorts of oddly shaped styrofoam packing material. Your children can use it for sculpture and collage work.

3. *Outside sources.*
   - *Teacher centers.* Many cities have teacher centers where you can get free or very inexpensive materials. Often the centers sponsor workshops to show you what you can make with these materials.

     Organize yourselves so one teacher has the job of stopping by the teacher center each month.
   - *Small businesses.* Local wood shops, newspapers, printing companies, and other small businesses are often willing to let you have surplus materials. See the end of this chapter for a list of ideas.

     Again, it's helpful to set up a rotating schedule so different teachers are responsible for contacting these businesses regularly.

PUTTING BEAUTIFUL JUNK TO WORK

Now that you're collecting mountains of marvelous junk, what are you going to do with it? Of course, most of you are aware of the time-honored collage boxes, and the ubiquitous baby-food paint jars. But let's take another look at how these materials can go to work for you and your children.

The child's choice
- Put out selected materials to be used in a free-form individual project:
  - yarn bits and punched cardboard circles for collage
  - styrofoam and popsicle sticks for sculpture
  - fabric scraps to be pasted on the child's own outline for "clothes"

- Watch for opportunities for a group project:
    - a large collage by the whole class
    - a "map" of the neighborhood with houses made from shoe boxes, jewelry boxes, milk cartons
- Put a few simple materials in an activity area and see what happens!
    - a cut-up egg carton in the block corner (people, hydrants, houses, basketball hoops!)
    - a roll of theater tickets in the dramatic play area (bus tickets, money, spaghetti!)

The teacher's choice
- Create "shoe box labs." Collect empty shoe boxes and fill each one with materials for a self-created learning kit. Label each shoe box clearly and store in the classroom to challenge children's curiosity.
    - a large magnet and assorted objects
    - assorted beads, string, and cards with pictures of bead patterns
    - a repair shop with an old radio or clock, and two screw drivers
- Invent your own games with found materials: lotto, sorting games, matching games, puzzles.
- Have some "make your own toys" parent workshops. Help parents look at the *purposes* of toys, and see that they may be even better providers by *not* spending a fortune! They may even try some ideas at home: making blocks out of milk cartons, puzzles out of magazine pictures, etc.

IDEAS

Here is a list of other possibilities for using your found treasures.

- *Boxes*
    - tunnel
    - store
    - box collage
    - box mobile
    - lacing box
    - nesting boxes
    - sorting game
    - feel box (with objects to guess)
    - letter box
    - obstacle course
    - telephone booth
- *Egg cartons*
    - containers for sorting
    - painting
    - anything
- *Wood*
    - wood designs
- *Toothpicks*
    - pea and toothpick building
    - toothpick and clay building
- *Playing cards*
    - matching games
    - sorting games
- *Film cans*
    - sound cans (beans, gravel, sand, etc.)
    - smell cans (orange peel, cloves, etc.)
- *Beans* (of different kinds)
    - sorting
    - separating
- *Milk cartons*
    - table blocks
    - garages
    - planters
- *Styrofoam*
    - nailing
    - printmaking
    - painting
    - stringing

RESOURCES FOR GROWTH

- *Baby food jars*
  - color jars
  - "smell" bottles
  - planters
- *Magazines*
  - cut-outs
  - puzzles
  - collage
- *Dress-up clothes*
  - buttoning
  - zipping
  - shoe lacing
  - dramatic play
- *Juice cans*
  - stacking
  - stilts
  - crayon cans
  - musical instruments
- *Bottles*
  - pouring
  - jars and lids (matching)
  - piggy banks
  - size sorting
  - music (strike or blow across)
- *Food containers*
  - store
  - classification

When you actually get the found materials back to the classroom, remember to sort them into carefully marked containers that are easily accessible to children and are located in an area where they can be used. If you want to save something you have collected, put it away for future use.

Buying Materials

If you need something and can't make it or get it free, you *will* have to buy it. When you go shopping, here are some guidelines to help you decide which materials to buy.

Guideline	Why	Example
1. The material or equipment should *actively involve* the child.	Just because children love flashy, entertaining toys doesn't mean they're good for children. Children learn by *doing* things with materials, not by sitting passively and being entertained.	Using this guideline, you'd pass up a wind-up car with a siren in favor of a car the children would have to push around themselves—and they'd have to be their own siren!
2. The material should have *multiple uses*.	Children learn by doing many things with one piece of equipment. This kind of play stimulates their creativity and problem-solving ability.	Using this guideline, you'd pass up a climber that looks like a fire engine in favor of a basic climber that could be a fire engine, but could also be a fort, a rocket, a cave, or a house.
3. The material should be of *well-designed*, quality construction.	You want the materials you buy to last a long time. Simple, durable construction is not only practical but also	Using this guideline, you'd pass up a cheaply made, fancy trike with streamers and fluorescent headlights in

Guideline	Why	Example
	beautiful. It's part of our job as teachers to help children separate beauty from gimmickry.	favor of a sturdier, simpler model.
4. The material should be *safe*.	If you've ever seen a child injured on a poorly designed piece of equipment, you *know* why materials should be safe.	Using this guideline, you'd pass up a metal telescope with sharp edges in favor of one made of smooth rubber or unbreakable plastic.

However you come by a particular bit of material, or piece of equipment, remember that it is only as useful to your children as you make it!

SAVE IT!

Here is a sample of the kinds of things you and your parents will want to save. You might send such a list home early in the year.

- *Containers:* oatmeal, cornmeal, berry baskets, egg cartons, margarine tubs, milk cartons, cans of all sizes, cardboard boxes, styrofoam grocery trays, cardboard tubes from toilet tissue, towels, jars, and lids.
- *Scraps of* paper, ribbon, fabric, yarn, string, cardboard (keep a scrap box in your room and get children in the habit of recycling every snip).
- *Dress-up clothes:* shoes, old hats, ties and belts, jewelry, old dresses, skirts, shirts, scarves, vests.
- *Odds and ends:* buttons, bottle caps, spools, keys, rocks, stamps, post cards, straws, toothpicks, popsicle sticks, beans (dried), rice, macaroni, jar lids, corks, decks of playing cards, hangers, envelopes, company letterhead stationery, shirt cardboards, crepe paper, glass jars, index cards, aluminum pie tins, cotton and cotton swabs, magazines and catalogues, meat trays, feathers.

"SCROUNGE" LIST FROM SMALL BUSINESSES

Here are some suggestions for materials available free from local merchants. Your area may have many other resources. Many of these materials are normally discarded; if you contact local businesses, shops, or factories, they are often delighted to save them for you.

- *Contractors and building supply companies:* lumber, pipes and wire, wallpaper, linoleum, tiles, molding wood, sawdust, wood curls. (You can make

DO IT YOURSELF

Evaluate the quality of some of the purchased equipment and furniture you have in your room at the moment.

If you are doing this exercise on your own, skip steps 1 and 4.

1. Find at least one partner, preferably someone who works in your classroom.
2. List several pieces of purchased equipment, toys, and games down the left on both your sheet and your partner's.
3. Rate each item on these scales. (Don't talk to your partner as you do your ratings.)

    1 = Very little
    2 = So-so
    3 = Very much

4. Compare ratings. When you and your partner have rated an item differently, talk it over. Each give your own reason for your ratings.
5. What do the ratings as a whole say about your classroom?

	Actively Involves Child	*Has Multiple Uses*	*Well Designed and Constructed*	*Safe*
EXAMPLE 1. box of watercolor paints	3	2	2	3
2.				
3.				
4.				
5.				
6.				
7.				
8.				
9.				
10.				

FORM 8-3

arrangements to go to a construction site when they are finishing a job; they will let you collect the scrap building materials.)

- *Plastics companies:* trimmings, cuttings, tubing, scrap plastic, and plexiglass.
- *Electronics manufacturers:* styrofoam packing, printed circuit boards, discarded components.
- *Lumber supply companies and furniture factories:* scrap wood, damaged bricks, concrete blocks, doweling, sawdust, wood curls, wood scraps for carving or sculpture.
- *Hardware stores:* sample hardware books, sample tile charts, linoleum samples, wallpaper hoops, paint chips.
- *Rug companies:* sample swatches, end pieces from rugs.
- *Supermarkets and outdoor markets:* cartons, packing materials, fruit crates, large pieces of cardboard and materials from displays, discarded cardboard display racks, styrofoam fruit trays.
- *Department stores:* fabric swatches (drapery and upholstery samples), rug swatches, corrugated packing cardboard, packing boxes from appliances such as washing machines, refrigerators, etc.
- *Phone company* (call their Public Relations Department): colored wires, telephones (on loan), empty cable spools.
- *Electric power company* (call their Public Relations Department): telephone poles, wooden cross arms, steel ground rods, wire, large spools that can be used for tables, assorted packing materials.
- *Garment factories and button manufacturers:* a great source for accumulating a wide variety of materials—yarn, buttons, scraps, decorative tape.
- *Camera manufacturers:* cameras (on loan).
- *Leather manufacturers and leather craft companies:* scrap pieces of leather and lacings.
- *Ice-cream stores:* three-gallon ice-cream containers, great for storage.
- *Airlines:* plastic cups.
- *Architectural firms, upholsterers, textile companies, floor covering firms, kitchen counter and cabinet makers, wallpaper and paint stores:* Color samples, wood, linoleum, and tile samples, formica squares, wallpaper books and scraps of all sizes.
- *Bottling firms:* bottle caps, large cardboard tubes.
- *Cleaners and tailors:* buttons, hangers, scrap material.
- *Restaurants:* ice-cream containers, corks, boxes, and cartons.
- *Plumbers and plumbing supply companies:* wires, pipes, tile scraps, linoleum.
- *Tile and ceramics companies:* scraps of ceramic and mosaic tile, tile by the pound (inexpensive).
- *Paper companies:* Unusual kinds of paper are often available free in the form of samples, end cuts, or damaged sheets. Paper is delivered to paper companies in large cardboard tubes which are usually discarded. These make good chairs, tables, cubbies, etc. (See *Building with Tubes,* a publication of the Early Childhood Education Study.)
- *Junk yard and scrap metal yards:* unlimited possibilities! Wheels of all shapes and sizes, all kinds of gears, and moving parts from clocks, radios, fans, cars, irons, toasters, etc. Handles from doors and cars, knobs, broomsticks, hinges, and fittings.
- *Gas stations:* tires and inner tubes, ball bearings, car parts.
- *Travel agencies:* maps, schedules, posters.

RESOURCES

Ascheim, S., ed. *Materials for the Open Classroom.* New York: Delacorte Press/Seymour Lawrence, 1973.

>Helps answer questions about what to get and where to get it. Includes specific sources and emphasizes free or inexpensive materials as well as high quality "store-bought" items. Some more appropriate for elementary school.

Blaw, R., Brady, E.H., Bucher, I., Hiteshew, B., Zavitkovsky, A., and Zavitkovsky, D. *Activities for School Age Child Care.* Washington, D.C.: NAEYC, 1977.

>Although this book is specifically designed as a working notebook on planning activities for young school-age children, many of the topics, schedules, and ideas can be adapted or used as they are.

Croft, D.J., and Hess, R.D. *An Activities Handbook for Teachers of Young Children,* second edition. Boston: Houghton Mifflin, 1975.

>A sequenced presentation of activities with clear designations and lists of materials. A comprehensive and useful book, although the focus is on the activities themselves rather than on individual needs.

Hirsch, E.S., ed. *The Block Book.* Washington, D.C.: NAEYC, 1974.

>A fascinating example of the creative ways in which teachers can use activity areas to extend children's growth in many directions.

Holt, B.J. *Science with Young Children.* Washington, D.C.: NAEYC, 1977.

>Focuses on both the what and how of developing science awareness in young children. While concentrating on the individual child rather than the group, the author attempts to view science as a total awareness and preparation for the world now and in the future.

The Scrapbook. Ann Arbor, Mich.: Friends of Perry Nursery School, 1972.

>A very usable recipe-like book containing a wide variety of activities for preschool children in all kinds of home and school settings. Delightfully, the materials required for most of the activities are household scraps and discarded odds and ends that teachers and students can develop.

Stauffer, R.G. *The Language in Experience Approach to the Teaching of Reading.* New York: Harper and Row, 1970.

>Provides a clear and systematic approach to developing language, prereading, and reading through the children's experiences. A concrete way of examining and expanding language activities in the classroom.

9

Supporting Children's Growth

THE MANY WAYS OF TEACHING

CHALLENGE YOURSELF

You may believe
- Children learn through personal relationships. But how do you use *your* relationships with children to encourage learning?
- There are many ways to "teach" children. But can you describe what those ways are, and the advantages and disadvantages of each?
- Children ought to solve their own problems. But do you have specific ways to help children learn this skill?
- Children should be free to work with materials in their own way. But can you see when to step in with a question, a direction, a new experience?

SKILLS IN THIS CHAPTER

- Instructing
- Setting problems
- Providing experiences
- Helping with feelings and behavior
- Managing routines and rules

CHILDREN LEARN THROUGH PEOPLE

A great environment isn't enough. Many so-called "open classrooms" have failed because the teacher thought all he or she had to do was set up exciting activity centers and let the children loose. Children need more than blocks and sand and crayons. *They Need People, Too.*

While growth is something that happens *within* people, it comes about partly because of what goes on *between* people. From the time a baby sits on its mother's lap handing a rattle back and forth, good learning happens through *personal support* from concerned adults. As a teacher, you grow through your encounters with children and other staff. Children grow through their contacts with you and with other children. One of a teacher's jobs is to make his or her strengths and ideas available to children in a way that benefits both the giver and receiver. How to do this varies from teacher to teacher—the "how" is often called "teaching style." Your "style" is the special stamp you give to whatever you do. You may be vivid and energetic or low-keyed and calm. You may be physically affectionate with children, or more formal.

But no matter what style a teacher uses, the goal is the same: to support children's urge to learn and grow. All children need the acceptance and support of an adult who is concerned with understanding them, not judging them. They need the approval of those around them so that they can learn what they can do and who they are. They need the opportunity to achieve with an adult who will help them when they are ready to be helped.

There are many ways, then, for you to support children's growth. We think they are all a part of the teaching process. Here are some examples of "teaching" in action.

1. Ms. Bond is looking at a book with a small group of children.
   "What's this?" Ronald asks.
   "That's a dinosaur," Ms. Bond answers. "They were animals that lived millions of years ago. Sometimes you can see their bones in museums."
   Ms. Bond is giving factual information, or *instructing*.
2. Ms. Alexander sees Joe making a snake with a ball of clay. She sits down beside him.
   "That's a big fat snake, Joe. I wonder if you can make it thinner."
   Joe rolls the snake.
   "Can you make it thinner than *my* snake? Which is longer?"
   Ms. Alexander is challenging Joe to think for himself. She's *setting problems.*
3. One winter morning there is a fresh snowfall. It's too cold to play outside all morning, but Mr. Spencer, the teacher, brings in a large dishpan of snow and sets it on a table with some cups and spoons. The children play with it until it's a big puddle.
   Mr. Spencer is enlarging the children's world by *providing experiences.*
4. Suddenly the air is filled with wails as Sharon comes running over to Ms. Kelly.

SUPPORTING CHILDREN'S GROWTH

"They won't let me be the mother!"

"You look really sad," says Ms. Kelly sympathetically, taking tearful Sharon under her arm. "I wonder what else you might want to be in that house?"

Sharon thinks for a while, sniffling. "I could be the doctor coming to see the baby," she suggests.

"Let's go see if the stethoscope's being used," Ms. Kelly says, taking Sharon's hand.

Ms. Kelly is *helping* Sharon with her feelings.

5. "I want to pass the cups!" Keith bellows.

    "Let's look at the list," says Ms. Sanders. "Whose turn was it yesterday? Whose name begins with B?"

    "Mine!" shouts Bart.

    "And whose name is next on the list? It starts with D."

    David looks up. "That's me!"

    Ms. Sanders turns to Keith. "Your turn is coming up soon, Keith. See where your name is?"

    Ms. Sanders is providing guidance to help Keith *manage rules*.

Which anecdote reflects the approach to teaching you rely on the most? You probably feel that you incorporate all to some degree; most people do. Yet you may overuse some, and shortchange others. Keep your own teaching in mind as you read about the teaching techniques described in the next section.

WHAT IS TEACHING?

Teaching is creating a social and physical environment where children learn by doing, by deciding, and by discovering.

Teaching is personal support of children's growth through:

1. *Instructing*. You can support children's learning by *instructing*—giving children helpful information, explanation, or directions.

    "This is a giraffe. It lives in Africa." "Here is how you make an A."

2. *Setting problems*. You can support children's learning by *setting problems*—asking a question to start children thinking for themselves.

    "How many ways can you use that paintbrush?" "What else will we need to make our cookies?

3. *Providing experiences*. You can support children's learning by *providing experiences*—giving them activities and materials to stretch their minds and whet their curiosity.

    "Here are some little animals for your farm." "I thought we might walk to the store today."

4. *Helping children with feelings and behavior*. You can support children's learning by *helping with their feelings and behavior*—giving them the support they need to solve their own problems through a language that communicates caring and understanding.

    "I can't let you hit Ray. Can you tell him what you want?" "You look really sad. I wonder if you would like to just sit here a bit?"

5. *Helping children manage routines and rules*. You can support children's

learning by *helping them manage routines and rules*—fostering competence and comfort by carefully planning routine times of the day.

> "The paper towels belong in the wastebasket. Billy will show you." "Annie, you really worked hard on that zipper!"

No teacher is ever entirely satisfied with his or her skill in all these areas, so there is always room to grow. But you may feel frustrated in using this chapter as a map for growth—you may feel that it "skims the surface"; it's "too superficial." Good. If you feel frustrated, that means that you can see how much more there is to teaching than what's presented in these few pages. However, you can use the ideas here to stimulate your thinking and to guide your observation of your *own* classroom behavior.

Since there *is* so much to learn about "teaching," we hope you'll pay special attention to the numerous "Do It Yourself" sections and to the "Resources" at the end of this chapter. Use them to:

- *practice* the skills you're acquiring
- find books to read (and discuss with the rest of your staff) that will increase your understanding of effective teaching.

But let's start with the basics, by looking at each of the five kinds of teaching more closely.

Instructing

> "I can't pump!" moans Carl, slumped on the swing.
> "Let me help," Ms. Nugent says, giving him a push. "*Pull* on the chains now—that's right! Make your legs go up too! Pull and *up* . . . pull and *up*! There you go, you're getting it. *Pull* . . . *up*! Now push . . . back."
> Carl grins as he sails back and forth.

GOAL

Your goal in *instructing* is to give the child specific information, explanation, or directions. Some people think instructing is the *only* way to teach. Most of us had lots of instructing as children—probably too much! But don't throw out the baby with the bath water. Every form of teaching can *support* or *hinder* learning, depending on how and when you use it.

Instructing Will Support Learning When You

- Fit the instructions to the child's interest and ability
- Have ways of finding out whether the child is learning
- Break instructions down into small, clear parts.

But Instructing Will Hinder Learning When You

- Overwhelm the child with a mass of unwanted information
- Give the child the idea that there is always one "right" answer
- Tell the child things he or she could find out for him- or herself.

SUPPORTING CHILDREN'S GROWTH

If Used Well, This Form of Teaching Can Help You

- Tell a child how to work the record player
- Show a child how to hold a pair of scissors
- Answer Henry's question about how to turn a somersault
- Teach a child the difference between a square and a rectangle
- Explain rules and procedures about fire drills, crossing the street, running indoors
- Get a frustrated child out of a temporary difficulty with the block house he or she is making.

Guidelines to Follow

In theory

1. Decide what you want the child to learn (your objective).
2. Decide what size group is best for what you want to teach.
3. Get the child's attention by removing distractions and capturing his or her interest.
4. Whenever possible, use concrete objects in instructing young children. They learn better when they can touch, look, and listen.
5. Break down material into small parts. Teach step by step.
6. Reinforce learning with praise for effort as well as for actual accomplishment.
7. Evaluate the success of the instructional activity:
    - Short-term: can child *demonstrate* that he or she has reached the objective?
    - Long-term: does child *remember* what was taught and apply it in other situations?

And in practice

1. "A few of the children are still having trouble identifying basic shapes," Ms. Beatty thought. "I'll give Ellen and Barrett some extra help today."
2. "Maybe I'll take them out of the room. Otherwise the children who know it all will take over."
3. "Ellen and Barrett," she says, "I have a special game to play out in the hall. Would you two like to come with me?"
4. "Here are two pieces of paper. They're different shapes, aren't they?"
5. "This one is called a circle. Ellen, can you find another circle? Barrett, can you find another one and put it on our pile?"
6. "Good! You both did it the first time. . . . Now here's a different shape—it's a square. Can you find another? Look again, Barrett, and keep trying. Great! You found it. . . . Let's mix them up now. Can you point to a circle? How about a square? Ellen—what shape is this? Fine."
7. Ms. Beatty thinks, "Tomorrow I'll put that shape puzzle out and see how they do with that."

It Sounds Easy, But

- *My children get so restless—they won't sit still to listen.* Maybe you need to balance instruction with more active kinds of learning. Or you might need to shorten the time you spend this way.

DO IT YOURSELF

Let's follow Ms. Beatty into the next day. Ellen was working on the shape puzzle that Ms. Beatty had put out on the table. She tried to fit in one shape after another, but she was having no success. Ellen's face showed her frustration as she angrily pushed the pieces into the frame.

If you were Ms. Beatty, what would you do? Use steps 1 through 6 of the guidelines for instructing to organize your thinking.

Step:

1.

2.

3.

4.

5.

6.

FORM 9-1

SUPPORTING CHILDREN'S GROWTH

- *These children forget as soon as I tell them something!* Try breaking it down into smaller parts—and give them time to *use* what they've learned.
- *They grab material and use it before I can tell them how.* Maybe they know how *already*! If so, let them go. If not, you may need to work on establishing clear "ground rules" about times for listening and times for doing.

Setting Problems

Ms. Unger watches Chuck at the art table. He's been scribbling with crayons for a few minutes but he's looking a bit bored. Ms. Unger sits down beside him. "Chuck, I wonder what would happen if you drew with the side of that crayon?" Chuck tries tentatively.

"It's a wide line," he says.

"Sure is," Ms. Unger agrees. "Will the red crayon make a wide line, too?" Chuck looks.

"Can I take the paper off it?" he asks.

"Just that one," his teacher says. "Then you might make a red and green picture with *all* wide lines."

GOAL

Your goal in *setting problems* is to encourage thinking and creativity. You want to help the child wonder about things, to find many ways of doing things, to ask questions as he or she uses the materials in the room.

Setting Problems Will Support Learning When You

- Focus and direct the child's own explorations
- Put emphasis on the child's ideas, not just the teacher's
- Encourage unusual and creative solutions.

But Setting Problems Will Hinder Learning When You

- Make the child feel he or she's being tested or quizzed
- Interfere with the child's own investigations
- Ask questions that are too hard or confusing.

If Used Well, This Form of Teaching Can Help You

- Challenge a child who is bored with an activity
- Find out whether Claudia understands what she's doing with the number cards
- Develop an understanding that there are *many* ways to climb a tree, paint a picture, or settle a fight
- Find out whether Molly understands the difference between "yesterday" and "tomorrow"
- Draw a group together by working on a common task—how can we move the bookcase through the doorway?

Guidelines to Follow

In theory

1. Decide on what you want the child to learn or think about.
2. Make sure the problem or question is of interest to the child.
3. Wait until children have had a chance to explore the material or issue before jumping in with questions.
4. Encourage *many* answers and solutions to problems. Before you begin, decide on some question you can ask to start the children thinking. Later, you and the children can decide which idea you want to use.
5. Encourage participation but help the child save face if he or she doesn't know the answer or wants to stop.
6. Evaluate the success of the problem-setting activity:
   o Short-term: can the child think of solutions to the problem?
   o Long-term: is the child beginning to challenge him- or herself, to think of questions and answers on his or her own?

And in practice

1. "Martin's mother is giving us a pair of guinea pigs on Monday," Ms. Plunkett remembered. "I'd like the children to figure out how to get ready for them."
2. "Guinea pigs!" everyone yelled at circle time. "Where will we put them? What will they eat?" Everyone was talking at once.
3. "I like guinea pigs," Ethel said. "So do I," said Will, "but mine died last summer."
   "Are they going to oink?" Addie asked.
   "They're a different *kind* of pig," Hannah answered disdainfully. "They're little and fuzzy like gerbils."
4. "Let's think about what we need to get ready," said Ms. Plunkett. "What could the guinea pigs live in?"
   "A box..."
   "A cage..."
   "A dollhouse!" The answers came fast.
5. "Jenny, you might have some ideas about what guinea pigs could eat," Ms. Plunkett said. Silence. "Maybe you want to think about it some more."
6. Ms. Plunkett thinks it over. Most of the children were successful at contributing a suggestion about what the guinea pigs would need. She was looking forward to seeing how the children would do on Friday when faced with the problem of building the cage with scrap materials.

It Sounds Easy, But

- *Every time I ask them a question, they answer something else!* Be sure the question tunes in to the children's interests and level of understanding.
- *One child just clams up when I ask her something.* Try more nonverbal methods of setting problems—e.g., draw a circle and then just hand the pencil to the child to see if she can copy it.
- *Danny cries when I ask him to do something and he fails.* You may need to go easy on this technique for a while. Is it possible that you *sound* as if you're testing him?

DO IT YOURSELF

Put yourself in Ms. Plunkett's place. You want to set up the activity of building the guinea-pig cage in a way that will involve the children in problem solving.

You know that they are eager to get started. In fact, just this morning you were besieged with suggestions and requests:

"Can we build a house for the guinea pigs today?" Jenny asked.
"We want to do it at the workbench," shouted Martin and Lucy.
"I want to use the blocks from the block corner," said Will.
"Can't we take the guinea pigs outside?" Ethel asked.

How would you handle this, using steps 1 through 4 of the guidelines for setting problems?

Step:

1.

2.

3.

4.

FORM 9-2

Providing Experiences

It's a gloomy Monday morning. The children in Ms. Bellini's group are working in several activity areas. Arnold, who's at the puzzle table, is tapping his foot in a distinct rhythm. Ms. Bellini goes to the closet and gets her guitar. Quietly she seats herself in a corner and begins to strum in Arnold's rhythm. Some children continue with their work; others begin moving to the sound of the guitar. Ms. Bellini plays louder and faster as two children start to dance together.

GOAL

Your goal in providing experiences is to give children activities and materials to think about, play with, and wonder about.

Providing Experiences Will Support Learning When You

- Tailor the experience to the child's level of ability and interest; start where he or she is and then build on what the child has mastered
- Help the child connect this experience with others
- Plan ahead to avoid chaos.

But Providing Experiences Will Hinder Learning When You

- Force a child to participate
- Overwhelm the child with newness, without letting him or her really work with old, familiar things
- Constantly quiz a child on what he or she has learned.

If Used Well, This Form of Teaching Can Help You

- Let children experiment without a lot of directions or instruction
- Introduce something new—a sand table, Cuisenaire rods, finger paint
- Let a child work off energy alone—hammering, throwing beanbags
- Give children something to think about—a good story, a film
- Open their eyes to all kinds of possibilities—painting with soap, blowing bubbles, rolling down a hill.

Guidelines to Follow

In theory

1. Decide what you want the children to get from the experience.
2. Consider time of year, interests, and other experiences of children.
3. Decide on rules and other arrangements.
4. Prepare children as necessary beforehand.
5. Be prepared for—and welcome—unexpected use of, or reactions to, the experience.
6. Evaluate the success of the experience:

SUPPORTING CHILDREN'S GROWTH

- Short-term: did children enjoy it? what expected or unexpected benefits did they get from it?
- Long-term: what carryover of the experience have you seen in their play, talk, or other learning?

And in practice

1. Tomorrow would be beautiful, the weatherman said. Ms. Allen thought about her class. Thomas and Joe had been awfully itchy lately, and David couldn't seem to find a friend. An outdoor activity made sense.
2. Still, it was too early in the year to think of a complicated field trip. How about taking just those three children for a walk in the park? Joe loves birds—they could try to look for some.
3. Mr. Smith and Ms. Pringle could look after the others for half an hour.
   "How would you three like to go for a walk with me?" she asked first thing the next morning. To the others she promised that they, too, would have walks and made a note to remind herself.
5. As it turned out, birds didn't interest the three boys in the slightest. They did find dozens of pine cones to bring back to school.
6. The rest of the day seemed easier. Thomas and Joe were more relaxed, and Ms. Allen felt pretty refreshed herself.

   David still found it hard to make friends, but over the next few days he'd approach Thomas and Joe to remind them of the "neat hike" they'd taken together. Ms. Allen helped them make a "construction" using their pine cones.

It Sounds Easy, But

- *The children seem bored with what I give them.* Maybe you need to provide more complex or unusual experiences. Or you might add other teaching techniques, like *setting problems.*
- *My children get confused and overexcited by new things!* Slow down. Keep guideline 2 above in mind. And don't always feel an experience has to be for the whole group. Most of the children can be working in familiar activity areas while you work with one child or a small group.
- *There are so many things I could do with the children—how do I decide?* Again, think of the time of year, the individual needs of the children, the resources of talent, money, and time you have. Try planning a *sequence* of experiences (in cooking, let's say, beginning with simple uncooked foods and progressing to bread baking). For more help, see Chapter 7, "Places for Growth: Activity Areas."

Helping Children with Feelings and Behavior

Ms. Tyrone reached out to keep Keith's arm from striking Pam. "I can't let you hit Pam," she said firmly, as Keith struggled to get away. "I think maybe you're angry because she told you to get out. What could you say to her—*in words?*"

DO IT YOURSELF

Ms. Allen would like to plan another experience for the children which will build on the "discovery" of pine cones. She has three possibilities in mind: another walk, a collection of seeds from various fruits and from local plants, or a trip to a natural history museum.

How would you choose and plan the next experience? Use steps 1 through 4 of the guidelines for providing experiences.

Step:

1.

2.

3.

4.

FORM 9-3

SUPPORTING CHILDREN'S GROWTH

GOALS

You have two main goals in *helping children with feelings and behavior:*

1. To help children feel good about themselves and cope with their own feelings.
2. To help the children find fair, realistic, acceptable alternatives when they find themselves in a tight spot.

This Technique Will Support Learning When You

- Accept the child's feelings, respecting each child just as he or she is
- Help the child find other ways of getting what he or she needs
- Let the child know you will stop him or her if he or she goes too far.

But This Technique Will Hinder Learning When You

- Make the child feel bad or unloved by scolding or comparing him or her to others
- Make the child completely dependent on you to settle problems
- Behave inconsistently about limits and rules.

We call this way of talking to children *the language of support—*

- not of blame
- not of criticism.

If Used Well, This Form of Teaching Can Help You

- Give a child a secure foundation for learning through a trusting relationship with an adult
- Help Mary find a way to play with Sarah
- Make Peter understand how other children feel when he hits
- Stop yelling at the children; stop saying "Don't" all the time
- Decrease fighting and arguing in your class
- Help children work together on a project.

Guidelines to Follow

In theory

1. Get physically at the child's level—stoop or squat. Don't call from across the room unless you're free to follow up.
2. Restrict a child's actions when an immediate danger is present or when the child has lost all self-control.
3. Deal with the most *distressed* child first, then deal with the most *misused* child. (*Not* "Whose fault was it?")
4. Set realistic limits on *behavior,* not on the child.

5. Help a child verbalize what happened by asking questions that will help the child interpret his or her own feelings.
6. When the child understands what happened, help the child find alternatives or more comfortable ways to get out of the situation.
7. Always show a child (by what you *say* and how you *act*) that he or she is a worthwhile person and that you are concerned with his or her well-being. Positive and supportive language is both verbal and nonverbal.

And in practice

1. "I had it!"
   "Well, *I* had it!"
   Tim's and Rico's faces were red. Ms. Bradley crossed the room and knelt down beside them.
2. "I'm gonna get you!" Rico yelled, raising his hand to hit Tim. Ms. Bradley put her arm around Rico to restrain him.
3. "Rico, you're really mad, aren't you?" Ms. Bradley asked.
4. "I can't let you hit Tim, though," she added.
5. "He won't give me it," Rico roared.
   "Give you the truck, you mean?" Ms. Bradley asked.
   "Yeah!" said Rico. "Gonna get him!" Tears were beginning to roll down his cheeks.
   "You look sad," his teacher said. "How did it make you feel when Tim wouldn't give you the truck?"
   "Sad...," Rico admitted.
   "And then you wanted to hit him," Ms. Bradley added.
6. "Tim *was* playing with the truck," Ms. Bradley said. "Rico, would you like to get another truck and play with Tim, or do you want to ask him to give it to you when he's finished?"
   "Can I have it when you're finished, Tim?" Rico asked.
   "OK," said Tim. "But I may not be finished for a long time."
   "We'll come back and see," said Ms. Bradley.
7. "Maybe you'd like to help me fix snacks while you're waiting, Rico," Ms. Bradley asked "I need a helper."

It Sounds Easy, But

- *I spend all day settling arguments.* Begin helping children think of their *own* solutions instead of providing an instant answer.
- *But Brad IS mean—why shouldn't I tell him?* Saying he's "mean" doesn't give Brad any help in knowing how to change his behavior, and it makes him feel even meaner!
- *I can't just let those children work out their own solutions—they'd kill each other.* It *is* a slow process! Certainly you need to prevent children from harming themselves or others. But if you *start* helping children find their own solutions in noncrisis situations, the crises may become fewer.

Helping Children Manage Routines and Rules

There was a lot of shoving going on near the door to the play yard. Ms. White, the teacher, came over to see what was happening. "I think you forgot our rule," she said.
"Oh, yeah," Dave groaned. "Stand back from the door till you come."
"Right!" Ms. White said. "Let's go."

DO IT YOURSELF

Later in the day, Will and Susie were playing together in the housekeeping corner. Suddenly, both children began tugging at a stuffed animal. Susie started crying. Laura ran over to the other two children and joined the fray.

Before Ms. Allen could move to the situation, Susie had grabbed a block and was starting to swing it at Laura.

What would you do and say to help these children? List some things you could try, using steps 1 through 6 of the guidelines for helping children with feelings and behavior.

Step:

1.

2.

3.

4.

5.

6.

FORM 9-4

GOALS

Again, you have two goals in *managing routines and rules:*

1. You want to keep children safe, secure, and comfortable so learning can take place.
2. You want to use routines as times for growth—learning independence, developing memory, making connections.

This Technique Will Support Learning When You

- Build self-concept by encouraging independence in routines like toileting, eating, dressing
- Involve children in planning and thinking about rules
- Use routine times for important intellectual and social learning

But This Technique Will Hinder Learning When You

- Hand down arbitrary and rigid rules that make no sense to children
- Think of routines as unpleasant times to be gotten through so "real" learning can start
- Make children feel miserable when they break a rule or forget a routine.

If Used Well, This Form of Teaching Can Help You

- Keep destruction and waste of materials to a minimum
- Avoid having to tell children what to do all the time
- Develop a way for children to wait for parents without chaos
- Have children help each other with routine tasks
- Give children the security of knowing what is expected at certain times of the day: snack, lunch, nap, dressing, picking up, etc.

Guidelines to Follow

In theory

1. Decide ahead of time *when* you need rules, and *what* the rules will be. When children's safety and learning are at stake, clear rules and routines are necessary. But rules for the sake of rules are stifling.
2. Introduce children to rules and routines in a clear, step-by-step way. Children respond best when they know what's expected.
3. State rules or directions about routines *positively*: "I expect you to . . ." or "Let's," not "Don't."
4. Make routines a growing time by incorporating intellectual and social learning.
5. In handling routines and enforcing rules, consider each child's needs and personality. Expect only what is possible for that child.
6. Evaluate rules and routines periodically, giving children increased responsibility for managing routines themselves. Change rules that are unnecessary or unworkable.

DO IT YOURSELF

"It is a few minutes before lunchtime," Mr. Hunter announces. "It is time for us to get ready."

The children in his group busy themselves with putting the table toys away and proceeding to do the jobs on the "job chart." Scott gets the napkins and cups, Lucy sponges the table, and Tony begins to put the plates and forks on the table in front of each chair. Nickie is new to the group. Instead of reading a book in the library area with the other children who have no jobs today, she begins to pull out the blocks, run around the room, and cause general disruption.

If you were Mr. Hunter, what would you do about Nickie? Consider steps 2 through 5 of the guidelines for managing routines and rules in making your decisions.

Step:

2.

3.

4.

5.

FORM 9-5

DO IT YOURSELF: SHARED TEACHING TECHNIQUES

Work with another adult who teaches in your class. Spend a few minutes each day *really watching* each other. Jot down positive examples of one another's teaching techniques and share them.

1. *Instructing:*

2. *Setting problems:*

3. *Providing experiences:*

FORM 9-6

4. *Helping with feelings and behavior:*

5. *Helping children manage routines and rules:*

Additional comments:

If you are alone: Take a few moments at the end of each morning and think back. Jot down any examples you recall.

PUTTING IT TOGETHER

Let's be realistic. You seldom use one teaching technique *all by itself*. If you're really observing your children and planning for their needs, you'll be constantly shifting back and forth from one technique to another, depending on such things as:

- the needs and personality of each child
- the kind of materials being used or concepts being learned
- the sequence: what's been going on before and what you plan to do next.

Here's an excerpt from the teaching day of Ms. Keohane.

> Paul and Sandy are sitting on the rug with a box of dominoes.
> "We don't know how to play, teacher," Sandy says.
> "Let's look at this one," says Ms. Keohane, sitting down and holding up a domino. "We want to make a road with these. But the rules of the game say that you have to find another one that has the same number of dots on the end. This one has two. Do you see another domino with two dots?"
> "I see one!" shouts Paul.
> "I had it first!" Sandy complains. They struggle over the domino.
> "Paul, you need to let Sandy use the one she has. Can we find another for you? How many dots should it have on one end?"
> "Four," Paul says, picking one from the pile.
> "Good," says Ms. Keohane, getting up. "I think you have the idea of the game now. You have five minutes more to play before circle time. I have a special record I want to play for you then."

In this episode, Ms. Keohane has actually used all five ways of supporting learning:

- Instructing
- Setting problems
- Providing experiences
- Helping with feelings and behavior
- Managing routines and rules.

FORM 9-7

DO IT YOURSELF: QUESTIONS FOR YOU

1. Why did Ms. Keohane begin by *instructing* Paul and Sandy?

2. Where does she begin to set the problems rather than instruct?

3. How does she help Paul find a way out of the struggle over the domino?

4. Where does she show skillful handling of routines?

FORM 9-7 (Continued)

DO IT YOURSELF: PRACTICING YOUR TEACHING SKILLS

Directions: Use role playing at your staff meeting or in your classroom in order to practice your teaching skills. "Act out" the following common situations. Take turns at playing children and teachers.

1. Ronnie is busy painting at the easel. He calls to his teacher, Ms. Allen, to see what he has done.
    Act out the conversation which might follow between Ronnie and Ms. Allen.
2. Mr. Hunter's children are all outside in the playground. He is playing catch with a few of the children while others are on the outside equipment. He suddenly sees Chris outside of the play area, walking toward the baseball field. He runs toward Chris and says . . .
    Role play the discussion which might come next.
3. Two children are arguing in the block corner. One child starts to cry after he has pulled a toy truck out of the other child's hands. Ms. Allen goes over to the two children. She says . . .
    Act out the scene between Ms. Allen and the children.

FORM 9-8

And in practice

1. After a week of school, Ms. Epstein had become concerned about the children's behavior at the outdoor swings. Hurt heads and hurt feelings were too common. She decided on some simple rules and gathered the group at circle time to explain them.
2. Ms. Epstein had made a poster with pictures illustrating these safety rules, which she discussed and rehearsed with the group.
3. Each rule began, "We're going to . . . (stand behind the line, etc.)."
4. "Turns" were to be counted as five "big pushes" by a teacher. They all practiced counting.
5. On the playground, most of the children obeyed the rules. Alec, whose parents had just separated, kept pushing ahead, calling "My turn!" Ms. Epstein tried to stay beside him to "help him wait."
6. As more children learned to pump on the swing, the rule about five "big pushes" by a teacher was changed to ten back-and-forth swings.

It Sounds Easy, But

- *Lunch is just one fight after another.* Again, this can be a real learning time. Try more teacher involvement, encouragement of conversation, responsibility for jobs.
- *Sam and Alec drive me crazy when it's time to come in from outside.* Can you give them more advance notice? Add a signal—ringing a bell, opening a door? Involve them in clean-up jobs, calling other children?
- *I wish they'd move faster after naptime. I'd like to get outside sooner.* Children savor each part of the day for itself, without rushing to the next one. And they learn all the time, even in those "in-between times" that you'd like to hustle through. Relax. Take fifteen minutes to chat, to listen to sounds outside—just to be!

RESOURCES

Croft, D.J. *Be Honest with Yourself: A Self-Evaluation Handbook for Early Childhood Education Teachers.* Belmont, Calif.: Wadsworth, 1976.
> Explores the feelings that both teachers and children have during "critical incidents" of the day. Lots of chances to work on actual situations.

Ginott, H.G. *Teacher and Child: A Book for Parents and Teachers.* New York: Avon, 1972.
> An easy-to-read, down-to-earth guide to coping with the inevitable conflicts between teachers and children.

Hawes, V.M. *Informal Teaching in the Open Classroom.* New York: Macmillan, 1974.
> Chapter 4, "The Teacher at Work," stresses the variety of roles a teacher must assume.

Stone, J.G. *A Guide to Discipline.* Washington, D.C.: NAEYC, 1969.
> Gives specific help in handling difficult incidents while preserving a child's self-esteem. Realistic and sensitive.

Tarnay, E.D. *What Does the Nursery School Teacher Teach?* Washington, D.C.: NAEYC, 1965.
> A short but useful pamphlet that answers the question it poses. Places emphasis on the teacher's responsibility for children's feelings of competence and self-worth. Will make you think about what lies behind those day-to-day activities.

10

Space and Time for Growth

THE ROOM ARRANGEMENT AND SCHEDULE

CHALLENGE YOURSELF

You may believe
- Children learn by independent exploring. But do you arrange materials so children can get them and put them away by themselves?
- Each child learns in his or her own way. But do you provide "quiet places" for the thinker to reflect and "noisy places" for the doer to let go?
- Children need a variety of activities. But does your daily schedule provide this kind of variety?
- Children are learning all the time. But do you help children use those "in between" times of the day for productive learning?

SKILLS IN THIS CHAPTER

- Becoming aware of the effect of space on children's behavior
- Making informed decisions about the use of space
- Evaluating and changing your room arrangement
- Planning and evaluating your schedule.

THE ROOM: PLANNING THE USE OF SPACE

It's easy to overlook two basic ingredients of a Growing Program: space and time.

Space = the physical arrangement of the room
Time = the arrangement of the daily schedule.

Often these two ingredients "just happen." Furniture is arranged a certain way because it's hard to push around; the day follows a pattern that was started years ago, and which no one has ever thought to question. We think these two ingredients deserve a lot more attention.

"Teacher! I need the scissors!"
Ms. Spinola turned to open the cupboard where the scissors were kept. As she reached up, she heard a howl of rage. Andy had knocked down Grace's building again, for the third—or was it the fourth—time that day. She really must do something about Andy . . . and about poor Howard, wandering around sucking his thumb. He looked like he just needed to curl up somewhere, but everyone was so busy, and naptime wasn't until two.
"Teacher! More paste!"
Ms. Spinola began to wonder if she was cut out for teaching after all.

Ms. Spinola was discovering that certain problems were interfering with her goals for the children:

- frequent, unprovoked aggression
- constant demands for help with routine matters
- children interfering with or destroying others' work
- children wandering or running around.

Perhaps you've had mornings like Ms. Spinola's.
We'd be oversimplifying things if we didn't admit that the roots of problems like these may be complex and difficult to understand. Andy's behavior may have its origin in a tension-filled home, or in a conflict with a too demanding teacher, or in an undetected physical problem. Howard may be feeling the effects of a new foster home, or television-filled evenings, or malnutrition. The demands for paste may be thinly disguised pleas for affection and attention.
But sometimes we look for complex answers when simple ones are right under our noses. The source of these and similar difficulties is often not in the children or the staff; it's in the room arrangement. Let's see why that is so.

How Children Learn through Space

All of us are affected by the physical space that surrounds us. Our homes are reflections of the kind of space we like, close and cozy or open and free. Some homes invite active socializing with their game rooms and beanbag chairs; others soothe with window nooks, soft music, and bookshelves.

In the same way, when we arrange space for children we are giving them certain messages—about themselves, about what they can and cannot do, about us. It's important that the actual physical setup of the classroom reflect our beliefs about children just as much as our objectives and activities do.

But sometimes we send mixed messages.

We may believe
- Children are innately curious. But the room is full of "don't touch" areas.
- Children have different learning styles. But we provide no place for the quiet "thinker" to be alone.
- Children learn by independent exploration. But materials are stored out of reach or inconveniently.
- Play is the child's work. But we set things up so as to invite interference with that work.

How can we make sure that the room in which our children spend most of their day is *really* reflecting and implementing a Growing Program? Here are a few questions to ask.

- *Does the room provide privacy for individual children, as well as places to be with a group?* Part of growing is learning how to be alone, as well as to be with others. It is important for each child to recognize his or her own wish to be by him- or herself at times. Children need to be able to find a quiet corner in a busy classroom. To get started, try
    - an old sofa, turned to face a wall
    - big sheets of cardboard and sawhorses to build a private "house"
    - an empty appliance carton furnished with pillows, and a window to peek out of
    - the bottom half of a closet, again softened with pillows or carpet squares
    - a rocking chair!
- *Does it keep interference with play to a minimum?* It is difficult for a child to build confidence and a sense of mastery with activities when he or she has to begin again every few moments because of distractions. To get started, try
    - a few tables placed in corners with chairs facing the wall for quiet activities
    - portable bookcases or dividers made of triwall cardboard
    - a block-building area located in a corner where special buildings can be kept up from one day to the next
    - a labeled shelf where unfinished projects can be kept.
- *Does it provide easy access to materials?* Children grow in independence and

self-confidence when they can do things for themselves, and having the right materials visible nearby really helps. To get started, try
- a wheeled cart for storage of frequently used art materials and collage supplies
- open, low shelves for paper and scissors
- a clothesline with clips where children can hang their own paintings to dry
- small pitchers for juice; baskets of crackers for each table.

- *Does it provide a sense of order?* Children can relax and feel more in control when there is a sense of order in the placement of materials and in how different areas are used. To get started, try
  - printed signs—"scissors," "rulers," "paper scraps"—to show where these supplies are kept
  - for younger children, pictures or shape outlines indicating where cars, blocks, dress-up shoes, etc., are stored
  - arranging paper by definite categories—size, color—and by shape if for collage
  - a masking-tape outline on the floor, indicating boundaries of, for example, the area where cars may be played with.

Making Decisions about Space

Ideas are useless without practical applications. How can you use the ideas we've suggested for room arrangement to get the most out of the space you have?

Everyone would like to start from scratch with a new building and ideal equipment. But most of us are stuck with certain basics:

- the dimensions of the room
- its furnishings
- immovable fixtures (sink, toilets, shelves, etc.)
- a fixed and often inadequate budget.

We might as well be realistic and accept these limitations. There's still a lot that can be changed.

Thinking about Activities

Let's say it's the beginning of the year and you're about to set up the room. One way to begin is to think about all the activities for which the room will be used. These may include:

- solitary play
- one-to-one contacts between teacher and child
- small-group activities, with and without the teachers
- whole-group times
- lunch
- naps.

You can probably think of others specific to your group. The next step is

DO IT YOURSELF: ANALYZING A SAMPLE ROOM

Before

Figure 10-1 shows the way one teacher organized the activity areas in her classroom. Picture some real children in this space and see how well you think the arrangement would work.

We've pointed out some of the disadvantages (and a few advantages) of this particular arrangement. Use the questions above to guide your own evaluation of the plan.

BEFORE

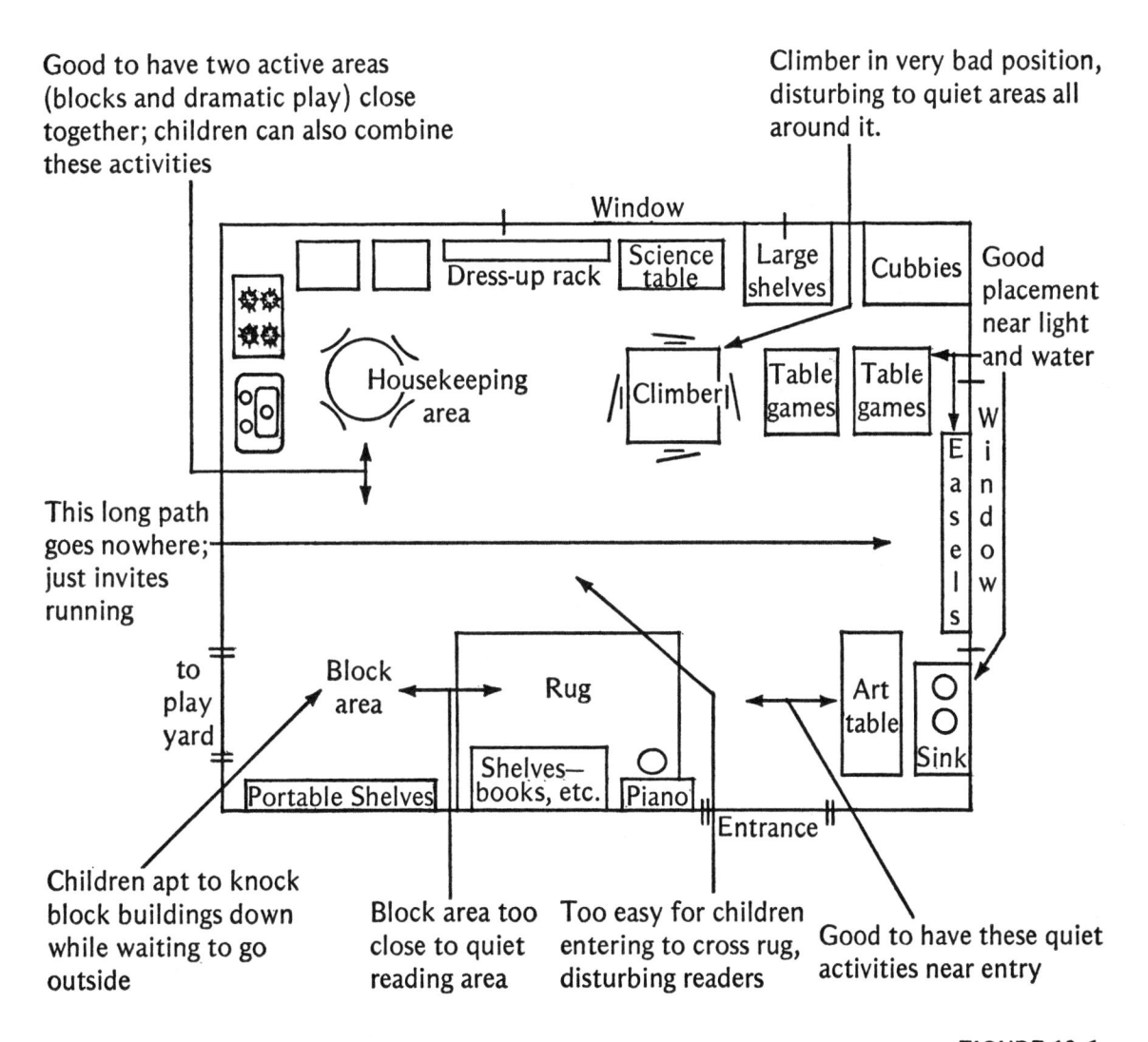

Good to have two active areas (blocks and dramatic play) close together; children can also combine these activities

Climber in very bad position, disturbing to quiet areas all around it.

Window — Dress-up rack — Science table — Large shelves — Cubbies — Good placement near light and water

Housekeeping area — Climber — Table games — Table games — Easels — Window

This long path goes nowhere; just invites running

to play yard — Block area — Rug — Art table — Sink

Portable Shelves — Shelves—books, etc. — Piano — Entrance

Children apt to knock block buildings down while waiting to go outside

Block area too close to quiet reading area

Too easy for children entering to cross rug, disturbing readers

Good to have these quiet activities near entry

FIGURE 10-1

183

And After
The first arrangement didn't work very well. Below is another arrangement of the same space, with no equipment added except some low dividers.

The arrows pinpoint new arrangements; can you take over and describe their *advantages*? A few disadvantages remain; see if you can pick them up.

AFTER

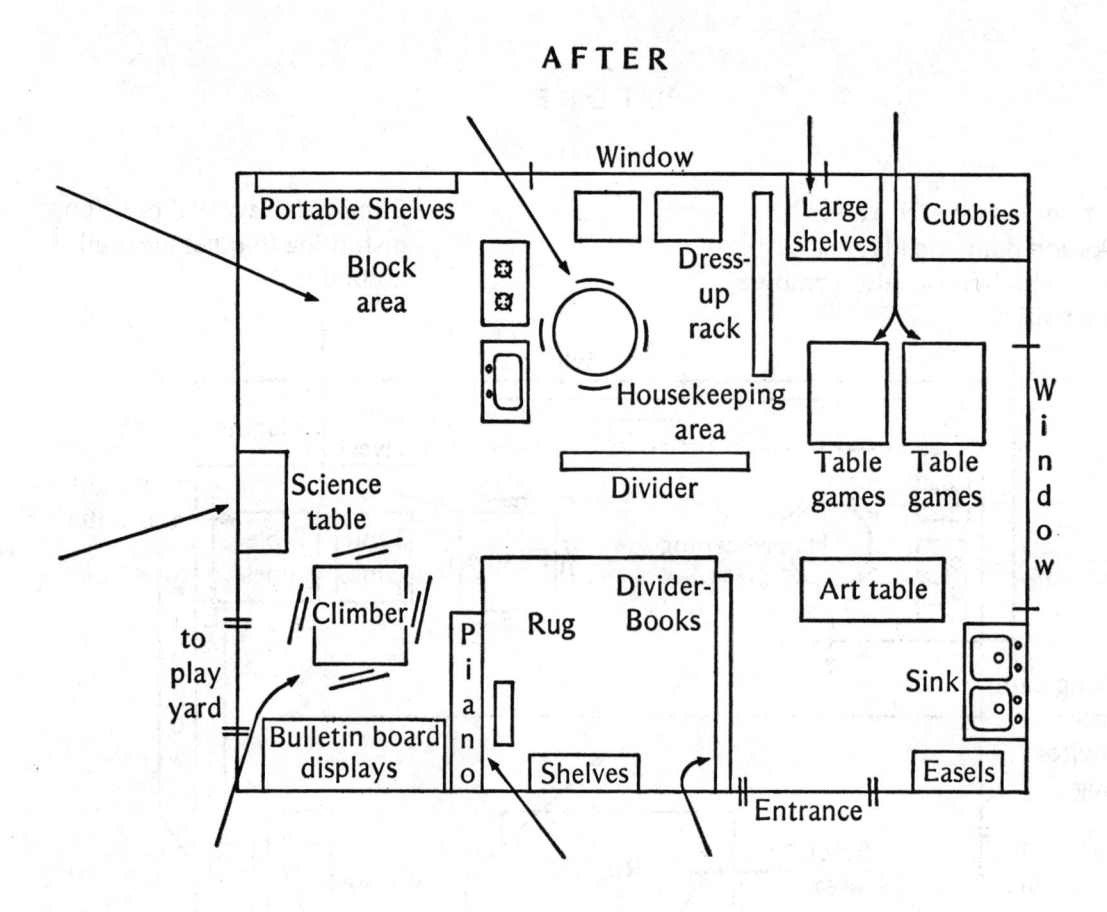

FIGURE 10-2

SPACE AND TIME FOR GROWTH

to get more concrete about the demands that each kind of activity will make on your room: for materials, for storage, for space, light, etc.

Table 10-1 shows one way to organize your thinking about the needs of each activity. In this table the activities are listed on the left, and the requirements for each on the right. Table 10-1 is filled out for an imaginary classroom. As you read through it, keep your own room in mind. You may get some new ideas.

Let's look more closely at the first item on this table (housekeeping and dramatic play), to understand the kind of thinking that goes into a worksheet like this. The staff recognized that the dramatic-play area needed to occupy a space large enough for "cooking," dress up, and rescue operations to go on simultaneously and peacefully. Orderly storage for clothes and small objects would keep the children's play more focused and make clean up easier. No special lighting is required for this activity, so the window space can be allotted to the art or puzzle areas. The bustle and constant conversation in this area make it a space with a particularly high activity level. The staff hoped to be able to have water nearby for the cooking and washing which this group of children particularly enjoyed.

Planning Your Room

On the room-arrangement worksheet you listed the activity areas you have, or plan to have, and analyzed the requirements of each. Now that you've made your list, what guidelines can you follow in deciding where to put all these things?

- First, work around immovable facilities (e.g., sinks, windows, toilets, doors).

  If the only sink is on the south wall, put the art and water play areas near it. Otherwise, you'll be toting water all day long.

- Group noisy or active areas together.

  Block building and dramatic play go well together; then their bustle won't interfere with quieter activities.

- Place quiet activities together, preferably in an area out of the main flow of traffic.

  The library corner and the puzzle table could go together.

- Create boundaries defining activity areas.

  Make dividers with existing structures (e.g., shelves, a coat rack, a piano turned sideways) or build them out of triwall, pegboard, or plywood. Dividers should be low enough for teacher supervision, but high enough to give children a feeling of privacy.

- Avoid large areas of "dead space" in the center of the room, or paths that go nowhere. They only invite aimless running.

  Fill in the "dead space" with a table or divider. Give children an outlet for that physical energy with a clay table, a climber, or a gym mat.

- Foster independence by storing materials where children can reach them and put them away easily.

  Put aprons on low hooks; crayons and paper on a low shelf. Help children learn while they're cleaning up by

	Requirements and Characteristics				
Activities	*Space*	*Extra Light*	*Materials and Storage*	*Activity Level*	*Other Comments*
1. Housekeeping and dramatic play	Large area		Rack for dress-up clothes. Storage for dishes, doll things	High	Good to have near water source for washing babies, dishes, "tea"
2. Reading and quiet listening	Small, cozy	Lamp?	Shelves for books, records. Record player	Low	Plug for record player
3. Art	Washable Large Near water	Yes	Storage for paints, clay, paper, etc. Need tables, easels	Moderate	Need rack or wall space for drying paintings
4. Water and sand play	Small Near water		Storage for accessories	Low	Make sure floor covering is easy to wipe up
5. Table games/ manipulative toys	Small, private	Yes	Accessible storage for puzzles, lotto, math games, etc.	Low	Nice to have near entry so children can "ease in" via quiet activity
6. Science investigations	Small, quiet		Cages, food for animals. Table space	Low	Near wall for bulletin board displays?
7. Block building	Large		Well-marked shelves	High	A rug would be nice to keep noise down
8. Large-muscle activity	Large		Indoor climber	High	Keep away from quiet work areas. Don't surround with high barriers; teachers need to see and supervise
9. Group meetings	Cozy Large enough for all		Rug needed; place for flannel board, calendar, lists	Moderate	Can combine with reading area
10. Naps	Large but with private areas	(*Dim*)	Cots stored nearby; blankets	Low	Need separate area for reluctant napper, even if just a screen
11. Music activities	Large		Piano; instruments on shelves	High	Need both cozy space for sing-alongs and large area for dancing

TABLE 10-1

DO IT YOURSELF

The room-arrangement worksheet which follows will help you organize the activities you have, or plan to have, in your own classroom. If the year is just beginning, list both the activity areas you plan to start with and those you may add later on. Use the example on page 186 as a guide. Of course, your worksheet will be tailored to your special activity areas. Maybe you and the children love plants and need a large scrubbable area for sprouting, potting, and pruning, or maybe you need a huge open area for dancing. Set your own priorities.

Student teachers: You will have two jobs in this chapter:

1. Apply the ideas in this chapter to the setting in which you are placed.
2. Start thinking about how you would like to set up your own classroom one day.

Complete the worksheet for the activity areas in the classroom in which you are working. If there are additional activity areas you would want to have in your *own* classroom, put them on a second room-arrangement worksheet.

FORM 10-1

ROOM-ARRANGEMENT WORKSHEET

| Activities | Requirements and Characteristics |||||
	Space	Extra Light	Materials and Storage	Activity Level	Other Comments

FORM 10–1 (Continued)

SPACE AND TIME FOR GROWTH

color coding small objects and games (to match color on shelf where they are stored), or having outlines of block shapes or kitchen utensils on proper shelves.

If You Work Alone

The "solo" teacher has some extra problems in planning the use of space. You need to be able to supervise the entire room at once. But you also need an arrangement that makes it especially easy for children to do things for themselves.

- You can achieve separation of areas without loss of ability to supervise if you use many *low* dividers or low, open shelves. Don't block off a whole area with a high divider.
- Label every storage space with a sign or a picture. Provide a clear place for everything, with plastic dishpans, wicker baskets, empty ice-cream buckets, contact-paper-covered cardboard boxes used for neat storage.
- Be firm and clear right from the start in establishing routines and limits for the use of the equipment in the room. You will be able to allow much more independence if children understand the ground rules for using and putting away materials.

A Trial Floor Plan

By this time you may be eager to try out your planning skills on something closer to home—your own room arrangement. To get you started, we've provided a grid in the following worksheet. Since your room may be rectangular or L-shaped, you'll need to draw its boundaries to scale.

We've also provided some samples of furniture to cut out (adjust size and number as necessary for your own situation).

Next, using your room arrangement worksheet (p. 188) and guidelines (pp. 185, 189), begin moving the paper "furnishings" around until you find an arrangement that fills the needs of children and staff. As a reminder, some of these needs are:

Needs of children
- Privacy
- Lack of interference with play
- Easy access to materials
- Sense of order.

Needs of staff
- Easy supervision
- Minimizing conflict and overstimulation
- Access to materials
- Places to work with one child or small group.

DO IT YOURSELF

1. Measure your classroom (children might help!). Draw its outline on the graph paper. A useful scale may be one foot to one square. Indicate the placement of doors and windows.
2. Check to be sure the furniture models on page 191 are the correct scale for your center. Cut out the appropriate ones and make more where necessary.
3. Try out different arrangements by shifting the furniture around on the graph paper. Use the guidelines we've developed so far to help you decide on the best ones.

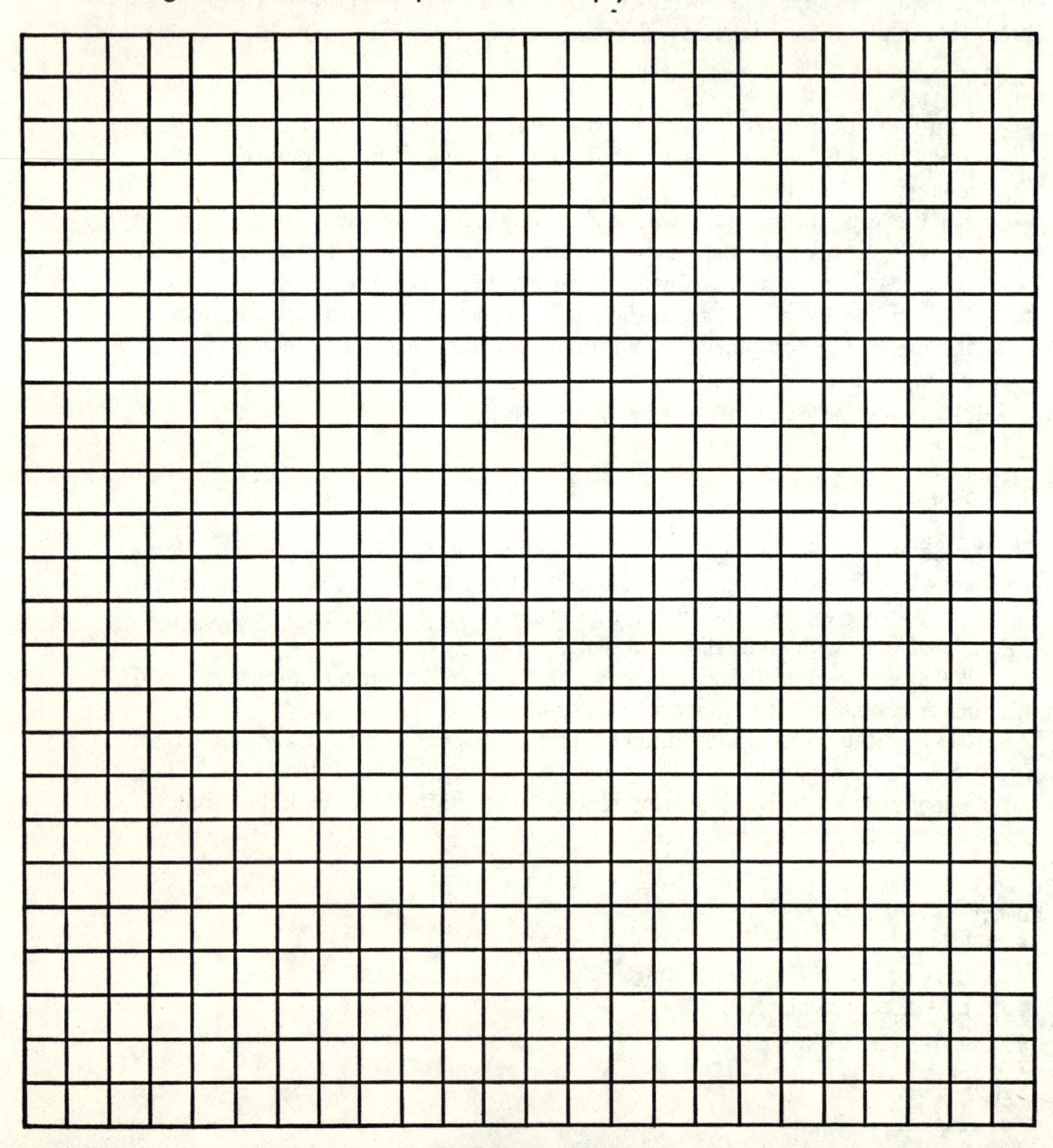

FORM 10-2

Tables

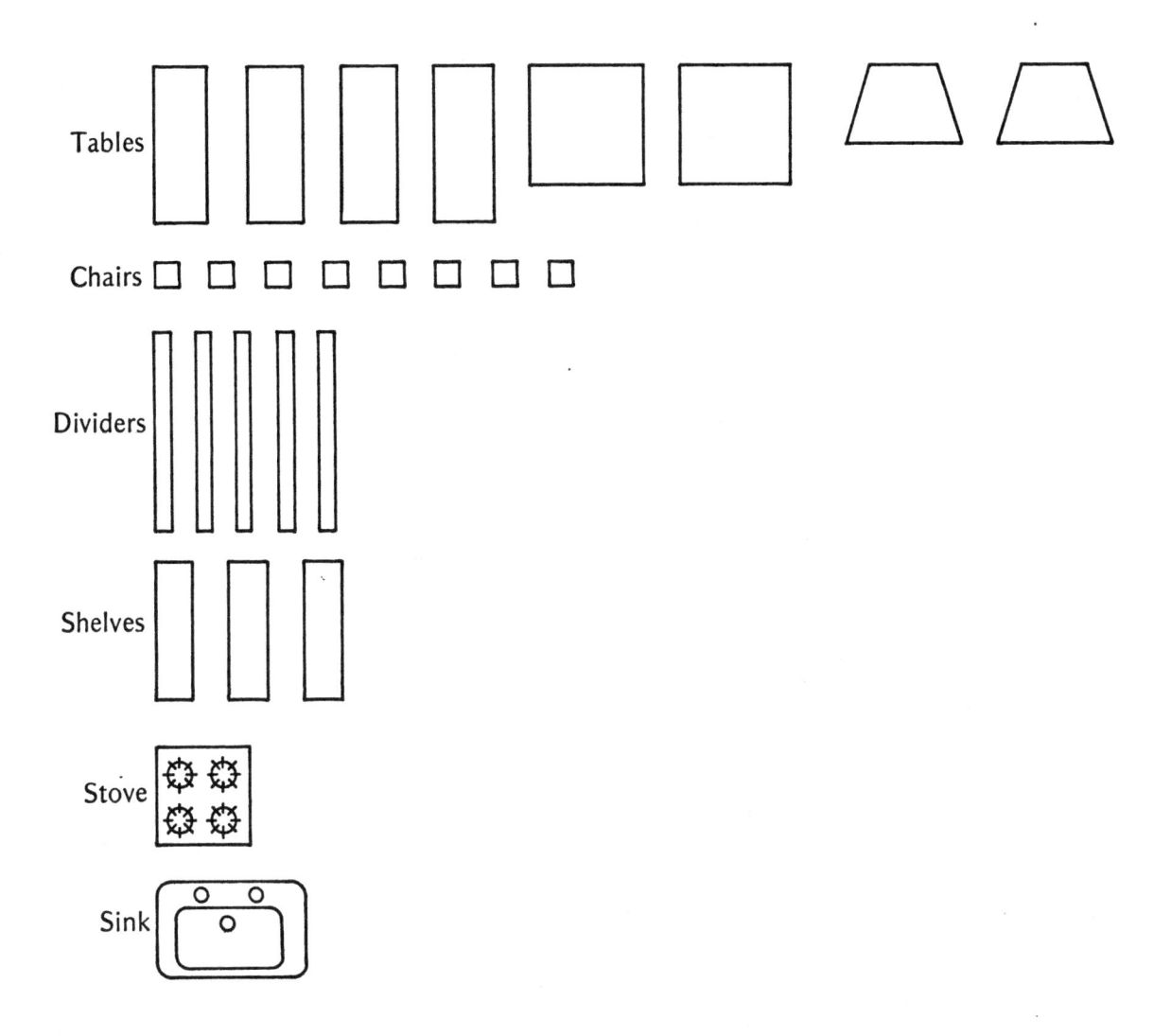

Chairs

Dividers

Shelves

Stove

Sink

FIGURE 10-3

FORM 10-2 (Continued)

"Impossible" Rooms

Some of you may look at the floor plans we've just provided and turn green with envy. You'd love to have a nice, big, rectangular room where you could arrange things just the way you wanted. But that's not always the way it is. Some teachers have to cope with physical space that's inadequate—small and cramped, cut up into several rooms, or even used for another purpose on weekends. These teachers need an extra dose of ingenuity. Here are a few suggestions for making those "impossible" rooms more livable:

1. *Living in a small box.* A room that's too small for the number of children you teach creates all sorts of difficulties. You may find yourself having to put severe restrictions on the activities that are permitted. And, even so, fights and whining may be common. Things may improve if you can try one or more of these ideas:
    - Make a "quiet corner" with soft cushions, a divider, an easy chair turned catty-corner to the wall. You may feel you can't spare the space in such a tiny room, but children need privacy *more* in a small, overcrowded environment, and arguments may diminish if a child has a good place to wind down.
    - Carpet at least some of the floor (especially in the block area!) The noise level will diminish and the room will feel bigger. Indoor-outdoor rugs are inexpensive and easy to maintain.
    - Think in terms of multiple-purpose movable units. With limited space, you'll have to get maximum mileage out of every inch. For example, a sand table on wheels with a sturdy cover can be used for sand play, water play, and snow play with the cover off. When the cover's on, the table can be used for snacks or table games. The cover alone can be a ramp for small cars, or a "roof" for a play house.
    - Use the "air space." Since young children are only about three feet tall, the upper atmosphere of your room is probably wasted. There are several ways to take advantage of this space.

      Use your carpentry skills, or those of parents, to construct a loft or platform area at one end of the room. It can be only a few feet off the floor (with storage space abounding underneath), or it can be a full-fledged second level, with stairs going up. One classroom has a cozy but well-lit reading area in such a loft; underneath is the dramatic play area, a low-ceilinged space just right for fantasy.

      You can also build a great deal of storage into the spaces near the ceiling, especially for rarely used items.
    - Expand beyond the room. You may have a hallway that could be used for a reading area or a puzzle corner—almost anything that doesn't require close supervision. Look outside, too; in milder climates you can move many activities to the play yard—easel painting, building with large blocks, much dramatic play.
2. *Living in a rabbit warren.* Rabbits thrive in warrens of tiny, interconnected rooms. But teachers find it difficult. Sometimes you're faced with arranging, not *one* big (or even small) room, but several. How to cope?

DO IT YOURSELF

Here are a few more trouble spots. After reading about each one, see if you can create an imaginative and practical solution (or a start toward a solution). If possible, discuss your answers with another student or staff member. Which solution do you think would work best?

Problems

1. This room is too noisy. Every sound reverberates off the cinder-block walls and the linoleum floor.

2. This room is used by two very different groups: in the morning, by a toddler group and in the afternoon by a kindergarten. The groups have different teachers.

3. This year, this room houses a group of exceptionally active four-year-olds. Their teacher is constantly stopping them from running around the tables and climbing on the book case.

Possible solutions

1.

2.

3.

FORM 10-3

- You can't be everywhere at once. For this reason, group the activity areas which need the most supervision where you can watch several at once. You'll often station a teacher in a doorway. If, from this spot, she can look after the climber to the left and the blocks to the right, she'll feel more in control and the children will be safer.
- Specialize. If you have several staff members to spread around, designate each room for a special purpose. One school has a small "quiet room" with no chairs, only rugs, pillows, books, and a record player. It needs little supervision, but it's a continual magnet. Another is blessed with a "block room" lined with shelves of blocks, cars, and rubber people and animals. Rich, imaginative play goes on in such a setting.

3. *Living in a hotel.* Some teachers feel as though they live in a hotel. From Monday to Friday they "rent" space. But come the weekend, they must pack up and clean out so that another organization can use the space for Sunday school or meetings. Again, there are things you can do to help yourself survive this nomadic arrangement.
    - Plan combined facilities for play and storage, so as to make the putting away job easier. For example, use the large rolling carts mentioned earlier for paints and other art supplies. When Friday comes, the whole art center gets rolled into a closet. Store dress-up clothes on a rolling rack, cardboard blocks in a trunk on casters. Children's art can be exhibited on movable triwall display stands, or pinned on large pieces of cloth.
    - Involve the children in the Friday pickup. Try a number of ways to make the job interesting: a graph showing how long it takes each week, a sign-up sheet for special duties, a chance to dance or parade in the newly cleared spaces.
    - Make up for the impermanence of your setting with little "homey" touches. A small fuzzy rug, some curtains at the windows (perhaps potato-printed by the children), a bright felt banner at the door—all these things say to you and the children, "This is *our* place." And they can all be tossed in a basket on Fridays.

Evaluating and Changing Your Room

Even the best plans need to be evaluated—and changed if necessary.

Once your program is underway, and the "paper" room arrangement has become alive with piano playing and clay and children feeding gerbils, it needs to be watched and evaluated.

These "danger signals" should warn you that your room arrangement needs a checkup:

- Under-used areas: parts of the room that children seldom gravitate toward, or that they actively avoid
- "Battlegrounds": parts of the room that seem to be a focus for arguments, fights, tears.

There may be a number of reasons for these problems. Here are some, and the ways that others have tried to deal with them.

SPACE AND TIME FOR GROWTH

- Materials may be unavailable, in short supply, or inconveniently stored.

    Ms. Baker's children were constantly arguing at the craft table. She noticed that many of the squabbles started over possession of the one large bottle of glue. She collected a lot of small containers and divided the glue among them.

- Space may be too small for the needs of the group or activity.

    A science corner stood empty most of the time. Mr. Pinella had noticed that his very sociable group avoided solitary activities. When he got a larger science table and added two more low stools to the one that had been there, his number of "scientists" suddenly increased.

- Area is too public.

    Ms. Billingham found her reading area was not being used except at story time. After some observation, she noticed that children who sat down to look at books were easily distracted by others in the house corner. The addition of a portable divider-bookcase and a few cozy pillows soon increased the length of time children would spend there.

- Boundaries are poorly defined.

    One group of four-year-olds was having a love affair with small cars. Unfortunately, the wildly zooming vehicles seemed to be taking over the entire room, getting underfoot and disturbing children engaged in other activities. The teacher helped the "automobile club" lay masking-tape "roads" in one corner, build a barrier out of hollow blocks, and make a printed sign to help define the area.

Even if there are few problems, no room should look the same in June as it did in September. Just as your goals and interests change, the "look" of the room should change, too. Some of these changes will be planned in advance, to reflect your changing goals as the year goes on. For example:

- Children have become more independent and capable as the year has progressed.　　So you put paints in pitchers (with lids) on low shelves, rather than pouring them yourself.
- The group can spend more time outside now that the weather's warmer.　　So you take down the indoor climber, which has been an important "safety valve" for the winter months.
- In the spring, some of your kindergarteners are ready for more formal readiness work.　　So you rearrange one end of the room with more tables and chairs, a portable blackboard, and a collection of appropriate games and materials.
- Several children in your group really need to let off steam in acceptable ways.　　So you get a gym mat or large foam pad, put it at one end of the room, and allow supervised "tumbling" for a while.

Other changes will be spontaneous reactions to an unexpected addition to your room, or to the changing interests of one or more children. For example:

- A few boys decided they wanted to "fish."　　So now your room has a large paper lake taped to the floor, complete with drawings of inhabitants ranging from a turtle to a giant squid.
- Two children have spent an entire　　So you create the real thing by con-

morning making play-dough cookies to sell.	verting the indoor climber into a bakery, and baking real cookies and doughnuts for "selling" and eating. Everyone gets involved.
• You are offered a piano.	So you enlarge the music area, stick numbers on the keys—and prepare for lots of noise!

Once a month, take a closer look at your room arrangement. If your program is growing, the room should be "growing," too.

Arranging the "Outdoors Room"

Even a small classroom has more space than meets the eye, if you include outdoor areas in your measurements. However, many teachers think of the classroom as the only possible setting for "real" learning. Outdoor time to them is a break for the teacher and a chance for the children to let off steam. But learning *does* take place outdoors; in fact, for many children "outdoor time" is the time of greatest learning—in social relationships, in language development, in exploring their environment. Let's see how to get the most out of the outdoors.

In planning the use of this space, exactly the same beliefs and goals should guide your thinking as helped you decide how to arrange your indoor space. Outside as well as in, children need to feel a sense of order, security, privacy (when needed), and independence.

But there are differences, too. Outdoor space invites racing, shouting, and daring feats. The expansiveness of the physical space—the sky, the wind, the horizon—call to children to be equally expansive. So your space arrangement should *encourage* vigorous physical play with large areas (or as large as possible!) for riding and running. As you do inside, though, you'll need to separate these active areas from quieter ones, and be particularly aware of safety hazards. Here are some other suggestions.

- Away from the riding areas, you need to provide quiet sheltered spaces, too. Make sure that your outdoor living area makes it possible for the "watcher" to retreat a bit, away from the noise and activity.
- Think about juxtaposing and combining certain areas to encourage richer, more imaginative play. If the sandbox is next to a packing-crate play house, and if you provide the "props," you'll soon have a stream of cakes and loaves of bread going in to "parties." And a nearby wagon will be pressed into service to deliver the finished products. Or if you store a collection of large, hollow blocks next to the riding area, you'll begin to see less aimless racing about, and more building of garages, fire stations, and gas stations.
- Use your outdoor space as an extension of the classroom. If you have more than one teacher, there's no need for everyone to troop out together at the end of the day. Send your five most active children outside with one adult first thing in the morning, either just to play or with a special task (finding leaves for rubbings, following fresh tracks in the snow, counting the number of cars going by).

DO IT YOURSELF

What kinds of changes would you make in your room to respond to the following interests and goals? If you're teaching now, think about your own classroom; if you are a student, imagine a "basic" room with standard nursery/kindergarten equipment. Discuss your answers with another person if you can.

Interests and Goals *Possible Changes*

1. A group of children has begun to do a lot of dancing. Right now, the space isn't arranged so that they can put on the "shows" they're eager to perform.

2. Your children love woodworking, but the "official" school workbench is only open to you one morning a week. How could you rearrange your room to create a class workshop? Keep safety and supervision requirements in mind.

FORM 10-4

Another way to integrate the outdoors into your day is to move certain "indoor" activities outside in good weather. Few things are more satisfying than working with clay while seated under a tree on a warm Spring morning. Easel painting, water play, story or music time, dancing—all these activities flourish in the fresh air.

The "Resources" at the end of this chapter will provide additional help in arranging this outdoor classroom.

THE SCHEDULE: A TOOL IN YOUR PROGRAM

Some teachers hate schedules. The very word reminds them of time clocks, loud buzzers, and nagging parents.

Other teachers love schedules. They love schedules so much that they feel uneasy when every golden moment isn't planned to the last detail.

Both groups of teachers are probably missing out on some of the benefits they could provide for their children through *well-planned* and *flexible* use of time.

By itself, a schedule is neither good nor bad. It's a tool, a tool which can be important and effective in helping to implement your program, your goals, and your plans for children.

It's one thing to make a *plan* for the day, including activities to meet the needs of individual children and the group. It's another thing to put that plan into action.

- What will the children do first?
- Will they all go outside together?
- When should you have a story time?

A schedule takes the pieces of your daily plan and puts them into a sequence that makes sense to you and your children.

Like the room arrangement, a good daily schedule should be consistent with your beliefs about the characteristics and needs of children, and should change in response to those needs.

To Fill These Needs of Growing Children	*The Daily Schedule Should Provide*
• order	• predictable sequence
• a stimulating variety of activities	• balance of active/quiet, indoor/outdoor, new/familiar, teacher-directed/child-centered, group/individual times
• involvement in their own learning	• a chance for children to help plan their day
• recognition of their individual differences	• flexibility

SPACE AND TIME FOR GROWTH

Scheduling According to Needs

Special Needs of Children in Day Care

Children in full-day group programs have all the needs listed above. But they have other needs, too, which a thoughtfully planned schedule can meet. They need:

- serene, low-keyed times at the beginning and end of the day
- a pleasant, quiet naptime
- a change of pace in the afternoon program
- additional physical activity
- time to be alone
- time for a hug, a lap, special individual attention.

Special Needs of Younger Children

The younger children you teach (three-year-olds and some young four-year-olds) have special needs, too. Their daily schedule should provide for:

- shorter whole-group times; more small-group and individual activities instead
- more opportunities for physical activity, both indoors and out
- a greater variety of activities, to respond to their shorter attention span
- more predictability in the routines of the day.

Looking Behind a Schedule

No one can hand you a perfect schedule—there's no such thing. We *can* give you an example of a schedule that has worked well for one group. We've labeled the parts of the schedule that would apply to full-day programs, and we've included notes explaining the reasons behind some of the parts of the schedule.

	Time	Activity	Notes
Full day	7:00 – 8:30	Children arrive a few at a time; free choice of quiet activities—books, crayons, etc.	Day begins quietly and peacefully—a chance for children to wake up and ease into the day
Full day	8:30 – 9:00	Most children have arrived; active play outside	Introduces variety after quiet start
	9:00 – 10:00	Indoor free choice—blocks, dramatic play, easel, etc.; special table activity (cooking, craft, game)	Lower-key time after outdoor activity Period long enough for children to become involved in an activity and complete it to their satisfaction Special activity provides variety

	Time	Activity	Notes
	10:00 – 10:20	Clean up Preparing for snack Snack time	Allows time for leisurely clean up without rushing to next activity Flexible—children go out as they finish snack
	10:20 – 11:00	Outdoor free choice	Again a change of pace back to active, large-muscle activity
	11:00 – 11:30	Indoors; group time with songs, dance, conversation, concept games, etc. Story time	Settling in after active play Provides chance for whole group to be together, sharing experiences of morning (younger groups will have shorter group time) A quieter activity
	11:30 – 12:00	Preparing for lunch Some children leave	Again a leisurely pace
Full day	12:00 – 12:30	Lunch Clean up after lunch	Flexible—children move to rug as they finish lunch
	12:30 – 1:00	Quiet listening activities Preparation for naptime, youngest first	Winding down before nap Considers differences in age, pace
	1:00 – 2:30	Naptime Lullaby music	A necessary "quiet time" for children in group care (even those who never nap at home)
	2:30 – 2:45	Up from naps Snack set up buffet style	Sleepy children shouldn't be rushed into group activities
	2:45 – 3:30	Special afternoon activity—art project, special dress-up boxes, etc.	Makes afternoon program different from morning, yet not too teacher-directed
	3:30 – 4:30	Choice of outdoor play or indoor quiet activities—cozy reading with teacher, etc.	Meets needs of children for free choice, individual attention at end of day
	4:30	Late afternoon craft—sewing cards, magic markers, etc.; child free to do or not Light snack available Little rugs, special books available Children gradually leave	Ends the day with special but not demanding activities Chance for child to rest or be alone if he or she wants

This schedule should show the need for thinking about the "why" of a schedule as well as about the "what." It isn't meant to be a rigid model; other ways of organizing the day are just as good or better for your group.

Adapting to Special Needs

In a Growing Program, each group has special needs and considerations which will affect your daily planning. For example:

- You might have a group where some of the children come very early so you eat lunch earlier so the morning won't drag on, or you provide a buffet snack rather than a group snack so the hungrier children can eat first.
- You're lucky enough to have two assistants so in nice weather, you station one outside for most of the afternoon so children can go in and out as they please.
- Your children get involved in a building project one day so you skip story time (or read during snack) to allow them to carry out their plans.

Evaluating Your Schedule

It's hard to tell how a daily schedule will work out until you've tried it for a while.

If the year has begun and you're already putting your schedule into practice, you'll need to watch for the following symptoms of trouble:

Symptom	*Possible cure*
• Fidgety, "hyperactive" children at large-group times	• Shorten length of group time
• Frustrations with cutting, coloring, puzzles	• Alternate with large-muscle things; give more free choice
• Whining and confusion about "What do we do now?"	• Discuss schedule at group time and informally during day; make day more consistent, predictable
• Tears, fighting at the end of the day	• Provide more soothing, simplified activities

If your diagnosis of trouble spots suggests that you need to change your schedule, fine—but go slow! Children (like many of us) are resistant to change; for some of them it's positively scary. Involving the children in planning and rehearsing for changes will alleviate a lot of anxiety.

There are positive reasons for changing a schedule, too. Like your room arrangement, your daily schedule will look different in June than it does in September. Generally, children need more predictability early in the year. As their attention span lengthens, you can think about longer activity periods or group times . . . and so on.

DO IT YOURSELF

Here's a chance to look carefully at your own schedule. Use the space below to write in your usual schedule, or one you plan to use in the future. Check it against the reminders on the left side of the page. If you find yourself checking any "no's," consider rethinking that part of your schedule. You may decide not to change it, but be sure your reasons are clear and are based on the children's needs. (*Student teachers:* You can use the schedule of the classroom in which you are working for this activity.)

Yes	No	Reminders	Time	Activity
☐	☐	Do you give children a chance to begin the day at their own pace?		
☐	☐	Do you alternate quiet/active, individual/group, easy/challenging activities?		
☐	☐	Do you have a time for the group to be together for a story and conversation?		
☐	☐	Do you have time scheduled *between* activities so children can clean up, finish a special project, etc.?		
☐	☐	Do you offer several activities at a time so children can choose?		
☐	☐	Do you provide different activities in your afternoon program?		
☐	☐	Does your schedule allow for quiet relaxation and personal contact at the end of the day?		
☐	☐	Do you freely change your schedule depending on the weather, the mood of the group, a special event?		

FORM 10-5

Helping with "Hard Times"

Some parts of the daily routine are especially difficult for teachers and children. A list of these "hard times" would vary from one group to another, but would probably include snack or meal times, and nap time in all-day programs. They're difficult times of day because they don't allow much choice, either for teachers or for children. Everyone must sit down and eat lunch at 12; everyone *must* be on their cots by 1:30. It's hard to allow for individual differences at these times, and when the group is all together, a few disruptive children can create chaos right before your eyes.

Here are some ways to handle the problems presented by the "hard times."

Snack or meal times

- Create small, family-style groups rather than one large table. The noise level and excitement will be less; the atmosphere more "homey."
- Have an adult seated at each table, to really talk with the children about their morning, their plans, the food, etc.
- Arrange the food and drink so that children can serve themselves. Small pitchers of juice make pouring easy. Children can pass bread, help themselves to carrot sticks, etc.
- Establish clear lunch routines, and stick to them. Jobs such as setting the table, collecting cups and napkins, calling other children to the table can be posted on a chart and rotated daily or weekly.
- Involve children in the planning and preparation of meals. In all-day programs, we want to create as noninstitutional an environment as possible. At home, children often help choose the menu for lunch or snack, and assist in some part of its preparation. Whenever possible, the classroom should allow this kind of involvement. To start, perhaps one lunch a week could be planned, shopped for, and prepared by the group.

Nap times

- Take children's natural rhythms into consideration. Children in a half-day program don't really need a "rest period" to recover from easel painting and block building (though maybe the teacher does!) They might welcome a listening time on the rug, though. Children in all-day programs, even those who don't nap at home, will probably be ready for a rest after lunch.
- Recognize and accept the fact that not everyone will fall asleep. Provide a "resting bag" of small toys for each nonsleeping child—a little car, a few miniature people, a book, a set of magnets; and make it clear that these are only for resting time, and that they are "quiet toys." Provide the same bags to those children who wake up early.
- Create a restful environment at naptime. Everyone needs time to grow sleepy. Begin by pulling shades or curtains. Speak softly! Play a quiet record, or read a story when everyone is lying down.
- Encourage parents to allow children to bring a favorite teddy, blanket, or pillow from home. It's easier to fall asleep with a familiar friend nearby.
- Create privacy for those who have difficulty withdrawing from the stimulation of the group. If you don't have a separate room, a folding screen can make a cozy corner.

Making the Most of Transitions

Every teacher knows that the hardest times of the day aren't in the schedule at all.

The schedule says: 10:15 – 10:30 Snack, 10:30 – 11:15 Outdoors.

What it *doesn't* say is how fifteen four-year-olds (with different rates of eating and dressing, and different tolerances for delay) manage to get themselves smoothly from the snack table to the play yard.

Why Transitions Are Hard

Why are transitions—those "in-between times" of the day—so difficult for children and their teachers? Let's look at such a time (say, the end of clean up, right before story time) from the point of view of Charlie, a five-year-old, and Ms. Burns, his teacher.

> *Charlie:* "Clean-up time"? But my building isn't finished, and it's got to have a tower on this side. Ms. Burns sounds grouchy today.
> I *hate* to clean up.
> There are millions of blocks on the floor—and all this other junk, too.
> Harry's already sitting on the rug with Bill. He likes him better than me. More of those dumb blocks! Harry likes Bill better anyway.
> I *hate* to clean up!
>
> *Ms. Burns:* . . . That Charlie! He never wants to stop what he's doing. Look at him—still piling blocks—seems like he does it just to annoy me. What a mess! I *hate* to clean up.
> Seems like it's more trouble than it's worth to get these children to help—they don't know what to do. Better get over and make those boys sit down for story. There they go, racing around again. But Charlie's still dawdling over the blocks, and Linda's off in a corner. I really can't stand this confusion. Where's that book I was going to read to them?
> I *hate* to clean up!

THE CHILD'S VIEW

Transition times are hard for Charlie and other children for many reasons:

- Usually children don't have much choice about ending one activity and beginning the next, and they are often interrupted before they feel finished.
- Often transitions involve necessary but not particularly enjoyable routines—cleaning up, toileting, getting dressed.
- Children's need for order and clarity is shaken by the confusion that usually surrounds transition times.
- Children may need staff members *most* at these times, just when staff are *least* accessible because they're so busy.

THE TEACHER'S VIEW

Teachers aren't so different. Transition times are hard for them, too:

- Teachers resent having to push and boss the children, though it often seems that if they didn't, nothing would get done.

SPACE AND TIME FOR GROWTH

- Usually teachers feel as if they have to be everywhere at once. They're tugged by conflicting demands.
- They sometimes find transition routines (putting crayons away, helping with mittens and boots) boring and demeaning.

Improving Transition Times

Now that we've agreed on the difficulty of transition times, and the reasons for that difficulty, what can be done to make these in-between times a more positive part of the day?

USE TRANSITIONS FOR LEARNING

The most important step you can take to better transitions takes place inside yourself. If you can begin thinking of transitions as *important learning times* for children, your attitude toward them will change. Children can learn all kinds of things at so-called "in-between" times. And once you see transitions as a time to learn, ways to use them come easily to mind.

Here are some things you can do to help children learn during transitions:

- How to plan

    (While sitting at snack) "Geri, what are you going to do when you get outside today?" "Jeff, who are you going to ask to help you buckle those boots today? Maria and Del are both good boot helpers."

- How to handle uncertainty

    "Marty, it looks like you are done picking up here. Do you know what to do next? No? Well, when you don't know you can always ask me, and I'll help. OK?"

- How to think about "before," "after," "next"

    "Who can think of what we do right before lunch? Then what comes after that? And what do we do next?"

- How to sort and match objects

    "All the cups go here. See the picture of the cup? They all go here. All right?"

MAKE SPECIFIC PLANS

Here are some things you can do to smooth transition times:

- Establish clear transition routines and procedures at the beginning of the year.

    Ms. Miller's class knows that, after each child finishes snack, he or she gets his or her coat and boots and finds a chair to sit on while dressing to go out. The first six children dressed go out with Ms. Miller, while her assistant gives special help to the rest.

- Use singing games or other musical cues to signal children that transitions are coming.

    Ms. Zella calls children to snack with a "Let's sit at the table" song which includes the names of children who are sitting down—"Here's Helen, and David, and Mario . . ."

- Provide quiet "transition activities" so that children who finish an activity early (snack, nap, dressing) have something to do.

- Have "rehearsals" of transition-time jobs and procedures.

- Make clean up a learning experience by organizing it in advance.

- Recognize that each child has his or her *own* difficult transition times.

The children in Ms. Arioso's group often hurry to wash up before naptime so they'll have a chance to sit on pillows and listen to a quiet record while the others are getting ready.

At circle time, Ms. Butler's group occasionally plays "picking up." Each child pantomimes how he or she would put away each item and what he or she would do when finished.

Ms. Sanchez does some casual picking up during the morning so the job won't be overwhelming for her three-year-olds. She also places outlines of block shapes, cars, and kitchen utensils on the right shelves so the children will be able to match the object with its shape. Color coding and labeling are helpful, too.

Danny is always disoriented and frightened when he wakes up from his nap. Ms. Little sits with him quietly until he is ready to join the others. Paula has a hard time moving from one activity area to another; Ms. Little helps her plan what she will do next.

A FINAL WORD

While not every "rough spot" in your school day can be smoothed out by rearranging your room or by making the most of transitions, you will find these are important foundations for a Growing Program. The healthiest of plants—or of programs—will soon find it difficult to flourish without a comfortable environment in which to grow and a reliable schedule of sunshine.

RESOURCES

Baker, K.R. *Let's Play Outdoors.* Washington, D.C.: NAEYC, 1966.
    Outdoor play space needs as much thought as indoor space. This pamphlet contains many useful suggestions, supplemented with excellent photographs.

Housing for Early Childhood Education: Centers for Growing and Learning. Washington, D.C.: Association for Childhood Education International, 1968.
    Articles on facilities planned to enhance human needs and learning programs.

Kritchevsky, S., Prescott, E., and Walling, L. *Planning Environments for Young Children: Physical Space.* Washington, D.C.: NAEYC, 1969.
    Provides the teacher with some basic principles to consider when planning room arrangement and outdoor play space. "Before" and "after" case study shows the effect of good planning on children's feelings and learning.

Palmer, R. *Space, Time and Grouping.* New York: Citation Press, 1971.

Good for those concerned with the wider implications of the education of young children. It provides a model for alternatives in the classroom.

Sargent, B. *The Integrated Day in an American School.* Boston: National Association of Independent Schools, 1970.

A good room arrangement is a flexible one. *The Integrated Day* describes how this teacher's classroom changed to adapt to the children's developing interests and the teacher's goals for them. Includes floor plans.

11

The Growing Staff

MAKING THE MOST OF YOURSELVES

CHALLENGE YOURSELF

You may believe
- Every child has unique talents and potential. But do you believe the same thing of your staff?
- Children should be allowed to learn through their mistakes. But do you allow yourself the same freedom?
- Children learn from each other. But do you, as a staff, learn from each other?
- It's important to teach children to resolve conflicts by problem solving instead of fighting or complaining. But do you use the same problem-solving approach in staff relationships?

SKILLS IN THIS CHAPTER

- Using your talents in your program
- Working together in staff meetings
- Working together in the classroom

Sometimes we're nicer to children than we are to each other. In a Growing Program, we let children

- be themselves
- make mistakes
- figure out their own answers to problems.

That's the way children learn and grow. Adults are growing, too, or they should be. Ask yourself these questions, to see if your staff is growing in the same way that you're helping your children to grow:

- Do you find opportunities to use your special talents or interests?
- Are your staff meetings varied and challenging?
- Do you feel free to speak up if something is bothering you?
- Do you usually feel you've accomplished something by the end of a meeting?
- Have you changed some of your ideas as a result of reading, listening, and talking to others on the staff?
- Do you feel free to try something new, even if it might not work?
- Do you feel your work with the children has improved because of discussions and planning with other teachers?

If you're like most of us, you probably feel pleased with some of these areas and dissatisfied with others. The purpose of this chapter is to help you make the most of yourselves as a staff, to create opportunities for your *own* personal and professional growth just as you create opportunities for your children's growth.

USING YOUR TALENTS IN YOUR PROGRAM

You are special. Whatever your job title, from director to cook to student teacher, each of you has skills and talents that can contribute something unique to your job and to the children you teach.

You know that

- Penny loves plants
- Barb is a gourmet cook
- Zella has a certain way with shy, scared children
- Steve knows just how to get that chip off Benny's shoulder

THE GROWING STAFF

- Maura always seems to get things done more efficiently than anyone else
- Ed is a great singer.

But sometimes these talents aren't put to good use.

- Maybe no one has thought to plan some gardening activities that will really let Penny use her "green thumb"
- Maybe no one thinks to give Ed a chance to sing with the group because he's "only a student" and is supposed to clean up during music time.

What are some of the skills and interests that might fit especially well into a Growing Program? Here are a few.

- Cooking
- Gardening
- Sewing
- Carpentry
- Playing an instrument
- Craft skill
- Sports skill
- Story telling
- Puppetry; theater
- Dancing
- Photography

In planning how to use these skills, think beyond one-shot demonstrations. Think of these skills as a continuous resource that you can draw on to enrich your program. Switch or combine groups occasionally to widen your children's horizons.

How do you make sure that the children get the most out of these experiences?

The problem with being good at something (like playing the piano) is that you forget what it's like *not* to be good. You forget that children want to participate, not just to watch; they want to try out their own ideas, not just copy someone else's.

Let's say you're a trained dancer. How do you share that talent with your children? There are many possibilities.

- You could demonstrate a dance to them—put on a "mini recital." They'd probably love it (if it wasn't too long). But entertainment is only a small part of learning.
- You could teach them a dance. The problem with this is that you may wind up with some reluctant children hating the whole thing, and with some creative spirits frustrated because their additions don't fit into the performance.

What else?

- You could use your training in movement and rhythm to help the children respond to music in spontaneous ways. Play a short selection of classical music and have the children just listen at first. Then give them room to spread out and move with the music. With older children, you could stop from time to time and ask a child to repeat a particularly interesting movement for the rest of the group. They might want to try it before returning to their own interpretation.

The key to using your grown-up talents effectively is to fit them to the interests and learning patterns of young children. That means sharing your skills through activities which are within children's abilities and which give them room to experiment, to develop their *own* ideas (not just follow a teacher-made pattern), and to learn by trial and error.

You can use these special interests to help your children reach goals in every growth area and curriculum content area. Here are some examples to start you thinking.

Teacher's Interest	Possible Goals	Some Activities
Carpentry	• to learn units of measurement • to make a plan and follow it • to develop coordination • to explore concepts of sinking and floating • to explore sensory concepts: rough, smooth, hard, soft • to cooperate in a joint project • to learn names of tools and their uses	• repairing classroom furniture • building a rabbit hutch • making wood sculptures • making boats for the water table • sanding splinters off the wooden blocks
Sewing	• to match patterns • to learn color names • to develop eye-hand coordination • to estimate quantity • to develop concentration • to develop spatial concepts: inside/outside; back/front	• making doll clothes • repairing stuffed animals • making a quilt • creating yarn pictures on burlap • cutting cloth scraps for collage

There's one more benefit to bringing your "extracurricular" interests into the classroom. You are a person, not just a "teacher." It's important for young children to see teachers, and all adults, as individuals with particular skills like weaving or gardening to share. If you feel you have no special hobbies or skills to share, share part of yourself. Show the children pictures of your spouse (or bring him or her to school some day). Bring your cat to school. Read your favorite old children's book to your group. Let them know that you love spaghetti and oatmeal cookies. The richer and more inviting you can make the adult world, the more children will want to get ready to enter it.

How can you take this assortment of individual talents and put them to work helping children grow? There are two situations in which you will need to work together as a team: in the classroom and in staff meetings. Let's see how we can use your unique resources in both situations.

DO IT YOURSELF

Think about your own staff. Use this space to jot down their names and the special abilities they have. (Include yourself!)

Name			
Talents or interests			
Skills with people			

    If you don't know, ask and observe. You may get some surprises.

    Now put a check beside those talents and skills which are *really* being used in your program. Are there some left over?

    As with the rest of your Growing Program, you need to be *flexible* in using the resources of your staff. If people are given a chance to do what they like and what they do well, they feel better about themselves and their work. And the children benefit, too!

    As a start, use the space below to make some specific plans to use the special abilities of at least one staff member. Use the guidelines on pp. 211-212 to make sure the activity fits with children's ways of learning.

Staff member(s):

Special interest or skill:

When to use:
  date(s):

  time:

What to do:
  activity:

  work with one child or group:

FORM 11-1

WORKING TOGETHER IN THE CLASSROOM

Many of you work in a setting with two or more adults assigned to each group. We think this kind of "team approach" to teaching young children can benefit everyone. The children get more individual attention, and teachers can support and learn from each other. In this section, we'll help you get the most out of "team teaching."

"But I'm All Alone!"

Although most early-childhood programs require that there be more than one adult in the classroom, there are exceptions. The teacher in a small private nursery school may be responsible for fifteen three-year-olds; many kindergarten teachers find themselves coping with twenty-five or thirty children with no help. "Team teaching" is only a fantasy for them.

Even if your setting has only one paid group teacher, there are ways that you can get help, so that you, too, can take advantage of the flexibility offered by the team approach.

1. Parent Volunteers. Parent cooperative schools have always used this kind of help. Many parents would love to give a few hours a week to help at "their" school. Kindergarten teachers are often especially successful at generating this kind of involvement. For many proud parents, their child's kindergarten year is their first encounter with school. They're excited and eager to be a part of it.

   Send a note home early in the year (or at the end of summer); buttonhole parents at coffee hours; post a sign-up sheet on your door. Once you get a group of parent helpers, see Chapter 12 for additional suggestions on how to train them and use their help successfully.

2. Retired persons in your community. Many communities have organizations through which retired persons contribute their services to day-care centers, schools, and hospitals. Try calling such an organization or running an article or advertisement in your local paper requesting "foster grandparents."

3. Students. In addition to student teachers from college early-childhood programs, student help can come from several other sources. Many colleges have service clubs which give time to helping others. Call local colleges to see if your setting qualifies under this kind of program. High schools have begun to develop work-study programs in which juniors or seniors spend four to ten weeks working in their field of interest. Again, a telephone call to the school is the first step.

4. Teachers in other classrooms. Although you may not be able to "push back the walls" and combine groups, the teacher next door might be interested in occasionally sharing responsibilities and activities. Start small; for example:

   o   have one teacher take over both groups for a joint story or singing time, to free the other teacher for planning or individual work with a child
   o   invite each other's groups to special events: a "bake sale"; a look at the new rabbit; an impromptu circus performance

THE GROWING STAFF

○ avoid duplication by setting up certain activity areas in each classroom (you, for example, might have a sand table while Ms. Petersen has a great collection of magnets) and letting children move back and forth to selected areas at certain times of the day.

Organizing Yourselves

Now that you have the people, you need a plan. Here are some suggestions for putting people to work.

- Have each teacher (or volunteer) responsible for certain activity areas—planning them, supervising them, keeping records, etc. Rotate these jobs.
- Have one adult work with a small group or individual child while the other adult supervises the rest of the children.
- If one adult seems to work better with a certain "difficult" child, have that adult stay with him or her during hard parts of the day—at nap, at story, at the snack table.
- If a few children are restless during a group time, one adult can take them outside or into another room.
- If one adult has a special talent or interest, he or she can plan some small-group activities around that interest.
- With a group of very young children in all-day care, each adult can be the "primary caregiver" for a small number of children.

Finding Ways to Improve Teamwork

Beyond these general guidelines, you can do a number of things to make your team function more smoothly:

Steps	How-to	Teamwork in Action
1. Define responsibilities	In your planning, agree on *who* is to do *what* jobs *when*. If the work is divided clearly and fairly, no one will end up feeling disgruntled or martyred.	Alva, Pat, and Vinnie felt that the transition from story time to snack had not been going well. They needed a new plan. Alva suggested that she begin reading the story while Pat washed the paint brushes and prepared snack. Vinnie would sit in the story circle with Mark, who listened better with an adult close by.
2. Help each other	When you're dividing up responsibilities, get into the habit of asking, "Will it be a problem for you to take on this job? What can the rest	When Pat was asked if her new job would create problems, she admitted that she'd feel rushed trying to wash brushes *and* get snack ready

Steps	How-to	Teamwork in Action
	of us do to make it easier?" Then see what you can work out.	before the end of the story. Alva suggested that Pat simply soak the brushes and let Alva finish them at naptime.
3. Discuss problems	You can't anticipate every snag that might come up. So be sure to check with each other every day about how things are going—what was hard to do that day; what went wrong. Problems are easier to solve when they're small. If you let them go, they'll probably get bigger.	Once they put their plan for story time into operation, a few problems came up. Children would hear Pat fixing the snack and wander away from the story group to "help." Pat didn't know what to do. They decided to have one child be the snack helper each day and made a list to keep track.
4. Share information	One of the great benefits of team teaching is the chance to get another adult's point of view about the children in your group. Share information casually and informally as well as at weekly "staffings."	Vinnie began to develop rapport with Mark from sitting with him at story time. He found out that Mark loved to talk to him about animals, and he passed this information along to Alva and Pat. Because of this, Alva planned to read some animal stories and to let Mark help pick them out.
5. Use skills and interests	In dividing up jobs in the classroom, ask what people *like* to do and are good at—and give them a chance to do it!	Vinnie told the others that he likes reading aloud and misses doing it. Alva suggested that they take turns reading.

Roles in the Team

Although in the classroom we'd like to think all adults are equal, in reality, as George Orwell said, "Some are more equal than others." Sometimes two of you really *will* be equals—co-teachers of a group. But more often you'll be part of a system in which there are hierarchies of status and responsibility. You may be called a director, an aide, a head teacher, a paraprofessional, an assistant teacher, a student intern. You may be responsible for supervising others, or you may be in the position of being evaluated. These kinds of role relationships can help things function smoothly, if everyone's clear about what's expected of them.

In any role relationship, the person occupying each position has certain *rights*. But along with those rights go certain responsibilities or *obligations* to others.

A director or head teacher, for example, has the *right* to

- make final decisions about key matters

THE GROWING STAFF

- insist that staff implement those decisions
- evaluate the work of the rest of the staff.

But he or she also has *obligations* to the rest of the staff. He or she should

- consult with staff before making major decisions
- explain reasons for rules and decisions
- show respect for the feelings and experience of staff
- give criticism in a constructive way.

A student teacher or aide has *obligations*, too. He or she should

- conform to the regulations and policies of the setting
- consult with the supervisor before taking action on major issues
- carry out jobs that are assigned by the supervisor
- work to understand the philosophy and goals of the program.

With those obligations go some *rights*; for example, the right to

- expect an adequate and courteous explanation of decisions
- receive helpful and frequent suggestions for improvement
- express honest dissatisfaction or disagreement with policies and goals.

Even when these mutual rights and obligations are clear, role relationships can sometimes be the source of real problems. The following "case studies" illustrate some of these difficulties.

> Ms. Webster is the new head teacher in a kindergarten group. She has a teacher aide in the class who's been in the school for *years*. Today Ms. Ball, the aide, is sitting with Kim and Charlotte, who are building towers with the table blocks. Ms. Webster sees the girls joyously pushing over the towers. Blocks are all over the floor.

There are a number of ways that Ms. Webster could handle the situation. She could:

- confront Ms. Ball on the spot and tell her not to permit that behavior
- wait until after school to tell her what she did wrong
- say nothing, but feel angry that the aide was letting the children get so out of control
- over an after-school cup of coffee, ask Ms. Ball how *she* felt about the incident, what she thought the children gained from it. Ms. Webster may get some new ideas or she may still have reservations, which she can share with Ms. Ball.

The last alternative is probably the best. It illustrates some guidelines that may smooth the way in the difficult job of criticizing or evaluating someone you are responsible for.

- Whenever possible, make your rules and goals clear in advance.

- Avoid criticizing another staff member in front of the children, unless prompt action is absolutely called for.
- Create a good interpersonal climate right from the start. Have coffee together, find out about each other's families, interests. Criticism is easier to take from someone who genuinely cares about you.
- Ask for the other person's opinion whenever possible, rather than giving yours right away. There often are aspects of a situation of which you may not be aware.
- Word criticisms so as to give positive, workable suggestions for improvement. "You might try going around to each group of children to tell them it's clean-up time" is more helpful and pleasant than "You shouldn't shout 'Clean up!' across the room!"

Cynthia is a new student teacher. Today her supervising teacher asked her to help a group of children mix their own paints. She soon found herself in the middle of a mess. Paint was on the children and the floor, and one child was starting to pour all the colors together. Cynthia thought that the supervisor's idea was terrible.

Again, Cynthia could handle the situation in a number of ways. She could:

- say nothing
- tell the teacher that the project was a disaster
- pretend everything was fine, but feel like a failure
- tell the teacher her feelings, and ask what she could do to make it go better next time.

This last solution has the best chance of succeeding. It may be that the head teacher's project *was* a poor one for this group, but again an exchange of ideas is more effective than either direct criticism or avoidance.

Here are some more guidelines for student teachers and paraprofessionals.

- Ask questions. Ask what to do, where things are, what the rules are. But ask (whenever possible) ahead of time, not when the head teacher has three children also asking her questions.
- Watch and listen for a while before making judgments. It's tempting to find fault with those who are in control. But you may find out that there's a good reason for the routine that bothers you so much.
- Share your feelings before they get too big to handle. If you're feeling overwhelmed, or you're eager to do an art activity, or you're angry about a child's behavior, say so now. Don't save it up for two weeks!

Solving Problems in Team Teaching

Any time people have to work together, there are bound to be problems. Even if the mechanics of staff meetings and classroom organization are running smoothly, subtle irritations and tensions can make your work harder.

Sometimes it seems that people who are comfortable and successful in helping

DO IT YOURSELF

Pick a time of day that's particularly hard on everyone in your classroom. Perhaps it's lunch, or settling in for naps, or getting ready to go outdoors, or late afternoon. With the other members of your teaching team, plan some concrete changes in staff responsibilities. Check back in a few days to see how it went.

Time of day:

Problems:

Proposed changes:

   who:

   what:

   when:

Feedback:

FORM 11-2

three-year-olds settle their differences have a hard time solving the interpersonal problems that arise when adults disagree.

We can't give you a magic formula for every staff problem, but here are some constructive steps you can take.

1. *Identify* the problem. What is bothering you? Is it really Ms. Babcock's nasal voice (which she can't do anything about) or is it her way of interrupting you?
2. *Create* a constructive climate for discussion. As we've said before, conflict and criticism can best be handled when people feel basically liked and accepted. A concerned question about a sick child or an offer of a cup of tea can create this accepting atmosphere.
3. *Describe* what's been happening and how you feel about it. Avoid blaming or accusing. Say "I feel . . ." not "You are . . ."
4. *Invite* the other person to work with you in solving the problem. Take time to discuss it thoroughly.
5. *Commit* yourselves to a specific goal that can be a first step in solving the problem.

Let's see how these five steps can help a few teachers solve some sticky—and probably familiar—problems.

The Novice and the Know-It-All. "I've been thinking about what to do after lunch tomorrow," Anita said hesitantly. "Perhaps I could take the children for a walk to the store and buy some fruit for snack time."

"That won't work," Pam replied firmly. "What you don't realize is that we tried that before. When *I* did it last year . . ." Anita began to seethe inside. Every time she had what she thought was a creative idea, Pam made her feel stupid.

1.	*Identify* the problem	Anita decided that Pam's tendency to give the "right answer" was at the heart of the problem. She really resented being stopped before she got started on an idea. She wanted a chance to attempt some new things herself, even if they didn't work out.
2.	*Create* a constructive climate	Anita waited until she and Pam were walking to the subway after school, a time they both usually enjoyed.
3.	*Describe* your feelings	Anita told Pam that she'd felt discouraged when Pam squelched her idea about the walk. She said she was really feeling the need to try things out.
4.	*Invite* discussion and problem solving	"Can we work out a way for me to take some more responsibility for planning activities?" Anita asked. "We can talk about them afterwards to see how they turned out."

THE GROWING STAFF

5.	*Commit* yourselves to one specific goal	Pam and Anita agreed that Anita would plan the art activities for the following week and that they would meet on Friday to see how things went.

Here's another example of the problem-solving approach in practice. This situation introduces another kind of conflict.

The Rivals. Molly looked over at the reading corner where Angela, the other teacher, was sitting on the floor with three children on her lap. Somehow Molly felt left out. Angela was telling them a story while several other children stood around listening. "Beth and Steve!" Molly called. "Come and see what I have!"

1.	*Identify* the problem	Molly sees that she and Angela have fallen into a familiar trap: competition over children. Each wants to be the favorite, and they shower attention on the children in order to win their allegiance. No one wins.
2.	*Create* a constructive climate	Molly asked Angela to stop for coffee after work so they could have time to talk.
3.	*Describe* your feelings	Molly said, "Look, Angela, I think there's a problem in our group. I'm wanting these children to like me so much that I'm almost bribing them with too much attention and entertainment. I wonder if you feel the same way sometimes."
4.	*Invite* discussion and problem solving	"I wonder what we can do to get ourselves out of this pattern. I don't think it's good for anyone. I'd really like your help in thinking up some ideas."
5.	*Commit* yourselves to one specific goal	After talking it over, Molly and Angela began to see that by their competition, each was interfering with the other's work—and with the children's independence. They decided to try two things: 1. not to interrupt if the other was involved in doing something with a child 2. try to direct the children into more independent activities, rather than entertaining them all the time. They planned to keep a record of these activities.

Now test your own problem-solving skills on the hypothetical situation on page 222.

DO IT YOURSELF

Here's another situation that frequently causes problems. We've listed the five problem-solving steps. Beside each, write down what Jeffrey could do to put them into practice.

The Soft and The Strict. "But Ms. Spelman always lets us!" Jody wailed as Jeffrey, a teacher, lifted him down from the tree. "Well, *I* don't," Jeffrey said firmly. "You could get hurt up there." Inside he thought, "Terry should have more sense than that. She's always giving in to these children."

Jeffrey could . . .

1. *Identify* the problem   1.

2. *Create* a constructive climate for discussion   2.

3. *Describe* your feelings   3.

4. *Invite* discussion and problem solving   4.

5. *Commit* yourselves to one specific goal   5.

FORM 11-3

WORKING TOGETHER IN STAFF MEETINGS

Staff meetings are another place where you can apply your problem solving. Let's look at some things you can do to help get results from these meetings.

Many people groan when staff meetings are mentioned. "They're dull," they say. "They waste my time...." We think they don't have to.

Think about the worst meetings you've ever sat through.

Did you feel powerless?
Did one person dominate the meeting?
Were you confused about the purpose of the meeting?
Did the meeting drag on endlessly?

You could probably add half a dozen complaints to this list.

But staff meetings don't *have* to be bad. In fact, they can and should be enjoyable and thought provoking. What they're like is up to you.

Staff meetings give you a chance to improve your program in many ways. You can do this by using meetings to discuss individual children or the whole group, to plan specific activities, to develop your teaching skills, to increase your knowledge of how children grow, to solve day-to-day problems that concern the whole staff.

Finding Time

For all these reasons, it's absolutely essential to find time for regular meetings. They are basic to developing a Growing Program. Despite their importance, some programs have no scheduled time for staff to get together. It's the responsibility of the director, supervisor, or head teacher to arrange things so that time *can* be found. But it can be hard, especially in an all-day program.

- Try having parent volunteers take over the group at quiet times once a week for an hour or so. It might be at naptime or lunch or during a film.
- Plan the weekly schedule so that everyone comes early on one day. Use that time for meetings.
- Rotate responsibility for supervising outdoor activities or naps, freeing most of the staff to get together on a weekly basis.
- If possible, close early once a week, and use the last hour to talk.

Planning Ahead

Once you've found the time, you need to fill it usefully. You'll need to plan a regular schedule of meetings, with a clear-cut *purpose* for each one.

What to Plan

DAILY MEETINGS

We can see the eyebrows go up. "Who has daily meetings?" *You* do, if you're teaching with someone else. You don't call them meetings, but that's what they are. Early in the morning, you talk as you set out materials, planning who'll supervise what, and how to interest a particular child in an activity. Halfway through the day, you exchange impressions of a child's painting as you clean up. At the end of the day, you look back at what's happened. Was it a "good day"? How? And why?

If you don't do this kind of talking now, begin to get into the habit.

WEEKLY MEETINGS

Besides these daily chats, teachers of one group of children should meet "formally" once a week.

The most important part of weekly meetings is the "staffing process" described in Chapter 6. This kind of individualized discussion and planning is what keeps your program responsive to the needs of children.

In addition to evaluating and planning for individual children, you should spend time talking about general goals for the following week and deciding on activities and materials. You can kill several birds with one stone if, at the same time, you actually prepare some materials (cutting collage shapes, making play dough, arranging a new activity center).

MONTHLY MEETINGS

The entire staff should meet at least once a month. The monthly meetings you have can be divided into two basic types:

1. "Learning" meetings where you gather information about children and teaching (sometimes with an outside resource person)
2. Problem-solving meetings where the staff discusses and finds solutions to situations involving children, staff, parents, policies.

Often you may combine the two, using the first part of the hour to solve the problem of late-arriving carpools and the last part to listen to a guest speaker on learning disabilities.

How to Plan

Whether it's a "learning" meeting or a "problem-solving" meeting, there are things you can do ahead of time to help things go better:

- *Vary the format of the meetings.* Weekly meetings usually have to cover the same ground (discussing children, planning activities), but there's no reason for each monthly meeting to follow the same pattern. Varying the format from a speaker to a workshop to a discussion keeps everyone interested.
- *Share responsibility for getting ready.* If you've helped plan a meeting, you're more likely to try to make it go well. Every member of the staff should share in planning the meetings, perhaps by rotating the leadership role on a regular basis.
- *Create a pleasant setting for your meetings.* Some centers have meetings at staff members' homes; others have a comfortable teachers' room where they can meet. But even if you have to perch on tiny chairs in a hallway, staff can take turns providing something to munch on, and a hot drink is always welcome. The important thing is to create an atmosphere that invites discussion and open communication.

THE GROWING STAFF

- *Streamline discussion of routine business.* Delegate some decision making to individual staff, list business items on a written agenda, and limit the amount of time for discussion. That way you won't subject yourselves to an hour-long analysis of the benefits of peanut butter versus jelly.
- *Post an agenda beforehand.* Let people know what to expect. If it's a meeting where a number of topics will be discussed, post a list of those topics a few days ahead. Leave a pencil handy so people will feel free to add items that they'd like to bring up. This procedure gives everyone a chance to think about the issues before the meeting begins and lets each person have a say in what will be talked about.

"LEARNING" MEETINGS

Somehow the word "meeting" suggests a formal speech. While you may occasionally want to listen to a speaker, there are other ways to get and share knowledge. Workshops, "hands-on" activities, role-playing sessions, films plus discussion —all are ways of involving staff in new ideas.

Sometimes one of your own staff may lead such a meeting. At other times, you may draw on community resources for help. Here are a few likely places for free or almost-free speakers to be hiding.

- *Teacher centers* often have speaker bureaus or workshop leaders
- *Art galleries or craft cooperatives* are good places to find local artists or crafts people who can develop art activities with teachers
- *Libraries* have speakers who would love to talk about books for children
- *Colleges* have teachers in psychology or education who will often speak for a small fee
- *Public school systems* have many resource people: teachers, psychologists, counselors
- *Hospitals or medical societies* may supply the names of pediatricians or other physicians to help you understand children's physical problems.

How do you decide what the topic of each meeting should be? The most important thing is that it be *interesting* and *relevant* to your day-to-day work. For instance, you may have recently accepted a mentally retarded child into your program. A speaker who's had experience integrating children with special needs into the classroom would be very helpful at that point.

To set your imagination going, here are some topics that others have enjoyed learning about and discussing. Most could be led either by a staff member or a guest, as a "speech," an informal discussion, or a demonstration workshop.

- "Pressures on Children Today"
- "Children's Ideas about Death"
- "Stimulating Children's Thinking"
- "Children's Fears"
- "The Hyperactive Child"
- "Sex and the Preschool Child"
- "The Meaning of Children's Drawings"
- "Play and Learning"
- "Patterns of Perceptual-Motor Development"

- "Intelligence Testing: What It Can and Can't Do"
- "The Gifted Child"
- "Reading Readiness: What and How?"
- "TV and Children"
- "Teaching Cooperation"
- "Behavior Modification: Pro and Con"
- "Recognizing Learning Disabilities"
- "Children as Scientists"
- "Math Activities for Young Children"
- "Getting the Most out of Table Games"
- "Building Furniture for the Classroom"
- "The World of Blocks"
- "Making Music and Musical Instruments"
- "Using Beautiful Junk"
- "Mud, Sand, and Water Play"
- "Outdoor Activity Centers"
- "Ideas for Group Times"
- "Books to Grow On"
- "Parent Conferences"
- "Involving Parents in the School"
- "Junk Food and Good Food"
- "The Young Carpenter"

"PROBLEM-SOLVING" MEETINGS

In some ways, these meetings are harder. You, as a staff, are trying to work together to set policy, resolve differences, work out dozens of minor crises. And you need to do it without becoming too bored, or frustrated, or angry. Here are some steps you can take to get the most out of the time you have for these meetings.

Steps	How-to	Taking Action
1. Define responsibilities	Have one person take responsibility for leading and summarizing the discussion. Another can take notes.	This time Lena was acting as the discussion leader. She asked Carol to take notes (which are kept in a notebook as a permanent record).
2. List agenda items	Some items will have been posted ahead of time; teachers may have added others. Ask the group what else they would like to talk about. Add these to the agenda and post it on the wall where everyone can see it.	Lena said, "There are only two things on the agenda this week—the problem about trikes and the field trip. Anything else?" "I'd like to talk about what we're going to do about the summer program," Parker commented. Carol added that to the agenda.
3. Determine priorities	You may not have time to discuss fully every item on the agenda. Ask the group which items are most important. Star them and discuss them first.	"What shall we discuss first?" Lena asked. "Since the field trip's in two weeks, let's begin with that," said Carol. Everyone agreed.

Steps	How-to	Taking Action
4. State goals	It's not enough just to kick a topic around. You need to decide what goal you're working toward: a specific decision? a draft of a letter? a list of jobs? If you begin this way, you'll focus your discussion, and you'll *know* when you're finished.	The group decided that their goal was to come up with two choices of places to go on the field trip in two weeks, and to appoint someone to check into the relative cost and time involved in going to each place.
5. Limit time	Parkinson's law wisely states, "Work expands to fill the time available." Unless you're ready for a marathon, set a time to stop—and stick to it.	Lena suggested that they stop at five o'clock. Parker had to get a train a bit earlier, so they decided to break up at 4:30 and give top priority to the summer program next month.
6. Brainstorm solutions	Every idea, no matter how unusual, should be welcomed. Allow enough time for this step before getting down to making a decision. The "secretary" can keep track.	The staff had many ideas for the next field trip, from the fire station to the library to a doctor's office to a bakery. All the suggestions were listed on the board.
7. Give approval	We sometimes forget the importance of positive reinforcement. Adults welcome a compliment on their work or ideas as much as children do. Get in the habit of giving each other specific, positive support.	Lena mentioned how successful Carol's excursions with the youngest group had been last year, and suggested that she write up a list of tips on field trips. Carol beamed modestly.
8. Focus the discussion	While brainstorming is helpful, irrelevant discussion only frustrates everyone and wastes time. Focus your talk on reaching the goal you've set. The chairperson can take primary responsibility for keeping on the subject, but it's really up to everyone.	At one point Parker started reminiscing about the time he had taken a class to the zoo. Lena reminded him that they only had a little time left to make a decision.
9. Use information to make a decision	Making a decision is never easy. It'll be easier if • the decision isn't imposed by one person • the decision is made on the basis of facts • the group agrees as to how it will decide the issue.	The staff looked at the list of field-trip suggestions and decided that the ones they chose should be tied in with previous group activities. Since the train station and the fire station would both add to the transportation games that had been going on, they decided to have Lena investigate these possibilities.
10. Summarize	Have one person summarize what was decided or accomplished. This gives the group a feeling of satisfaction and gives everyone a chance to see if they've understood the decision correctly.	Lena summarized what they'd decided and what she was going to do next. She also went over the items they didn't get to and listed them on the agenda for the next meeting.

Solving Staff-Meeting Problems

Even if you use these steps, problems will come up, as they do any time people have to work together. Here are some typical problems and possible solutions:

Problem	*Possible solution*
• You're finding yourself daydreaming about the movie you saw last night.	If you're off in the clouds, maybe others are, too. Why not say frankly, "I'm afraid I'm having a hard time keeping my mind on the discussion. Could someone summarize things?"
• You're mad. Inside your head you're disagreeing with everything that's being said.	If you *keep* it inside your head, you won't accomplish much. There are ways to disagree without coming across as aggressive or complaining. If you try to get at the facts and avoid personal attacks, disagreement can be productive.
• You haven't said a word in half an hour because another staff member is talking too much.	A discussion leader has a key role in cutting off monologues. He or she is expected to keep everyone involved and moving toward the goal. If you are not the leader, you might wait for a pause and direct a question specifically at another member of the group.
• You're going around in circles. The problem has been discussed and discussed, but the group's getting nowhere. It's all "*I* think . . . ," "Yes, but *I* think . . . ," "Well, *I* think . . ."	Again, nothing will happen unless you say something. Tell the group that you feel as if you are all going around in circles—maybe others feel the same way. Then *stop*; go back and look at your original goal; summarize what's been said; list what information may be needed to help resolve disagreements.

Working with others is never easy. We all have our private needs, wishes, frustrations. We have different personalities, different styles, different goals for ourselves and the children we teach.

A FINAL WORD

Throughout this chapter, the tool we've offered you in working effectively together is *communication*. By talking with one another, you'll start to share those private selves, those experiences and feelings. You may not agree, but you'll begin to understand each other's view of things. That's real growth.

RESOURCES

Brubaker, D. *The Teacher as a Decision-Maker.* Dubuque: William C. Brown, 1970.

    Part III, "Sources of Conflict in the School," contains a number of thought-provoking case studies of conflicts between teachers and between teachers and administrators. No easy answers, but helpful in thinking about how decisions get made.

Greenberg, H.M. *Teaching with Feeling.* New York: Macmillan, 1969.

    Teachers have feelings, too! Dr. Greenberg tells it like it is in chapters like "Colleagues: Friends or Foes?" and "Mood and the Teacher."

Newman, R.G. *Groups in Schools.* New York: Simon and Schuster, 1974.

    A perceptive and often humorous analysis of group life and group leadership in educational settings. A good chapter on "The Staff." Examples are drawn from elementary and secondary schools, but early childhood teachers would also find it relevant.

Simpson, R.H. *Teacher Self-Evaluation.* New York: Macmillan, 1966.

    Diagnose and improve your performance as a teacher, including your relationships with colleagues. Contains specific questions and checklists.

12

Growing Together

PARENTS, CHILDREN, AND STAFF

CHALLENGE YOURSELF

You may believe
- in the importance of good parent-teacher communication. But are you able to talk to parents without feeling defensive, worried, or insecure?
- that parent involvement is essential to your program. But do you offer parents a variety of options for involvement?
- that regular parent-teacher conferences are a vital part of the teaching process. But are you comfortable in handling specific conference problems?
- that parents need help with their problems, too. But do you have ways of helping "problem parents"?

SKILLS IN THIS CHAPTER

- Identifying parent-teacher communication problems
- Talking with parents about their child
- Involving parents in the program
- Helping "problem parents" and "problem teachers"!

GETTING PAST THE COMMUNICATION GAP

A parent and a teacher have a lot in common. They're both adults. They're both engaged in teaching and nurturing—at home or in school. They're both deeply concerned about the same child's growth. So why is it that they have such a hard time talking to each other? The teacher says

"Mary's been having a hard time making friends so far."

and the parent thinks

"Is she saying my little girl is unpopular? I've *tried* to help her with her shyness. I can't do everything!"

Or the parent says

"Are you going to teach them how to write their names?"

and the teacher thinks

"She's always criticizing this program. Her child has problems enough learning to pay attention without learning to *write*. I can't do everything!"

Communication Problem

It looks as if there's a real communication problem here. Often, when they talk to each other, parent and teacher both *feel*.

Teachers		*Parents*
because they feel parents are critical of their methods	DEFENSIVE	because they think teachers blame all the child's problems on them
because they don't know how parents will react to bad news	WORRIED	because they're afraid the teacher may tell them that something is very wrong with their child

232

GROWING TOGETHER

| because they wonder what parents really think of them | INSECURE | because they are often in awe of the teacher's education and uncomfortable in the "school" setting |

Because of these anxieties, parents and teachers sometimes lose sight of the most important link they have: *the child*.

Combining Strengths

After all, parents and teachers basically want the same thing. Their goal is to help the child grow and learn. If they focus on this common goal, they can combine their talents and energies to work *together* instead of against each other.

A parent and a teacher bring different but complementary strengths to the job of helping the child grow.

Parents
The parents bring a personal, intimate knowledge of their own child. They have watched the child develop from birth and have seen the child in every possible kind of setting. They also bring an intense love of, and identification with, the child, despite shortcomings or problems that are obvious to others.

Teacher
The teacher brings a breadth of experience with all kinds of children. He or she has a background of reading and training in child development and education. He or she is concerned with the child's well-being, but can be objective in assessing the child's strengths and needs.

The Child

FIGURE 12-1

When these strengths work together, everyone will benefit: parent, teacher, and child.

Let's see how we can bring this about. In this chapter, we'll look at a number of ways to use the strengths of parents in improving your program and your individual work with the child.

→ *Parents and their child.* Here we will share some ideas about how to decrease tension and improve communications between parent and teacher for the benefit of the child.

→ *Parents and the program.* Here we will share some ideas about how to use parents' talents and energies in improving your program—and improving parent-teacher relationships in the bargain.

PARENTS AND THEIR CHILD

All parents are interested in one thing: *their child.*

GOAL

Your goal is to help the child by establishing a comfortable, two-way exchange of information with his or her parents. That way, each of you—parent and teacher—can use this information about the child's growth to solve problems and make plans for the future.

Informal Contacts

Good communication with parents doesn't happen all at once. Like any other relationship, the parent-teacher relationship is nourished by lots of small, informal contacts. By the time you have a formal conference, it's not so threatening to either of you.

Every teacher should have a repertoire of informal channels of communication. Each is helpful for different purposes.

- *Informal talks at the beginning or end of the day.*

    "How was your weekend?"
    "Billy had such a good time with Chuck this afternoon—they really play well together."
    "Martha seems tired and weepy. I wonder if she's coming down with something."
    "Have you noticed that Eric can read a few words?"

    You can give a lot, and learn a lot, in brief, casual exchanges like these. You give parents the message that you care about them and their child; without prying, you often learn about home events that affect the child's feelings and behavior in your class. Just don't drop bombshells as the parent's walking out the door; if you think Carla may have a hearing loss, save the news for a telephone call or a conference.

- *Phone calls.*

    "Hello, this is Nan Youngman, Brenda's teacher. I just wanted to tell you about something that happened at school today. A large dog came into our play yard. He seemed friendly, but Brenda was terrified. I wondered if she had talked to you about it, and whether she's ever been badly hurt by a dog."

The telephone is a wonderful invention. Quicker than a conference, more personal and detailed than a note, a telephone call can put teachers instantly in touch with parents.

Sometimes, like Nan, you want to discuss a problem that calls for immediate action. Sometimes you're concerned about a sick child. At other times you want to keep in touch with working parents, to share their child's accomplishments. Many teachers have found parents more relaxed and communicative over the phone than in person.

- *Notes.*

    o from the teacher { "Adrian has had a wonderful week. He's really enjoying school now."
    "Big news! Florrie got dressed all by herself today!" }

    o from the parent { "Dave isn't too happy—he wanted to stay home today."
    "Wanted you to know our dog died over the weekend." }

    When the parent does not deliver the child to school, a note is often the easiest way to exchange brief pieces of information. Encourage parents to let you know about happenings at home (like the dog's death) which could affect your understanding and handling of the child's behavior.

- *Home visits.* Some teachers swear by home visits; others dislike them. Parents have the same mixed reactions, so you have to "play it by ear." Many teachers do find that a friendly visit (either before the school year begins or later in the year) is a great ice-breaker, as well as a way to learn something about the child's life outside the school or center. Other teachers feel very uncomfortable in this area. Although no one feels very comfortable about home visits at first, you should at least try a few where you think it seems appropriate and then decide if this kind of experience was worthwhile for you and the parents. Here are a few tips:
    o Don't use the home visit as a chance to tell the parent about the child's problems. Keep it happy and sociable.
    o You can put parents at ease by keeping the visit child-centered—you're there to see Bill, Bill's toys, Bill's cat.
    o Be warmly appreciative of the positive elements in the visit—the cookies, the new couch, the child's friendliness.
    o Some teachers feel more comfortable—especially before school starts—if they bring something to do with the child: a game, paper and crayons, etc.

You might also try inviting small groups of children into your home before you go to visit theirs. Through these visits children can see that teachers have normal families and homes much like theirs. This could be done two or three times a year on a Saturday afternoon.

Formal Contacts: Parent Conferences

If you've made a real effort to build a relationship through the informal contacts described above, parent conferences shouldn't be so difficult. Still, many teachers find conferences the hardest part of their job. Part of the problem is that oftentimes neither the teacher nor the parent is really sure what the purpose of a conference is.

Purpose

Like the rest of your program, conferences should focus on *helping the child grow*. A conference provides an uninterrupted period of time when parent and teacher *together* can

1. *exchange* information about the child's development and progress at home and in school, and
2. work to *solve problems* that the child is facing in his or her home or school life.

Getting Ready

Preparing for a conference is a two-way street. You, as the teacher, can prepare by:

1. Clarifying your own views about the purpose of parent conferences through reading and staff discussion.
2. Sharing those views with parents early in the year.
3. Just before the conference, going over the child's observation records, work folder, and planning sheets.
4. Preparing a conference report form (see p. 240), summarizing the child's progress and strengths. This may be given to the parent or simply used as a guideline for the teacher in remembering points he or she wishes to bring up.
5. Arranging a place for the conference that is private, comfortable, and pleasant. *Don't* be on one side of an imposing desk. (Coffee is nice, too.)

The parent can prepare for the conference by:

1. Thinking over and perhaps listing the things he or she wants to discuss.
2. Visiting the class to observe the child. Some centers arrange visits and conference times together, so that the parent can observe for half an hour or so and then talk with the teacher afterward. This arrangement gives parent and teacher something specific and objective to talk about.

Conference Time

Every conference is—or should be—different, if you're tuned in to each unique parent and each unique child. But even experienced teachers have certain recurring problems with conferences. Maybe we can think them through.

Q. How do I start? It's so awkward those first few moments.
A. The coffee *does* help here! Then, a general, *positive*—but honest!—comment about the child relieves the parent of that "I know she's going to tell me something awful" feeling.

"Susie is such a pleasure to teach."

"Jimmy has been telling us such interesting things about your vacation."

"We've all enjoyed Luke's sense of humor."

After that, the question "Does Tommy talk much about school at home?" is a nice lead-in to further discussion. The parent will usually say something like, "Oh, yes—he talks about his friend Mikey all the time." Then you can get into the great block building he and Mikey have been doing together, and from there move into his progress in other activities and areas of the program.

Q. How do I give a parent bad news about her child?

A. It's not easy. You need to tread carefully, because parents' identities are wrapped up very closely with that of their child—as they should be. This means that they will take personally any criticism of the child. Here are some suggestions:

1. *Let the parent say it first.* By asking "Is there any special way you would like us to help Dennis?" you will probably find that Mrs. Menace sees the problem, too—and you are spared the role of bringer of bad tidings.

2. *Describe what you've seen; don't diagnose or interpret.* Somehow, parents find a statement like "We've seen Joe get involved in a lot of fights lately" easier to deal with than "Joe is very aggressive" or "Joe never seems to have learned impulse control." A *label* like "aggressive" or "withdrawn" doesn't give the parent or the teacher anything to work with; these labels imply that there's a defect in the child's character which probably can't be changed. Behavior, on the other hand, *can* be changed, if parent and teacher work together.

3. *Don't give advice unless it's asked for.* People hardly ever follow unsolicited advice; it only makes them balky and defensive. Instead (as with children), involve the parent in the problem-solving process. "How do you think we could help Frankie with his speech?" or "Maybe we could try . . . ," NOT "You ought to. . . ."

4. *Encourage the strengths of the parent.* When you give parents bad news about a child, their own self-images are going to be affected. Rightly or wrongly, they are going to feel as if they've failed, at least in one small area. Often they will be feeling helpless to cope with this new difficulty. You can help by focusing on the forces of strength and adequacy *in the child* and *in the parents:*

"Ronnie's so determined. He never gives up no matter how hard it is for him."

"You must be a very strong person to have coped with all these illnesses over the years."

Q. I know a conference is supposed to be a two-way communication, but how can I get parents to talk about their home life without my seeming nosy?

A. Some parents *do* interpret any question about their homes as prying, and you certainly need to respect this sense of privacy. But most parents are glad to share this information if the focus is on helping the child. "I'm eager to know more about Zachary," the teacher might say. "How does he like to spend his time when he's home?" A question like this is friendly and nonthreatening; still, the parent's response gives the teacher

Q. Help! What do I do during those awkward silences?
A. Silences are only awkward if you think they are. Silence can be comfortable if you accept it as a chance for both of you to think a bit. During a conference, the teacher should be a good listener; there's no need for you to leap in with a comment at every pause. If the silence follows something the parent has said, you can often help by simply *reflecting the parent's feeling* ("You're really discouraged about Randy's behavior") rather than turning the conversation in a new direction. Of course, if the topic has exhausted itself, it's probably up to you to introduce a new one—or end the conference.

Q. That's another problem—how do I end it without making the parent feel pushed out—or without having it go on and on?
A. Ending a conference can be difficult. However, several things will help you finish up in a pleasant, satisfying way.
1. Make sure the parent understands the time limit of the conference. Then, five minutes or so before the time is up, you might say, "We'll need to finish up in a few minutes. Is there anything else you'd like to add?"
2. Avoid being drawn into discussing new issues as the parent is walking out the door. Perhaps he or she's waited this long to bring up the subject of Ray's nightmares because he or she's worried about them, but you won't be able to discuss them helpfully if your mind's on Mrs. Jones waiting in the hall. Instead, say something like, "I didn't know that was on your mind. Why don't I call you and we can set a time to talk it over soon?"
3. If specific plans have been made during the conference, it's useful to summarize them at the end. By asking *the parent* to sum up ("Can you help me review what we decided to do about Ricky's problem, Mr. Pine?"), you can assess the extent to which the two of you are in agreement. In addition, both you and the parent will feel a stronger commitment to the proposed plan if it's been put into words. If target dates will help get things done, set them ("I'll call you next Tuesday to see how our plans are working out, all right?").

A simple "Thank you for coming—I think it's been helpful to both of us" will usher the parent out the door.

Conference Report Forms

At the beginning of this section, we pointed out the need for the teacher to summarize the child's progress before the conference, as a way of organizing thoughts. Some centers give parents these written reports; others do not. There are good arguments on both sides.

Pro:
Many parents like to see written evidence of progress; they tend to forget what was said in a verbal exchange.

Con:
It's hard to give a personal, well-rounded picture of a child's development in a written report. Also, negative comments sound much worse in writing.

GROWING TOGETHER

In any case, the conference always comes first. While a written report may supplement a conference, it should *never* replace the conference. If you do give parents a written report, be sure to keep another copy for your files.

Immediately after the conference, take a few minutes to record information and impressions gained from the parents.

- Perhaps Mrs. Spivack told you that she's getting a divorce.
- Perhaps you got the feeling that Mr. Bimini expects a great deal of Timmy.

Keeping a record of these kinds of comments will be useful to you in your planning.

Whether you keep reports only for your own use or give them to parents, you should decide what you want the report form to accomplish before deciding what format to use.

GOALS

A good report form should give a picture of the child's strengths as well as needs. It should measure the child's progress against what *he or she* has done, not what others are doing. It should give emphasis to all growth areas. It should reflect the emphases and values of your program. It should be used as the basis for future planning, *not* as the "final word" on the child.

SAMPLE FORM

One sample report form that seems to meet these goals is presented in Form 12-1.

"PROBLEM PARENTS" AND "PROBLEM TEACHERS"

"Problem Parents"

Some parents have special difficulties in their relationship with the school program. To work successfully with these parents, you'll need to do some extra planning.

The Parent	*How to Help*
1. *The Complainer.* This parent criticizes everything about the program, from the food to the discipline. Nothing is right. Yet the child seems happy and well-adjusted.	Many times you'll find that this parent has a child who likes school very much—so much that the parent feels that the teacher is competing for the child. Arguing about the food won't help; sincere praise of the parent's child-rearing skills may.
2. *The Talker.* Every morning, the minute he or she walks in the door, this parent starts to talk—about everything under	It's hard to break away from this parent, because he or she seems to need you so much. Try a firm "I'd like to talk another time, but

Parent-Teacher Conference
REPORT FORM

Child's name _____ Date _____

Period from _____ to _____

Child's outstanding interests at school:

Child's outstanding progress or accomplishments at school:

Child's outstanding needs at this time:

Suggestions and future plans for meeting child's needs:

Questions about child:

Additional information (vision, hearing screening, other referrals or testing):

[Parent Comments]

Teacher's　　　　　　　Director's　　　　　　　Parent's
Signature _____ Signature _____ Signature _____

Perhaps this form may suit your purposes—or you may want to design your own, with the above goals in mind.

FORM 12-1

The Parent	*How to Help*
the sun! You try to listen, but others are arriving and the paint needs to be mixed.	I need to get back to the children now. Let's make an appointment."
3. *The Invisible Parent.* You never see this parent. His or her child is dropped off by a car pool, he or she never comes to meetings and seems totally uninvolved in the program.	The telephone is helpful here. Call about pleasant trivia—Eddie's lovely paintings— or to extend a personal invitation to a meeting. This parent may come if he or she feels someone really cares.
4. *The Denier.* When told that the child has a problem, this parent denies it: "Not my son!" He or she ignores suggestions about referrals and continues as if everything were fine, when everyone else knows it isn't.	You can't *make* this parent listen. Still, it's worth saying that you see a problem. The following year, when the kindergarten teacher says the same thing, he or she may realize there might be some truth in it.

"Problem Teachers"

Teachers aren't perfect, either. In your relationships with parents, do you sometimes fall into one or more of the following categories?

- *The Know-It-All.* He or she has an answer for every problem—whether the parent wanted it or not.
- *The Rescuer.* This teacher's job in life is to save children from their terrible parents.
- *The Buddy.* His or her need for friendship with parents gets in the way of a professional relationship.
- *The Doormat.* This teacher is so scared of parents' disapproval that he or she does whatever they want.

Solving Problems

You can begin to resolve these difficulties by using the following steps:

1. Observe the situation.
2. Identify the problem.
3. Make a specific plan and follow it:

> "I'll call Mrs. Edmunds tonight and invite her to coffee."
> "In my next conference, I'll try not to give one piece of advice unless I'm asked."

It works with children and staff—it'll work with parents, too.

DO IT YOURSELF

1. To sharpen your skills, role play a parent conference with another teacher or student. Reverse roles after a while.
2. Look over your present report form. If you're not satisfied that it reflects the goals of your program, revise it using the guidelines in this chapter. (*Student teachers:* Create a report form for your future use.)
3. Here is a series of statements to help you assess your use of formal and informal contacts with parents. Check the column that reflects your feelings. (*Student teachers:* This activity may not be appropriate for you.)

	Very Satisfied	*Fairly Satisfied*	*Dissatisfied*
1. I try to have a word with parents at the beginning and end of the day.			
2. I use the telephone as a way of keeping in touch.			
3. I send notes home and encourage parents to do the same.			
4. I feel comfortable making home visits.			
5. I schedule conferences once or twice a year.			
6. I prepare for each conference by gathering information and writing a summary.			
7. I encourage parents to observe just before their conference.			
8. I feel comfortable beginning and ending the conference.			
9. I know how to handle a discussion of a child's problems.			
10. I use the conference as a chance to learn more about the child at home.			

FORM 12-2

	Very Satisfied	*Fairly Satisfied*	*Dissatisfied*
11. If I give out written reports, they are well-balanced and clear.			
12. I make specific plans to help "difficult parents"—and to work on my own problems.			

Areas of least satisfaction

1. _____

2. _____

Specific plans to work on these areas

1. _____

2. _____

FORM 12-2 (Continued)

PARENTS AND THE PROGRAM

Twenty years ago, programs discouraged or ignored parent involvement in the educational process. Children "belonged" to the school during school hours and "belonged" to the parents at home.

But things are changing. Research is pointing the way to the benefits of a stronger link between home and school. Many federally funded preschool programs now require parent participation. Most of us have seen the good that can come when parents and teachers share educational goals, working together to solve common problems.

Let's be realistic, though. Not all parents are willing or able to participate to an equal extent in the educational program. The degree of their involvement is influenced by many factors:

- their feeling of comfort in the school setting
- their ideas about the proper roles of parent and teacher
- other demands on their time—jobs, younger children, etc.

Since there's so much variety in parents' interest and time, your goals for parent involvement should be flexible.

GOALS

- Each parent should be made to feel that he or she is *welcome* to participate, and that (like the child) the parent is *valued* for the unique attributes and skills that he or she possesses.
- Therefore, you should offer a *variety of options* to parents, without making them feel pressured to choose any particular one.

Options for Direct Involvement in the Daily Program

Parent cooperative nursery schools have always required regular, direct participation of "parent helpers" in the classroom. Even if your program doesn't call for this kind of involvement, there are many other ways to include parents in your daily program.

Show and Tell

Many parents are great resources—and they don't even know it! The jobs or hobbies that seem ordinary to them can be full of new ideas for children.

- *Job sharing.* "When I grow up, I'm going to be . . ." Any child loves to feel part of the real world of work—especially if the worker is his or her own mother or father. Parents who work at jobs that are interesting to children can be asked to come once a year to demonstrate their skill. Just make sure there's more *doing* than lecturing! Think about
  o a carpenter planing wood and drilling holes

- a nurse with a stethoscope
- a secretary demonstrating shorthand and typing to kindergarteners
- a policeman teaching how to direct traffic.
- *Sharing of hobbies and talents.* Many parents will be delighted to teach or demonstrate their special interest once a year, or more often if they have time. By including a question about hobbies and talents on your application, you can discover hidden—and free—resources to enrich your program. Who knows, you may uncover
  - a square dancer
  - a yoga enthusiast
  - a weaver
  - a Mexican cook
  - a guitarist
  - a photographer.

These sessions will be more enjoyable for everyone if you plan ahead. Talk with parents ahead of time to find out what they're going to speak about or demonstrate, and how long they expect to take. Some may need reminders that children's attention in a group is brief, and that children learn best by concrete involvement rather than by just watching or listening. You might want to consider having the parent talk with interested small groups or individual children. At any rate, keep it *short, simple,* and *concrete.* You can borrow additional suggestions from Chapter 11, "The Growing Staff: Making the Most of Yourselves."

Planned Participation in Classroom Activities

Some parents do not respond to large formal meetings. Your aim is to involve parents whenever possible. One way to make these parents feel more a part of their children's classroom is to invite them, a few at a time, to take part in special activities that their children have planned. Through this method, not only do you eventually bring parents into school, at some point during the year, but you also involve the children in making the visit a special time. It also gives parents a chance to see what is actually happening at school.

A small group of "chefs" invites their parents to snack on Friday to sample some pumpkin bread. Although not all the children have helped prepare the pumpkin bread this time, everyone partakes in the snack buffet with the parents that are visiting. The parents are able to sample the snack and get a copy of the recipe to take home. The following Friday another group of children will be making whole wheat and raisin bread and their parents will be asked to participate at snack time. At other times, parents may be invited to come and help prepare snack.

Children help make invitations to an art exhibit where parents can drop in during the morning to view the "junk sculpture" their children have constructed. Some of the children have prepared a snack, some act as "tour guides," and others hand out programs describing each work as dictated to the teacher. Activity areas are set up so that everyone has something to do. The entire exhibition may take no more than one hour on Tuesday morning and one hour on Thursday morning. For those parents who are unable to come, Ms. Morgan uses her camera to record the exhibit for the class picture album.

A group asks parents to come and see what they've been doing in creative dramatics. Some of the older children have especially enjoyed reading and acting out *The Three Billy Goats Gruff*. They decide that it might be fun to have their parents see their play one day close to dismissal time in the afternoon.

Again, if you keep it *small, informal,* and for short periods of time, everyone will have a good time.

Parents' Corner

Parents often feel uncomfortable in the school setting. The child-size chairs, the toys, the art supplies—all create a rather foreign atmosphere to some adults. They're reluctant to come in and relax. You can create a parents' corner with a few chairs, posters, a parent bulletin board, and a bookshelf with current readings on families and schools. An inviting spot like this, located in the hall or near the entrance to your room, will encourage parents to stop and chat.

Parent Pool

If you're lucky, you'll have a small group of parents who really want to help more often. They can be trained to work in the classroom on a regular basis (maybe once a week). They might

- read to one child or a small group of children
- do music or movement activities
- participate in block building or dramatic play
- supervise the workbench
- assist in the art area

These parents will need more training and help from you.

Prepare Your Parents

Although you'll be delighted to get this kind of help from parents, there are steps you need to take if you want to get the most out of these resources. Helping in the classroom should be a positive experience for everyone: the parent volunteers, the staff, and the children.

Preparation is the key to success in using parent volunteers. A carefully planned series of discussions, mini-workshops, and classroom observations will get parents ready for their classroom roles.

Let's follow Ms. Jones, a kindergarten teacher, as she works with a group of six interested parents.

	Guidelines
Ms. Jones decided that the parents would feel more comfortable if she trained them to help in specific areas and with specific tasks.	1. Give parents definite roles and responsibilities in the classroom.
She invited the six volunteers to meet at school on a Wednesday evening. At this first meeting, she began by outlining the areas in which they would be able to help, and asked each parent to	2. Be responsive to parent interests and talents.

select those activities in which he or she was most interested. Ms. Jones kept a list of these special interests.

Next, Ms. Jones began to give the group an overview of the activity areas in which they might be working.

Tonight, she began with the block corner, explaining the kinds of intellectual and social learning that take place in this area. She listed the classroom rules for that area (number of children allowed, clean-up duties, etc.), and suggested some specific things parents could do or say to extend children's learning (describing blocks as "longer," "shorter"; making suggestions without taking over; etc.).

The next day, the parents came into the classroom and informally observed the children's activities in the block corner. After the children went home, the parents discussed what they had observed with Ms. Jones. They had many specific questions: "Why did the teacher let Ronnie use all the long blocks? When—and how—should they stop an argument?" Ms. Jones answered some of these questions, and helped the parents think of their own answers for others.

When they'd had a little more experience, the parents felt comfortable enough to draw up a list of guidelines for helpers, which was posted in the block corner for future reference.

To build on what they'd learned, Ms. Jones gave each parent a copy of an article on block play.

The parents decided that they would develop skills in several additional areas: reading stories to children, working with music and movement, supervising the workbench, and helping in the art area. Ms. Jones set up dates for future workshops and classroom observations in these areas.

When the volunteer program got underway, Ms. Jones was disappointed to see

Guidelines

3. Help parents understand the underlying purpose or philosophy of the program.

4. Give parents detailed information on rules and routines, and specific techniques to use in working with children.

5. Allow time for observation.

6. Encourage open discussion, questions, differences of opinion—making it clear that these are to be reserved for after school.

7. Involve parents in problem solving.

8. Display written guidelines for volunteers.

9. Enrich parents' classroom experiences with readings, films, speakers.

10. Realistically accept the fact that, since parents *are* volunteers, some

that two parents dropped out. The other four, however, remained enthusiastic and committed to the program.

Guidelines

of them will be unreliable. Concentrate on keeping that number as few as possible, by preparation and training.

Options for Indirect Involvement in the Program

Many parents will not participate in your daily program. Some have jobs that conflict with school hours; others (perhaps because of earlier, unpleasant school experiences) feel inadequate or ill at ease in the classroom.

That's all right. There are still ways that they can be a part of their child's educational experience.

- *Maintaining and improving the center.* "Work parties" are a great way to cut maintenance costs and improve relationships between parent and teacher, especially if parents and teachers work together. You'll see different sides of the parents:
    o Mr. Platt, who seemed so aloof and superior at the open house, is great at making learning games out of almost nothing.
    o Quiet Ms. Wilson repaired the climber in less than an hour.
    o Ms. Santo, who can't speak English, beams with pleasure when everyone admires the curtains she sewed.
- *Fund raising.* Some people hate to ask for money. Others treat it as a challenge, and are resourceful and imaginative in organizing bake sales, auctions, and pot-luck suppers. They feel good about their contribution, and you improve the program with the money they raise.
- *Parent education.* Another way to involve parents out of school hours is to create a series of evening or weekend meetings. You'll be most successful if you enlist the help of *parents* in planning the program, rather than imposing your ideas about what they "ought" to know. Many groups have enjoyed
    o a "night at school" when parents can actually use the materials that their children talk about—blocks, clay, lotto, etc.
    o discussions of common child-rearing problems—tantrums, sibling rivalry, bedtime struggles—with no "right answer," but a chance for everyone to share ideas
    o a "toy workshop" so parents can learn how to use ordinary objects around the house (tin cans, milk cartons, old magazines) as learning materials; everyone brings something home
    o parent discussions around crucial issues involving parents, children, and staff: nutrition, health care, the single-parent family, effects of the long day at the center
    o a special guest speaker from the community.

Some of the suggestions for speakers in Chapter 11, "The Growing Staff," are also appropriate for parent meetings. Although these meetings will take place outside of school hours, it may be necessary to provide for some type of child care. Often, one or two high school or college students would be willing to supervise a small group of children. You may also want to help arrange car pools or other kinds of transportation so that parents can more easily attend an evening session.

Other parent-education suggestions include:

- a monthly newsletter produced with the help of parent volunteers. It might include news of the classroom, ideas for parents to try at home, and a special note or article by the teachers or director
- a special bookshelf in the parent corner filled with articles and books on parenting that parents can borrow to read at home
- a toy lending library where each week a small number of toys and games will be available for parents to use at home with their children. The teacher should provide any necessary suggestions or guidelines
- parent bulletin board in the parent corner with special notes of classroom or community activities.

Benefits of Involvement

Everyone wins when parents become enthusiastic and involved.

- *The teacher* gains added time and resources for the program; gets to know parents as *people.*
- *The parent* understands the program better through increased contact with the school and teacher; carries home ideas for new ways to create a "growing environment" for the child.
- *The child* feels proud that his or her mom or dad is part of "her" school; the child enjoys time in school more when parents are excited about it, too.

Getting the Message to Parents: You're Needed!

Parents won't volunteer if they don't know how much you need them. Early in the year, do some thinking about the ways in which you could use volunteer help to make your job easier and the children's experience richer. Share your list with others on the staff.

Then write a letter to every parent, explaining how—*specifically*—they could help, and asking for their participation.

A sample of such a letter is given in Form 12-3.

A FINAL WORD

"Parents are people, people with children," say the words of a song on the children's record *Free to Be . . . You and Me.* They *are* people, with the strengths and weaknesses, the hopes and worries of any other person—like you.

If you think of parents as allies, not antagonists, you are well on your way to using your combined insights and skills to help children learn and grow.

And that's what you both want.

September 20, 19--

Dear Parents:

As I begin to look at classroom needs this year, I could use your help in the following areas:

- ☐ 1. snack buffet
- ☐ 2. lunchtime
- ☐ 3. stories with individual children
- ☐ 4. art-area projects—assist teacher
- ☐ 5. listening-post activities
- ☐ 6. block area
- ☐ 7. outdoor play
- ☐ 8. water table
- ☐ 9. collecting found materials
- ☐ 10. helping with parent-teacher resource area
- ☐ Other interests (list) _____

Would you please check the area that interests you? Please also fill in the dates that you are available before sending in the form with your child.

I am available (dates, times) _____

_____
(signature)

Thank you.

FORM 12-3

DO IT YOURSELF

Plan a new parent-involvement activity, using the guidelines in this chapter.

Goals: What would you like the activity to achieve?

What: What kind of activity or activities would help meet your goal?

Who: How many parents would be involved? Who else? (other teachers, children)

When: What day (or days) and times can you set aside for this project?

Materials or equipment: What "things" do you need to actually do the activity?

FORM 12-4

RESOURCES

Benjamin, A. *The Helping Interview*. Boston: Houghton Mifflin, 1969.
> A useful book for anyone in the "helping professions"—doctors, counselors, ministers—as well as teachers. Wise and helpful.

Gordon, I. "Parenting, Teaching, and Child Development," *Young Children,* 31 (March 1976), 173-183.
> There are many similarities between good parenting and good teaching. Gordon documents them in a convincing and very interesting article.

Honig, A. *Parent Involvement in Early Childhood Education*. Washington, D.C.: NAEYC, 1975.
> Describes the importance of parent involvement and outlines some program models and methods to promote and achieve significant parent involvement in early childhood programs.

Parent Involvement Training Kit. Columbus, Ohio: Franklin County Welfare Department, 1977.
> A creative collection of activities and practical suggestions for implementation in the areas of parent discussion, creative dramatics, food and nutrition, and parent conferences.

13

Differences in Growth

MAINSTREAMING HANDICAPPED YOUNG CHILDREN

Samuel J. Meisels

INTRODUCTION

This chapter* differs in format from the preceding chapters you have read. It is a chapter devoted to giving general guidelines for planning and implementing a mainstreamed early-childhood program, that is, a program which integrates handicapped and nonhandicapped children in the same classroom.

This chapter is different from the rest of this book, but not solely because it is about children who are different from children who do not have special needs. Rather, it differs because it is meant to draw on and use all the information and skills presented earlier in this text.

As the forthcoming discussion will demonstrate, mainstreaming requires the development of a variety of new teaching skills. But primarily it is built on a fundamental competence in the regular classroom and an ability to modify and adapt competent teaching. Thus, this chapter assumes your familiarity with and understanding of the topics and issues presented throughout *The Growing Program*. In addition it:

- explores the meaning of "handicap";
- presents several justifications for mainstreaming; and
- identifies a number of critical issues that must be confronted when planning and implementing a mainstreamed program.

Although these issues are being raised at the end of this book, they should not be considered an afterthought. Rather, mainstreaming is presented in this book as the next logical step for early-childhood education.

*From Gunnoe, L.G. and Meisels, S.J. *Mainstream Challenges: A Manual for Early Childhood Educators.* Medford, Mass.: LINC Outreach, Tufts University, 1978.

HANDICAPPED CHILDREN

What comes to your mind when you think of the words, "handicapped child"? Do you conjure up an image of someone you know who is disabled? Or do you think back to children who were always in the "slow learner" class when you went to school? Possibly you might think of the Easter Seal's poster child—a child who is usually severely physically disabled, in a wheelchair, or in braces and crutches, but who is nevertheless cute, smiling, and enticing.

Most people who are not themselves disabled, or who do not have relatives, close friends, or neighbors who are handicapped, rely on faint memories or distorted stereotypes when thinking about handicapped children. Handicapped children and adults have been out of the way for a long time—in hospitals, institutions, special schools, segregated classrooms, or just at home.

But this isolation is coming to an end. As an early-childhood teacher, you can help put an end to the social and educational practices that have deprived millions of children and adults of their share of the equal and appropriate education guaranteed every United States citizen by the Constitution.

You can do this with the assistance of colleagues, administrators, parents, and a relatively new federal law, Public Law 94–142, The Education for All Handicapped Children's Act—a law which calls for the education of handicapped children in the "least restrictive environment."

Who Is Handicapped?

Bobby can't walk. When he was three years old he ran out into the street across from his house. He was struck by a truck. Bobby is lucky to be alive, but he'll never walk without crutches and braces; his spinal cord was permanently damaged.

When Saundra was born she looked a little funny. Her overall reactions were slow, her facial features somewhat peculiar, and she did not react very strongly to the noises and lights of the delivery room. Some time later it was determined medically that Saundra was born with a chromosomal defect known as Down's syndrome. Saundra is now five. She talks like a child who is younger than her age, learns some things with great difficulty, and has had several operations to correct a cardiac difficulty, but on the whole she's doing quite well.

Karen is four years old. Her parents have been separated for the past year and a half; divorce proceedings are about to begin. Recently, Karen's mother has been very busy looking for an apartment where she, Karen, and her two-year-old brother can live. Karen sees her father infrequently and misses him greatly. She has been very unhappy in school this year. She often cries, fights with other children, and just can't seem to settle down or make attachments.

Fred is hearing-impaired. When he was five years old an audiologist discovered that the auditory nerve in both ears was impaired. This is called sensorineural hearing loss. In addition, it was determined that he had a conductive hearing loss due to a buildup of fluid in his middle ear. The latter problem was corrected through a surgical procedure, but the sensorineural hearing loss is permanent. Fred is now wearing hearing aids in both ears and is beginning to develop language rapidly. He will always have some difficulty hearing, but he is catching up quickly.

All these children are handicapped. In this they are the same. Yet, they are also all different from one another. They differ in terms of their disabilities—Bobby is paralyzed from the mid-waist down, Saundra is intellectually slow, Karen is very anxious and is having difficulty forming relationships, Fred has trouble hearing and his speech is delayed. And they differ in terms of their strengths—Bobby has unusual artistic abilities, Saundra is motorically very advanced, Karen is an early reader, and Fred is a very warm, loving, and thoughtful child.

If we were to identify four other children with handicapping conditions similar to theirs, we would continue to observe this pattern of similarities and differences. For example, two children, both of whom have hearing loss, may differ greatly in terms of the severity of that loss, its potential for correction, extent of speech delay, and so forth. These two children would also differ in terms of their strengths, just as is true of any two individuals.

By virtue of having a handicapping condition children are not somehow made to be alike—not even if they share the same disability. All handicaps are *spectrum conditions:* they describe a continuum of disability and ability. In the case of hearing loss, the continuum ranges from permanent, profound deafness to temporary, partial loss of hearing (as when a child is just recovering from a cold). We all know people who wear eyeglasses to correct a mild vision problem; some of us also know people who are blind. Such individuals may be at extreme ends of the continuum with regard to visual ability; however, in terms of other characteristics, skills, and abilities, they may be very similar to one another.

Thus, to know that a child is handicapped is only to begin to make his or her acquaintance. You must also find out the child's name, age, something about his family and background, his likes, dislikes, interests, and concerns. This is, of course, what you do with any child, and, although one must usually make modifications in one's classroom in order to work effectively with disabled children, teachers generally find that handicapped children are more like, than unlike, children without special needs.

In recent years, educators have begun to call the inclusion or integration of handicapped children in regular classrooms by the name "mainstreaming."

MAINSTREAMING AND THE LAW

The Education for All Handicapped Children's Act (P. L. 94-142) was implemented across the country in the fall of 1978. This law represents landmark legislation for handicapped children. By national estimates, more than twelve percent of the entire population under the age of nineteen has some type of disability. P. L. 94-142 is a landmark because it guarantees to every handicapped child of school age, as well as to preschool-age children in states that provide educational services to three to five-year-olds, a free and appropriate education. No longer can a child be denied an education *because* of his or her handicap.

But the law goes even further. It requires that:

> to the maximum extent appropriate, handicapped children are [to be educated] with children who are not handicapped . . . . Special classes, separate schooling or other removal of handicapped children from the regular educational environment [should] occur only when the nature or severity of the handicap is such that education in regular classes with the use of supplementary aids and services cannot be achieved satisfactorily.

Some people have read these passages and have concluded that the law mandates mainstreaming, or that *all* handicapped children should be educated in regular classrooms.

But this is a mistaken impression. Many children, including Bobby, Saundra, Karen, and Fred who were described above, can do very well in a regular classroom. However, other children, with more severe and more multiple handicaps, should probably only spend a portion of their time in mainstreamed classrooms. For still other children, with other problems and disabilities, the regular classroom may be utterly inappropriate. Such placement decisions are extremely difficult to make, yet the critical point is that the regular classroom is but one possibility—albeit a potentially rewarding possibility—among the instructional alternatives for handicapped children.

In this chapter, we will focus on the mainstreamed classroom in order to better understand its role in a growing early-childhood program.

WHY MAINSTREAM?

Children with special needs have been integrated into regular classrooms from time to time for many years. However, it is only recently that the regular classroom has intentionally been sought as an appropriate placement for many handicapped children. This change in policy is reflected in P. L. 94-142 and it stems in part from legal deliberations concerning the issue of whether the rights and futures of handicapped children are protected when they are subject to potentially biased forms of diagnosis, labeling, and special-educational placement.

Several other justifications for mainstreaming have also emerged. From a *moral perspective,* mainstreaming can be regarded as a means of reducing isolation and prejudice while enhancing an understanding and acceptance of differences. Fundamentally, mainstreaming reflects human concern for human beings. For a teacher or parent who has never had direct contact with disabled children or adults, a mainstreamed classroom poses challenges to one's attitudes and to one's conception of justice and equality. Mainstreaming raises questions concerning the rights of one child versus the rights of many children. It forces confrontations with stereotypes and prejudices concerning people who are different in appearance and ability. And it challenges everyone to look beyond superficial differences to deeper, shared human qualities.

Another justification for mainstreaming is *socio-cultural* in orientation. In this respect mainstreaming is thought to increase the potential contribution of handicapped individuals to society at large. Children who are segregated at an early age in institutions or in special classes frequently spend their youth—if not their entire lives—in these specialized settings. Their ability to function as independent, self-sufficient individuals in the mainstream of society is not enhanced under such conditions. Adherents of mainstreaming intend to change this state of affairs.

The Educational Justification

A final justification for mainstreaming is educational. For many handicapped children—although certainly not for all handicapped children—the regular classroom provides an optimal educational setting. This is particularly true in the preschool. It is true because of three fundamental characteristics of early childhood programs:

1. maturation;
2. mastery; and
3. modelling.*

Maturation

Maturation refers to the wide range of normal behavior and activity demonstrated by children in most preschool programs. Children under the age of six mature at dramatically different rates. This difference justifies a range of behavior that is not typically expected in classrooms for older, elementary-aged children. Young children differ in terms of their language usage, speech articulation, conceptual sophistication, emotional stability, and fine- and gross-motor accomplishments.

This range of normality thus permits the integration of young handicapped children to take place without these children being isolated or highlighted as exceptionally bizarre or unusual.

Mastery

Another aspect of early-childhood programs that contributes to the success of mainstreaming is these programs' orientation toward mastery experiences. That is, most preschools and day-care programs encourage children to attain a degree of knowledge or level of performance that is appropriate for the individual. Children who display various levels of mastery are reinforced and respected for the abilities they can demonstrate. Such early-childhood programs grow and change with their children. They are not deficit-oriented; rather, they focus on what children *can* do. The wide range of activities that can therefore be considered mastery experiences in early-childhood programs has the potential of contributing to a handicapped child's sense of overall strength and competence even if that particular child's abilities differ from those of many other children in the class.

Mainstream Models

The integrated classroom also offers handicapped children opportunities to interact with positive role models as well as occasions to serve as positive models for other children. It has been shown that under certain circumstances negative behavior is modelled, or imitated, more readily and more frequently than positive behavior. This is one reason that classrooms composed entirely of special-needs children may have a negative impact on the children enrolled in those programs. Several researchers have shown that, *with systematic planning,* exposure of special-needs children to positive nonhandicapped role models will result in a marked increase in socially positive behaviors on the part of special-needs children. The integrated classroom, with its focus on normality and on "typical" behavior, is thus capable of providing special-needs children with positive educational experiences through exposure to positive peer models.

Integrated classrooms also provide opportunities for disabled children to

---

*For further discussion, see Meisels, S. J., and Friedland, S. J., Mainstreaming young emotionally disturbed children: rationale and restraints, *Behavioral Disorders,* 1978, *3* (3), pp. 178–185.

serve as positive role models for their nonhandicapped peers. Given that most children in an integrated program have the ability to respond favorably to positive, competent, purposeful activity, when special-needs children are given an opportunity to display mastery and effectiveness they are likely to be reinforced for these actions by their peers. Thus, there is an important place for handicapped children in early-childhood programs.

TALKING ABOUT HANDICAPS WITH CHILDREN: SOME GUIDELINES*

One of the primary goals of this chapter has been awareness: What is a handicapping condition? How do I feel about handicaps? How can I help all the children in my class talk about and deal with handicaps? The following is a list of strategies to use in talking with children about handicaps. Each strategy has illustrations.

1. Give simple, direct, and honest explanations.

    EXAMPLES
    Explaining a physical handicap
    - The kindergarten children were sitting around the snack table when all of a sudden one of them began to talk about Jean, a girl who is paralyzed from the mid-waist down. Jean was having snack at the time.

        Child: "Just because she can't walk, doesn't mean she's a baby."

        Teacher: "That's right. Jean's legs do not work. But she is five years old just like you. Jean, would you like to explain why your legs don't work?" (At the beginning of the year, Jean refused to talk about herself.) Jean explains in great detail how she was hit by a van ("dumb driver").

    Talking about aggression
    - A child was talking to the teacher about his classmate, Frank. Frank was frequently very aggressive and uncontrolled during school.

        Child: "I don't like Frank. He's always hitting."

        Teacher: "Frank has a difficult time when he's angry. We need to help him use words. You need to tell Frank how it makes you feel when he hits you."

    Explaining causes
    - To explain a child's outburst of angry hitting and subsequent removal for a time out, a teacher would say, "Sandy is very angry because he couldn't have the car. He needs to be alone to calm down." To explain a special choice-board system designed to help this child focus his attention on classroom activities, a teacher would say, "Sandy sometimes has trouble finding something to do at school. These cards help him to choose."

*From Gunnoe, L.G., and Meisels, S.J., *Mainstream Challenges: A Manual for Early Childhood Educators.* Medford, MA: LINC Outreach, Tufts University, 1978, pp. 53–56.

DIFFERENCES IN GROWTH

2. Explain the causes of disabilities simply and only at an appropriate opportunity.

    EXAMPLE
    Choosing appropriate times and simple explanations
    - One day Bobby arrived at school with a plastic model of the body of a man. He wanted to give a "lecture" on the human body, and did so. While discussing the legs he said, "Now, the legs are what make you walk, like this." (Putting one foot in front of the other.) "Unless, of course you're like Jean and break your legs. Then you can't walk unless they put you in a cast. Then she could walk."

        Teacher: "Jean's legs are not broken. Even if they were put in casts, she could not walk. Jean's legs cannot be fixed. They will never work. The only way Jean can walk is with her braces and crutches, but her legs will never work." When pushed for further explanations, the teacher showed the spinal cord on the model. She explained that the brain sends messages through the spinal cord to tell the legs what to do. "Jean's spinal cord was broken when she was hit by the truck, so the brain can send no message to her legs."

3. Use observable, behavioral terms.

    EXAMPLES
    For a problem of hearing
    - Tim, who is hearing impaired, had difficulty sitting or attending during group time. After observing this, the teacher began to wonder if his inattentiveness was related to his hearing loss. She gave Tim a special place near her and told him he needed to sit there because he would then be able to hear what was going on better.

    physical disability
    - To a child with a mild physical disability: "Sometimes, it's difficult to use your right hand, isn't it? It's hard to make it work just the way you want it to. Here, I'm going to help you hold this pair of scissors so we can help your hand practice to cut better."

    slow learning
    - To a child who is a slow learner: "It's hard for you to write these letters. You have to practice over and over. But look how beautiful that "s" looks—you really worked hard on getting that so good."

    impulse control
    - For a child with impulse-control problems: "I know it's sometimes hard for you to say, "I'm angry" and the first thing you want to do is hit. How do you think it makes Jenny feel to get hit? Let's try to see if she understands better when you *tell* her just how mad it makes you feel."

4. You don't need a "special language" for handicapped children.

    EXAMPLES
    - When Cindy starts to take a toy from another child, the teacher says, "I know it's hard for you, but you must use words." The teacher says the same thing to other children.

- When Phil cannot make himself understood, his teacher says, "I know it's hard for you, but say it again a little slower." The teacher tells other children that it is sometimes hard for Phil to talk.

5. Start where the child is.

   EXAMPLE
   Dealing with a physical disability
   - Art's handicap, cerebral palsy, was physical and visible. At the beginning of the year, discussions with Art about his handicap dealt more with the limitations of having cerebral palsy than with the specific details of the handicap. We helped Art to tell other children why he needs a walker ("My legs aren't strong enough for walking. I need my walker to help me walk."); to insist that his walker was for his use only; to set limits with other children when playing rough games; to ask for extra help when he needed it; and to express feelings of anger and frustration when he fell over unexpectedly or was left behind. Gradually we began to talk more specifically with Art about the treatment procedures he received weekly—physical therapy sessions, the transition from a hip brace and full leg supports to a heel to knee support to leg braces and crutches and discarding the walker. Art responded positively to these objective discussions of his disability; and other children shared constructively in these discussions also.

6. Allow opportunities to try out handicaps in a supportive environment.

   EXAMPLE
   - Mary's handicap, major surgery to remove a brain tumor, was physical and invisible. Mary had no surgery during the school year, but was in and out of the hospital for blood transfusions and because of illness. We did not talk with Mary directly about the nature of her illness, but we did provide many opportunities to talk about doctors, hospitals, being sick, being small, being weak, and feelings of loneliness, anger, and fear. Discussions occurred regularly throughout the year, initiated by Mary or teachers, or stimulated by school events, such as Mary's recurring hospitalizations and separation problems, the hospitalization of another child in the class for surgery and the presence of a child in the class whose father had died. Many opportunities were provided to play out doctor-patient-hospital themes using doctor props and a "hospital" set-up. Mary responded to discussion and stories and play props, but she was never preoccupied with these things and seemed more interested in the normal activities at school. Other children joined in the discussions mentioned above.

DIFFERENCES IN GROWTH

7. Don't confuse the child with his/her inappropriate behavior.

    EXAMPLES
    Separating
    the child
    from the
    behavior
    - With acting-out and aggressive children, it is important to clearly distinguish between the child's feelings and the child's inappropriate expression of those feelings.
    - The biggest problem area for Sandy was his lack of control over angry feelings and impulsive aggression. In talking with Sandy, we acknowledged and accepted his feelings, but not his out-of-control ways of expressing those feelings: "You feel angry because Adam took your car. It's all right to be angry, but you cannot hit. You have to use words to talk to Adam. Teachers will help you."

8. Don't try to ignore the obvious.

    EXAMPLE
    Reassuring
    the other
    children
    - We talked with nonhandicapped children about Art's handicap (cerebral palsy) in the same way that we talked with Art. The only differences were to assure other children that the condition had existed from birth, that it was neither contagious nor painful, but that Art's equipment was not a toy and it was no privilege to have to use it all the time. We were able to obtain an extra walker so that other children could satisfy their curiosity and allay their own fears by trying it.

ISSUES IN PLANNING AND IMPLEMENTING A MAINSTREAMED PROGRAM

Well before the first handicapped child enters your classroom, you should have completed a number of planning activities. Mainstreaming is not easy, but it can be made manageable by careful thought, training, support, and anticipation of problems. Some of the major planning and implementation issues are discussed below.

Who Should Mainstream?

Public-school programs no longer have the legal right to decide who shall or shall not be given educational services. Unlike private schools, public schools now must attempt to provide a free and appropriate education for every handicapped child within a certain age range who lives in the local school district. But the public schools, in conjunction with the child's parents, can make decisions about which children will be mainstreamed, and which children would be better served by receiving more specialized services.

Head Start programs are in a somewhat different position. By Federal law, all Head Start programs are required to fill ten percent of their enrollments with handicapped children. Head Start has other family and income restrictions which influence their intake process, but like public schools, they are required to provide services to handicapped children.

In contrast, private preschools and day-care centers are under no legal or statutory obligation to integrate special-needs children. P. L. 94-142 does not apply directly to them, nor do the Head Start regulations. Then, why get involved? Briefly, there are three reasons.

- First, the moral, sociocultural, and educational rationales that were detailed earlier constitute sufficient reason to justify a commitment to mainstreaming.
- Second, the private preschool and day-care sector is needed. Very few public-school systems offer preschool experiences for nonhandicapped children. This means that public schools which are under obligation to serve three- to five-year-old disabled children must either start new integrated programs or must contract for services with ongoing programs (Head Start or private) that are suitable for mainstreaming. The likelihood is very great that if the public schools are going to fulfill their responsibility to those handicapped preschoolers who can profit from mainstreaming, some arrangement will have to be created with the private sector. But for this to occur, preschools and day-care centers will have to prepare themselves, their teachers, and their parents in specific ways to be described below.
- Finally, there is another reason private preschools and day-care centers should get involved with mainstreaming. The reason is simple: it is exciting, it is challenging, and it is on the cutting edge of future developments in the field of early-childhood education. For professionals, it is the place to be.

Which Children Should Be Mainstreamed?

There is no easy answer to this question. Some people suggest that only children with certain handicapping conditions, e.g., deafness, learning disability, health-impairment, etc., should be mainstreamed. But this approach—by way of labeling—is generally very unhelpful.

It is unhelpful because no particular handicapping condition is better or more poorly suited to integration than any other handicapping condition. The difference lies in the child, not in the handicap or the label we attach to it.

In general, diagnostic labels such as developmental delay, epilepsy, hyperactivity, emotional disturbance, etc., are of limited usefulness to teachers. For one thing they usually encompass the whole spectrum of disorders that could be ascribed to a particular child. Hence, labels tend to be extremely vague.

More important, labels are static or unchanging; children are dynamic and in process. As a teacher works with a child, and as the child undergoes change and development, the labels begin to lose their usefulness. They describe incompletely and poorly, and they do not reflect the dynamism which the child is able to demonstrate.

So labels are not a fruitful route to take in deciding who should be mainstreamed. Another common strategy is to integrate only those children whose disabilities are at the mild or moderate end of the handicapping spectrum. While this approach may be useful in terms of certain disabilities—for example, retardation or emotional disturbance—it is just as frequently misleading as are diagnostic labels. Children who are deaf, blind, or paraplegic are often excellent candidates for mainstreaming. Yet, without question, they are severely disabled. Many other similar instances could be presented which show that broad categories are not very helpful in determining who should be enrolled in an integrated classroom.

Then, how should this decision be made? It should be made by looking at what the handicapped child can *take from* the regular classroom, and what he or she can *give to* that classroom. This is an interactive criterion that is meant to identify handicapped children who can both profit from and contribute to a modified regular classroom curriculum. Thus, the classroom has to be able to offer something to the child, i.e., provide significant educational and social opportunities and the child must be able to offer something to the class, i.e., effectively participate in the educational and social life of the school. If the child's educational needs are so specialized that the regular curriculum cannot be adapted to meet those needs, the integrated classroom may be inappropriate. Similarly, if the discrepancy in functioning between the special-needs child and his or her peers is very great, the handicapped child may be ignored, segregated, or scapegoated.

This is a very controversial issue. It is best settled by looking at individual children in particular classroom environments. The information potentially available from educational assessments performed by specialists, as well as the goals and objectives included in the child's Individualized Education Plan (IEP) are often greatly useful in making selection and placement decisions. These plans should be written so that they identify a child's strengths and weaknesses and permit the teacher to begin to anticipate the match between the child and the classroom.

How Many Handicapped Children Should Be Integrated into a Regular Classroom?

Although Head Start mandates that at least ten percent of its children be handicapped, there is no "ideal" ratio of handicapped to nonhandicapped children. However, if only one or two disabled children are integrated, it will be much more difficult to prevent these children from becoming isolated and segregated from the rest of the children than if there are three or four special-needs children. Efforts at helping non-handicapped children to recognize that all children are different from one another and that all children have some type of special need are weakened when only one or two handicapped children are present.

In contrast, a school must be careful not to overcommit itself by enrolling too many children who present social problems. Working with handicapped children does take a great deal of time, energy, and planning. Before making a decision about how many handicapped children to enroll, teachers should carefully consider the characteristics of the children who do not have special needs, the number of teaching staff and their experience, the extent of support services available, and the types of challenges likely to be posed by the particular handicapped children being proposed for integration.

Does Mainstreaming Require Teacher Aides?

Mainstreaming does not necessarily require the addition of teacher aides, but it does require various other kinds of aids, or support systems, for the teacher.

Although having another pair of skilled hands in an integrated classroom is useful, it is still possible to mainstream in the preschool without additional staff.

This conclusion is based on a number of assumptions. First, most preschools and day-care settings are staffed by two or more teachers. Thus, from the outset the teacher is not alone. Second, some children with physical disabilities, e.g. spina bifida, require assistance in toileting and other basic needs. When these children are mainstreamed, it will be necessary that someone be available to help them. However, it is important that these children not have someone "assigned to them" all the time, lest they be prevented from actually experiencing and participating in the regular classroom.

The third, and most important assumption regarding staffing concerns the necessity of teacher support, training, and consultation. If mainstreaming is to succeed, "teacher support systems" must be created and implemented.

What Are "Teacher Support Systems"?

The major sources of support for teachers beginning to mainstream are one's own colleagues, the school administration, and the parents in the school. Depending on your situation and your resources, any combination of one or more of these support systems will be extremely useful to you.

Support from one's own colleagues is critical whenever you attempt to implement a new and difficult program. This support can take the form of specific suggestions for what to do in the classroom, constructive problem solving, or just general "moral support."

The support of administrators is also critical. Administrators can plan parent meetings, coordinate outside resources, secure teaching aides, reinforce teachers for their efforts, and lend professional advice concerning individual children.

The parents of the children in the school are also key individuals in the mainstreaming process. The commitment of parents of nondisabled children to the program will ease the initial experience for the parents of special-needs children. Their commitment and activity, as well as that of the parents of the handicapped children, also provide support to teachers as they begin to modify their classrooms and to work with special-needs children.

Support can also be derived from other sources. For example, if someone on the staff has experience working with special-needs children, he or she may begin to fill the role of special-needs coordinator. Otherwise an outside consultant should be identified who is paid or who volunteers services through a clinic, university, or mental-health center. This individual should be prepared to answer questions about handicapping conditions, assist in arranging orientation sessions for parents, help with screening and intake, and provide consultation regarding program planning and coordination of services.

Finally, support can also come from inservice courses. Many state departments of education and state universities offer inservice courses at very low cost. The special-needs coordinator may also be able to lead a regular series of workshops and discussions. Mainstreaming inevitably entails additional training or retraining.

Will Mainstreaming Change My Teaching?

The answer to this question obviously depends on the kind of teacher you are before you begin to integrate special-needs children into your classroom. If you are someone who tries to teach to the average abilities of all the children in your class, if you are someone who is uncomfortable with varied responses from children instead of homogeneous responses, if you are someone who highly values compliant behavior, if you are someone who would rather not work with a team and would prefer to have as little as possible to do with parents—then either you are going to have to change a lot, or you should not try to mainstream.

Most early-childhood teachers do not fit the description given above. Young children are simply too individual, too spontaneous, and too complex to respond favorably to rigid or homogeneous modes of teaching. From this perspective, it is fair to assume that special-needs children will fit into individualized, responsive, active early-childhood classrooms without requiring immense changes in those programs or in teaching practices.

But it would be a serious error to assume that no changes need be made in your program. The type of changes or modifications in the mainstream that will be required are directly related to the needs and characteristics of the particular children who are integrated into your classroom.

For an intellectually slow or delayed child, you may have to learn how to break down complicated tasks into simpler steps. More repetition and one-to-one instruction may also be required. Speech-impaired children may profit from particular verbal activities and from suggestions of projects that they can work on with their parents at home.

For the teacher working with behaviorally disordered or disturbed children, his or her approach to limit setting may have to be modified. Limits, rules, and restrictions should be devised and applied with clarity, consistency, and attention to consequences. The teacher should also review the physical arrangement of the classroom. Some children who are impulsive and disruptive respond favorably to a classroom that contains a number of small, safe places in which activities are clear and boundaries determined.

The teachers in one school listed a number of skills that they had begun to develop as a result of mainstreaming. Their experience showed them that they had to learn some or all of the following:

1. how to talk to children about handicaps;
2. how to teach highly active children inner controls;
3. how to support parents of special-needs children;
4. how to talk about handicaps with parents whose children do not have special needs;
5. how to work with parents who deny their child's limitations;
6. how to assist parents and children through a period of hospitalization;
7. how to refine skills of individualization;
8. how to utilize prescriptive teaching techniques;
9. how to incorporate specialists into the classroom;

10. how to acquire familiarity with specialized medical terminology and diagnostic labels;
11. how to become sensitive to the effects of medication;
12. how to become acquainted with a number of formal and informal screening and diagnostic procedures;
13. how to acquire familiarity with state and federal laws concerning the handicapped; and
14. how to come to grips with one's own feelings concerning difference, deviance, and handicaps.*

Although this list may appear overwhelming, it represents a composite view of a wide range of experiences that several teachers had with a number of handicapped children over a long period of time. An individual teacher working with a specific group of children will have occasion to encounter only a portion of the issues raised above. Moreover, if mainstreaming is seen as a gradual process of learning for everyone involved, the skills that are needed can be seen primarily as adaptations of existing knowledge, rather than as impositions of foreign jargon or specialized techniques.

Remember: handicapped children are first and foremost children. They have "normal needs" as well as "special needs." The mainstreamed classroom is not a place that tries to mix two separate, unrelated groups of children—handicapped and nonhandicapped. Rather, it is a setting in which all children are given individualized attention and where specific modifications are made to meet the special needs of children who require unusual or sustained teacher attention.

One critical source of support for the teacher that has been mentioned already is parent involvement. The following section offers specific suggestions for enlisting the help of this important group of concerned individuals.

Enlisting Parents' Help in Mainstreaming

One of the most important experiences anyone can have in beginning to think about mainstreaming is actually to spend time with handicapped children. This is true for teachers and for parents.

"Parent helping" in the classroom is an excellent way for the parents of nondisabled children to begin to find out how similar to their own children are the children with special needs. As is always the case when parents volunteer their help in the classroom, the teacher should meet with the parent beforehand to discuss the class schedule and routines, the manner in which the parent wishes to be involved—for example, undertaking a specific project or offering more informal assistance—the possible responses of the parent's own child to the parent's presence, and any questions or concerns the parent may have concerning other children in the class.

Through directly working in the classroom, parents will begin to gain firsthand access to what mainstreaming involves. If appropriate, opportunities can be arranged for a parent to lead a group activity that includes a special-needs child

*See Meisels, S.J., First steps in mainstreaming: some questions and answers, *Young Children*, 1977, *33* (1), p. 8.

or to work one-to-one with one of the disabled children. The teacher should be certain to orient the parent to the child's particular strengths and disabilities. It is also very important that time be saved after class for the parent and teacher to discuss the parent's experience in the classroom.

A number of steps for introducing parents to the goals and objectives of mainstreaming can be identified. Strategically, these might take place in the following sequence:*

1. On acceptance of the child to the school, all parents should be informed that the program is mainstreamed, that the issues of mainstreaming will be discussed, and that their participation is needed in order to make the program work. Any questions parents have at this time should be answered.

2. In September, teachers should try to make visits to the home of each child. There, in a less hurried, more personal encounter, teacher and parent can discuss the school program. Time could be taken at this point to reinforce the school's commitment to mainstreaming and to talk about what parents can expect to see in the classroom. With parents of special-needs children, it is important to tell them that some information is being shared with other parents and to allow them to participate in the formulation of what they might want communicated about their child. At this point, it is important to stress the availability of the teaching staff to receive all concerns, including those relating to mainstreaming. In some programs, home visits are not feasible; parent meetings can be utilized instead.

3. In the early part of the year, at an evening room meeting, open dialogue on mainstreaming as well as other issues should be encouraged. It is sometimes useful to show a film or slidetape as an impetus to such a discussion. It could also be useful to solicit in advance the contributions of parents of special-needs and nonspecial-needs children in describing and discussing their responses to mainstreaming.

4. Throughout the year the teacher must maintain a great deal of flexibility with regard to individual and group issues. Extra parent conferences or room meetings may have to be scheduled to accommodate those needs. Informal communication between parents can occur by recommending that children play together after school. This brings together parents who have similar issues concerning their children or who can serve as resources for each other. Pot-luck suppers and informal social meetings for parents are another way to bring all parents closer together.

5. Regular parent conferences should always raise the issue of responses to mainstreaming. Too often it is assumed that if parents say nothing, they are feeling satisfied and informed. Frequently, just the opposite is true.

6. Parent meetings in individual conferences or in groups should continue to occur regularly. Although mainstreaming will not always be the issue, the commonality of parental concerns will.

7. Some parents will require special attention to help them express their feelings without being destructive to others. Teachers can model how to do this and may have to intervene in group situations. In the ideal situation,

---

*From Gunnoe, L.G. and Meisels, S.J., *Mainstream Challenges: A Manual for Early Childhood Educators.* Medford, MA: LINC Outreach, Tufts University, 1978, pp. 328-329.

parents who become comfortable as a group decide how specific and how deep they want their discussions and relationships to become. However, this type of situation is difficult to anticipate and it becomes the responsibility of the teacher sometimes to take an issue one step further and to analyze carefully the receptivity of the group.

Preschool teachers often discover that their strongest allies in the mainstreaming process are parents. However, in order to enlist their help, teachers must reach out to them in some of the ways discussed above. As is true throughout the teaching experience, honesty, flexibility, and advance preparation are critical for engaging parents' confidence and support. In the case of preschool mainstreaming, this involvement is all the more important because of the social and attitudinal aspects of the mainstreaming process.

IN SUMMARY

This chapter has only just begun to raise some of the issues entailed by mainstreaming. We have asked the question, "Who is handicapped?" but we have not discussed screening and identification. We have noted the need for "modifying the mainstream," but we have not detailed the process of educational assessment, planning, and curriculum adaptation. We have remarked that individualization is a key variable in the mainstreamed classroom, but we have not explored how informal assessment can contribute to the effectiveness of an individualized program. We have noted that "teacher support systems" can determine whether a mainstreaming program succeeds, yet we have not focused on a systematic plan for inservice training and development.

Many of the next steps that should be taken in order to begin filling in this missing information are to be found in this book. The chapters on child development, curriculum, staff collaboration, and assessment and record keeping will help you work on specific problems and particular issues.

In other words, although mainstreaming poses its own set of particular challenges, it is in many ways an extension of the kind of teaching you are currently doing or learning to do. Success in mainstreaming does not come easily, nor does it come without significant change and personal-professional development. But it can be achieved. You, the teacher, are the person who can make it happen—you, and your commitment to working with individual children in a carefully planned and carefully thought through Growing Program.

RESOURCES

Caldwell, B.M. The importance of beginning early. In Jordan, J.B., and Dailey, R.G., eds. *Not All Little Wagons Are Red: The Exceptional Child's Early Years.* Reston, Va.: Council for Exceptional Children, 1973.

> A helpful presentation of the historical antecedents of mainstreaming. Caldwell provides a justification for early intervention and critically analyzes contemporary educational programs for handicapped children.

Guralnick, M.J., ed. *Early Intervention and the Integration of Handicapped and Nonhandicapped Children.* Baltimore: University Park Press, 1978.

> A challenging collection of original essays concerning different conceptual and empirical models of mainstreaming. Includes chapters on open education, cognitive-developmental and behavioral approaches, and programs that focus on infants, toddlers, and preschool-age children.

Meisels, S.J., ed. *Special Education and Development: Perspectives on Young Children with Special Needs.* Baltimore: University Park Press, 1979.

> This anthology of original essays applies a model of human development to issues concerning the education of handicapped children. Contains detailed chapters on classroom design, teacher preparation, informal assessment, and program evaluation. The book also describes three developmentally oriented mainstreamed preschool programs and contains an extensive annotated bibliography.

Safford, P.L. *Teaching Young Children with Special Needs.* St. Louis: C.V. Mosby, 1978.

> A useful textbook focusing on educational provisions and strategies for handicapped children from birth through eight years of age. Presents a range of alternatives for developing programs for children with a wide variety of handicapping conditions.

14

An End...and a Beginning

This book, *The Growing Program,* is ending. But your own Growing Program will continue to develop and flourish long after you turn the last page.

If you've made it this far, you've changed. You couldn't help it. If even one idea has stayed with you, you have taken in something new. So, whether you've read the book through in one sitting, or used it in a course or workshop, or applied its ideas in a staff-development program at your own center or school, you are a different person than when you read the first page. But the book is also a different book because you've read it and made it your own.

When Barney plays at the clay table, two things happen at the same time. Barney molds and changes the lump of clay to fit his ideas about what the clay should become—perhaps he wants to make a boat. But his ideas are also changed because of his experience with the clay. He finds that clay boats are fine to look at, for instance, but they sink quickly. The result for Barney is growth.

Adults grow in much the same way. A new experience doesn't simply get added to what you already know like one more brick in a tower.

You are a person with a unique set of beliefs, attitudes, and habits. So in "taking in" an experience or an idea—or this book—you always change it a little bit, trimming off the corners or shaping or prodding it (like Barney with the clay) to make it fit better with what you already believe or know. That's one part of learning.

- Maybe you had to throw out many of the suggestions about scheduling because your "drop-in" center has children coming and going all day long.
- Or maybe you found that our ideas about planning activities fit perfectly with some things you just learned in a college course.
- Or maybe you picked over the suggestions for activity areas to find a few that fit best with the freewheeling outdoor life at your school.

So the book *is* a different book now. You've skimmed it, studied it, written in it, dog-eared some pages, and left others unturned. It's yours.

But no matter how you try to trim them and shape them, the new ideas never quite fit with the old ones—and a good thing, too. Because when things don't fit, you are forced to change and grow (again, like Barney!) Even if you don't "buy" a new idea completely, your comfortable stereotypes are shaken a bit. Some of the things you've read in this book may have caused you to rethink some old beliefs and try some things that are a little different.

- Maybe you changed your way of handling lunch time because of what you've learned about young children's need for order.
- Maybe the chapter on "staffing" has prodded you to set aside some time to discuss individual children with the rest of the staff.
- Or maybe you've decided to rearrange some of the outdoor equipment because of your new understanding of how physical space can affect children's behavior.

The kind of growth we're talking about is a gradual process. Because you do assimilate new ideas to your own personality and situation, and because your old ideas are only gradually transformed into new ones, it's sometimes hard to see that change has taken place.

Stop for a minute. Turn back to page 8 in the very first chapter, where you listed the things you liked about yourself as a teacher, and the areas in which you'd like to improve. Whether it's been a week or six months since you wrote that list, the chances are that you feel differently about it—and about yourself— now.

- It may be that you value your ability to notice little details of children's behavior even more now that you see its importance in the planning process.
- It may be that you can find more things to like about yourself after experiencing some solid successes.
- It may be that the changes you wanted (better organization, improved staff relationships) have begun to happen, almost imperceptibly.

A BACKWARD LOOK

You may be able to see your growth even more clearly if we take a systematic look at the pieces of *The Growing Program*—the chapters of this book. Each one had something different to offer you, and each one of *you* probably selected something different from what was offered. To help you summarize what you've created out of the ideas in this book, we've listed the skills that each chapter emphasized. Beside each skill, we've left room for you to record something you've done to apply that skill or understanding in your work with children, staff, or parents. (If you're a student, you might write down your plans for using a particular skill in the future.)

Here are some guidelines to use as you think about how you've tried to put these ideas into practice.

- Give yourself credit for trying! Failures can teach you as much as successes— about yourself and your children. If your attempt to organize an evening parent meeting got a turnout of three people, that's three more than you would have reached if you didn't try at all! And maybe next time you'll try a pot-luck supper.

AN END... AND A BEGINNING

- Remember the small steps you've taken. You may believe, for example, that you've really done nothing to apply the ideas we've offered about observing children. But stop and think. After reading Chapter 3, have you begun to notice how the children look when they walk in the door in the morning? Even if you haven't gotten to the point of writing it down, you've made a start.
- Recognize your own needs. There's no reason to feel guilty because you haven't developed every skill we've touched on. You—and your program—are unique. You *ought* to pick and choose from what's been offered. Remember, the whole idea behind this book was not to give you a ready-made plan, but to offer some tools, skills, and insights to use in your own way.

Chapter 1, "Your Growing Program," invited you to become an active participant in developing the skills described in the rest of the book.

Chapter 2, "Growing Your Own: A Teaching Philosophy," offered help in developing and implementing your own professional values and identity.

These skills were emphasized:
1. Identifying your own educational beliefs, goals, and values.
2. Planning experiences and activities to help you "grow your own" teaching philosophy.
3. Beginning to put your philosophy into conscious practice in daily classroom decisions.

An application:
1. _____
2. _____
3. _____

Chapter 3, "Patterns of Growth: Child Development and Teaching," offered a place to start in "growing" your program: with children themselves. It offered some help in understanding the process of development in young children, and suggested ways in which that understanding can help you in your work.

These skills were emphasized
1. Using developmental milestones
2. Becoming aware of the ingredients of healthy development: maturation, experiences, and people
3. Understanding individual differences
4. Anticipating changes in the four growth areas: social-emotional, perceptual-motor, cognitive, and language

An application:
1. _____
2. _____
3. _____
4. _____

Chapter 4, "The Growing Child: Observing and Recording," offered a system for keeping track of the development charted in Chapter 2. It gave you some places to look for indications of growth in children, and some ways to organize what you found out.

These skills were emphasized: *An application:*
1. Obtaining information from parents   1. _____

2. Collecting samples of children's work   2. _____

3. Observing children's behavior   3. _____

4. Getting answers to questions about children   4. _____

5. Recording children's behavior   5. _____

Chapter 5, "Directions for Growth: Goals, Objectives, and Plans," offered some assistance in putting observations of children to work by making program decisions based on each child's needs.

These skills were emphasized: *An application:*
1. Selecting goals   1. _____

2. Designing objectives   2. _____

3. Using goals and objectives to guide activity planning   3. _____

Chapter 6, "Setting Directions for Growth: Putting Goals, Objectives, and Plans to Work," offered some help with the day-to-day process of working with other staff to make those goals, objectives, and plans a reality for each child.

These skills were emphasized: *An application:*
1. Individualizing your program through staffing   1. _____

2. Implementing and evaluating the individualized plans you've made   2. _____

Chapter 7, "Places for Growth: Activity Areas," offered ways to use activity areas in your classroom to help you and the children reach the goals you've set.

AN END... AND A BEGINNING

These skills were emphasized: *An application:*
1. Setting up and evaluating activity areas   1. _____
2. Selecting activity areas   2. _____
3. Maximizing learning in each area   3. _____
4. Supervising activity areas   4. _____

Chapter 8, "Resources for Growth: Activities and Materials," offered guidelines for choosing materials and activities for your classroom which will make the most of children's urge to learn.

These skills were emphasized: *An application:*
1. Choosing activities   1. _____
2. Getting the most out of the materials you have   2. _____
3. Getting more materials   3. _____

Chapter 9, "Supporting Children's Growth: The Many Ways of Teaching," offered an overview of your role in helping children get the most out of the environment you have provided.

These skills were emphasized: *An application:*
1. Instructing   1. _____
2. Setting problems   2. _____
3. Providing experiences   3. _____
4. Helping with feeling and behavior   4. _____
5. Managing routines and rules   5. _____

Chapter 10, "Space and Time for Growth: The Room Arrangement and

Schedule," offered help in organizing an environment that reflects your growing understanding of children and their needs.

These skills were emphasized: *An application:*
1. Becoming aware of the effect of space on children's behavior 1. _____

2. Making informed decisions about the use of space 2. _____

3. Evaluating and changing your room arrangement 3. _____

4. Analyzing the reasons behind a schedule 4. _____

5. Planning and evaluating your schedule 5. _____

Chapter 11, "The Growing Staff: Making the Most of Yourselves," offered help in creating effective and harmonious staff relationships, so that you *and* the children will benefit.

These skills were emphasized *An application:*
1. Using your talents in the program 1. _____

2. Working together in staff meetings 2. _____

3. Working together in the classroom 3. _____

Chapter 12, "Growing Together: Parents, Children, and Staff," offered help in bringing parents and teachers into comfortable partnership.

These skills were emphasized: *An application:*
1. Identifying past parent-teacher communication problems 1. _____

2. Talking with parents about their child 2. _____

3. Involving parents in the program 3. _____

4. Helping "problem parents" and problem teachers! 4. _____

AN END... AND A BEGINNING

Chapter 13, "Differences in Growth: Mainstreaming Handicapped Young Children," offered help in understanding and implementing a program which integrates handicapped and nonhandicapped children in the same classroom.

These skills were emphasized: *An application:*

1. Becoming aware of the spectrum of handicapping conditions.   1. _____

2. Understanding the justifications for mainstreaming.   2. _____

3. Discussing handicaps with children and parents.   3. _____

4. Modifying the mainstream classroom   4. _____

5. Developing "teacher support systems"   5. _____

You can see that your own program has grown since you started working with this book. You've been putting theories into practice, trying new things, adapting suggestions to fit your own style and beliefs, rejecting some ideas and emphasizing others.

WHAT'S NEXT?

With these chapters, we've given you the pieces; you've begun to fit them together. What happens next is up to you.

At this point, you're probably full of determination to continue "growing" your program. That's great.

But we all know what happens to good intentions. New ways of doing things have a discouraging way of fizzling once the first enthusiasm wears off. The second five pounds is much harder to lose than the first five, and the second week of jogging isn't nearly as exhilarating as the first. Old habits have a discouraging way of hanging around, ready to take over at a moment's notice. Sometimes there just isn't enough payoff for the effort it takes to try new things. At work, no one even notices the five pounds you lost, and none of your neighbors laugh enough to see you start off in your new jogging suit. So you quit.

The same thing can happen to resolutions about professional growth. Once the book is closed, the course is over, or the workshop ends, you begin (despite your good intentions) to go back to your old habits—even if you never liked them in the first place.

We'd like to help you to resist that backward pull. Here are a few "tricks" that have worked for some people. Maybe one of them will work for you.

Make your decisions public. It's harder to go back to smoking if you've loudly announced your decision to quit. In the same way, if you're planning to start keeping notes on each child in your group, tell another teacher about it. You'll be more likely to do it if you know she might ask!

- Spend some of your own money. Once you've bought the note cards and file box, your thrifty self will probably make you use them.
- Write down your plans. A written reminder is a powerful push to action for some of us. Keep a notebook of goals and plans in the classroom, or post a list of group plans on your door (and if someone else sees it, you'll be even more inclined to follow through).
- Hold on to records. Sometimes it may seem that you aren't making any progress, but a rereading of notes from earlier in the year will show you how far you and the children have come. When a day of Jerry's arguing gets you down, read about the days in October when he'd scream rather than talk.
- Get the "one-a-week" habit. Set yourself some *modest* but *regular* goals. How about deciding to try one new thing every Friday? It may be an activity, an observation system, a different way of dealing with a difficult child. If you experiment even more often, that's fine.
- Don't use one failure as an excuse to quit. Often we're secretly looking for excuses to stop doing something that's hard. So when a failure occurs, we say, "See? I *knew* I couldn't do it." And the whole plan is hastily given up. Decide right now that you'll give yourself permission to fail—and to try again.
- Keep in touch with other professionals. Contact with others in the field is a great stimulus to growth. Try joining professional organizations. Go to meetings, read bulletins, volunteer your services. You'll make new friends and encounter stimulating ideas to take back to the classroom.

These suggestions will help you maintain the momentum you have right now. But there's one final suggestion we can make to keep this growth firmly rooted and vigorous: *Follow the children.*

Books will help. New materials will help. Other professionals will help.

But the children will help you the most. They'll help by being themselves: by living, laughing, fighting, building, running . . . growing.

They will show you what they need, and what a difference you can make in their lives. With their help, you'll be on your way to your own Growing Program.

We hope this book has helped, too.

Good luck.